THE PATH TO SERENITY

Dr. Robert Hemfelt, Dr. Richard Fowler,
Dr. Frank Minirth, Dr. Paul Meier

A
JANET
THOMA
BOOK

THOMAS NELSON PUBLISHERS
Nashville

The accounts presented in Parts One and Two of this book are fictional composites based on the authors' clinical experience with thousands of clients through the years. Any resemblance between the characters of Parts One and Two and actual persons is coincidental.

Published in Nashville, Tennessee, by Thomas Nelson, Inc., and distributed in Canada by Lawson Falle, Ltd., Cambridge, Ontario.

Scripture quotations are from the NEW KING JAMES VERSION of the Bible. Copyright © 1979, 1980, 1982, Thomas Nelson, Inc., Publishers.

Scripture quotations taken from The Holy Bible: NEW INTERNATIONAL VERSION are marked NIV. Copyright © 1978 by the New York International Bible Society. Used by permission of Zondervan Bible Publishers.

Library of Congress Cataloging-in-Publication Data

The Path to serenity / Robert Hemfelt . . . [et. al.].
    p. cm.
Includes bibliographical references.
ISBN 0-8407-7691-8
    1. Twelve-step programs—Religious aspects—Christianity.
I. Hemfelt, Robert.
BV4596.T88P38   1991
248.8'6—dc20   91-37811
                                       CIP

Printed in the United States of America

1 2 3 4 5 6 7 — 96 95 94 93 92

Contents

Contents

Acknowledgments

The authors are grateful to the friends, family members, and working companions whose contributions and assistance have made the publication of *The Path to Serenity* possible. We are especially thankful for Susan Hemfelt, Jerilyn Fowler, Mary Alice Minirth, and Jan Meier, whose graciousness and patience have eased the work. Many thanks also to Janet Thoma, for her tireless encouragement and editorial expertise; and to the in-house staff of Thomas Nelson for their diligence in producing the finished book.

PART ONE

Before You Begin

The Path to Serenity

Andy Thomson looked at the clock over his workbench and groaned. Seven o'clock. He'd promised himself he'd stop at five and go running. And he'd promised Jennifer he'd meet her for her birthday celebration dinner at their favorite restaurant at six. Would she still be there? He called "La Sierre" and asked the maitre d' to look for her. "A nice-looking blonde woman who was waiting a long time just left," the man replied. "I'm sorry."

Andy pictured Jennifer with her sleek, honey-blonde hair falling around her shoulders and her gentle blue eyes sparkling. They wouldn't be sparkling now—more like shooting darts. This was the third time this month that he'd kept her waiting for almost an hour. And today was her twenty-fifth birthday. He had been so sure it would be different this time. He was sure he could handle his workaholism on his own.

But he just couldn't seem to get it right with relationships. Well, he might as well finish reconnecting the circuitry on this computer. Half an hour later he covered the computer, turned to his telephone, and dialed Jennifer's number. After ten rings he hung up. She should be home by now. *That's a sign she's really mad,* he thought. He tried to reach Jennifer several times that evening but still no answer. The next day when he saw her at church, she made it very clear that their relationship was over. "I can't be very important to you, Andy, if you can't even remember my birthday celebration. I'd rather not go out with you again." Her voice had been sharp and her decision final, he realized in the next weeks as she refused to talk to him on the phone or at church. "It's over, Andy, remember?" was all she would say. Yet Andy knew Jennifer was the girl he wanted to marry. Two other girls had broken up with him in the last couple of years, but that hadn't hurt so much.

Andy Thomson's extraordinary efforts to ensure the success of his new business had become more than a habit in the last several years. It had become an addiction.

In our modern American culture, addictions have reached epidemic proportions. An estimated fifteen million Americans are chemically dependent upon alcohol or drugs. Each chemical addict severely affects at least four other people. That means that sixty million Americans are directly affected by ongoing chemical dependencies. In addition an estimated 28.8 million are adult children of alcoholics who may no longer be directly influenced by the addicted person but still bear the scars from childhood. Some experts put the figures as high as seventy-five to one hundred million people who are severely impacted by the alcoholic and chemical addictions alone, to which one must add the other addictions many people suffer, such as compulsive eating, gambling, working, or spending.

But that desperately gloomy picture is only one side of the coin. There *is* good news. In America alone it is estimated that more than ten million people attend as many as five hundred thousand self-help group meetings every week. So people are reaching out for help—and help is there for them. Not all self-help groups in America are Twelve-Step groups but the vast majority of them are, and this unique approach to spiritual and emotional healing often results in people living happy, peaceful lives. The best news is: we can overcome our addictions, our obsessive-compulsive behaviors.

Addictions and Obsessive-compulsive Behaviors

It is our experience that all addictions are fundamentally *control* addictions. In other words, all addictions are efforts to satisfy our internal needs or feelings by manipulating external events, people, or things. And here the great paradox is that *over-control* of events, people, and things sends our lives spinning dangerously *out of control.*

As we define *addiction,* it is important to note that all addictions have two components. The first component is the *obsession,* which is a mental preoccupation or craving. For example the workaholic may obsess about the tasks that need to be completed and the constant guilt feelings that whisper, "You need to be doing more." The second component of the addiction is the *compulsion,* which is behavior that lives out or acts out the mental obsession. The workaholic's twelve-hour days at the office are the compulsion dimension of his obsessive-compulsive behavior.

We often think that alcoholics and drug addicts are the only ones who are addicted to external substances. Yet you can see that the definition we just gave you includes addictions to events (like crises, for instance; we have one patient whose mother is a crisis junkie; every time things in the family seem to be peaceful her mother calls her with some new magnified problem) and people (like a spouse, boyfriend or girlfriend) and things (like the biggest house on the block or the fastest boat on the lake), and behaviors (such as compulsive cleaning or obsessive worrying). We call this obsessive-compulsive behavior. Many people fit this description—our next door neighbors, our mothers and fathers, our sisters and brothers, ourselves.

We counsel people with obsessive-compulsive behaviors at our sixteen clinics throughout the United States (in cities like Dallas, Texas, Washington, D.C., Chicago, Illinois, and Los Angeles, California). The most commonly treated compulsions at our clinics include dependency on alcohol, marijuana, cocaine, tranquilizers, and other illicit or prescription drugs, eating disorders, sexual and relationship addictions, religious addictions, and obsessions with work, achievement, and perfection.

And those who suffer from obsessive-compulsive behaviors are not just our patients. All of the authors of this book—Dr. Frank Minirth and Dr. Paul Meier, the two founders of the Minirth-Meier Clinics, Dr. Robert Hemfelt, a staff psychologist at the hospital in Dallas, and Dr. Richard Fowler, director of the Minirth-Meier Clinic in Richardson—have had bouts with some form of compulsive or driven behavior.

Dr. Rick Fowler openly discusses his tendency to try to control others at our seminars. "In the past I needed to be in control," he says, "because of my lack of self-esteem. As a kid I was programmed for failure. My parents were missionaries in the Central American interior, so I was home-schooled until I was nine. When we came back to the States, the public schools tested me and were horrified at the deficiencies that showed up on my test scores. From then on the pattern was set—special ed and remedial programs all the way through high school.

"The only thing I could do was play basketball. And being a starter in basketball was important to me. I couldn't be in the academic classes with the kids I liked, but if I was a basketball star, then they'd have to accept me.

"The change came in my junior year of college. My philosophy professor said, 'You've been sold a bill of goods. You're bright. You can do something academically!'

"My world changed. I'd never heard such a thing before. My grade point average went from 2.01 to 3.5, just because I found out I *could* do it.

"From then on I made my own rules. I didn't violate any of God's laws, but I quit paying attention to other people's expectations. I was in control. That was great for my self-image and my accomplishments, but not all the changes were good. I also found that I had to control other people.

"I entered a codependent marriage—my wife needed to be rescued, and I needed someone to rescue or control. I began coaching basketball and soon realized that if I could learn how to motivate athletes, we'd have a better team. So I registered for a graduate degree in social psychology. In graduate school I took a battery of psychology tests for a test and measurements course I was taking. One evaluation indicated that my flexibility score was zero.

"My professor asked me, 'Why are you in psychology?'

"I knew the answer to that question. I was planning to use psychology as a manipulative tool to win games, but I didn't admit that. I gave him a selfless version of my goal: 'I want to understand my players better so I can be a better coach.' I still had no idea, however, that my real goal was a symptom of my codependent personality. My self-esteem was validated by what I did. I could show everyone, 'I'm somebody,' if my team won.

"In the next year I began to realize that if my team won, I'd be cordial and gracious to my wife and kids afterward. I'd play games with the kids; I'd take Jeri out to dinner or do something special for her. But the reverse was also true. If we lost, my temper was short, my mind distracted.

"One day I realized that I was relating to my family just as an alcoholic does. Even though I never touched alcohol, my kids were suffering just as an alcoholic's did. I could see by the look in my kids' eyes when I came home that they were wondering, 'What's dad going to be like today?' Our home was unstable, I realized.

"Now I began to evaluate other areas of our lives. For ten years my control of my wife had been so extensive that I wouldn't even let her cut her hair without my permission. She had never been farther than ten miles away from our home on her own. She had never put gas in the car. I did everything for her.

"One day I came home from work as usual, but a major change had occurred. Jeri had cut her hair. That scared me. It was the first time she had ever done anything against my wishes. I felt out of control.

"That evening she wrote a letter to me, explaining that she cut her hair because it had become such a burden. 'I take the children swimming everyday, and it takes two hours to wash and style my hair afterward. That's interfering with the time I have with the kids. I knew you wouldn't agree to it, so I had to cut it without your knowing. I love you, but this is what I had to do.'

"For two weeks I hardly talked to her, except to quote every Scripture I could think of about how a wife should be submissive to her husband. She was disobeying God, as well as me, I told her.

"Then I came across a verse that said something different: 'Likewise you husbands, dwell with them [your wives] with understanding, giving honor to the wife, . . . and as being heirs together of the grace of life, that your prayers may not be hindered'.[1]

"As I thought about that verse I realized that husbands are never told to order their wives to submit, but to love and understand and honor them. I looked up the word *helpmeet,* which God uses to describe a wife in Genesis 2, and realized that the Hebrew translation was 'to go alongside of.' There was no doubt that I needed to change.

"The old patterns still crop up at times. Just recently I found myself turning to my wife and giving her an order. Fortunately she has also found recovery from her codependency, her need to be controlled, so she knows where to draw the line. She just smiled at me, and I realized what I'd done. Then I did myself what I'd unthinkingly ordered her to do."

In this book we are formally renouncing the myth that counselors and psychologists sometimes propagate: We have our lives arranged in textbook precision. Instead we too suffer from the dis-ease of some compulsions.

Dr. Paul Meier has battled his compulsion to overeat and has lost thirty-five pounds in the last year, by applying the principles in our earlier book *Love Hunger*.

Dr. Frank Minirth and Dr. Robert Hemfelt are constantly aware of their tendency toward workaholism. They know that obsessive-compulsive behavior can be a never-ending cycle.

The Never-ending Cycle

The dependent person who overspends, overworks, gambles, drinks, abuses sex, or whatever in response to internal pain finds that indulging that addiction causes more pain, and he must run ever faster and faster in an attempt to stop the pain with more material goods or more winnings or more sexual conquests or more alcohol or more whatever. Emotional pain brings the addict to the addiction, but the practice of the dependency generates its own new pain. And so, the need for the addiction "security" or "anesthesia" grows ever greater.

Soon the addict is caught in the terrible paradox of not being able to hang on, but not being able to let go either. Dr. Hemfelt recalls a most vivid picture of this. His young daughter, Katy, was enjoying a gentle merry-go-round ride with several children her own age. Then some older children came and began spinning the merry-go-round faster and faster. Katy was shrieking frantically by the time her daddy could rescue her. When she was safe in his arms she sobbed, "Daddy, Daddy, I couldn't get off, but I couldn't hold on." Those of us caught on the spinning wheel of the addiction cycle echo her words. We can't live with our addictions because they are destroying us, but seemingly we can't live without them. We're trapped.

If you are struggling with the question, "Am I addicted?," the important point to remember is that it's not entirely a question of how much you spend or how hard you work or how often you have sex or how much you drink. The key question is: *Why* do you do these things?

An addiction is anything that is done to change reality. It is an effort to alter interior moods and feelings by manipulating or incorporating substances, people, and events on the outside. The problem is not food or material goods or sex, the problem is the underlying spiritual or emotional hunger, which causes you to reach for the addictive agent.

Are you suffering from some of the symptoms of this spiritual or emotional hunger? Is your life plagued by the chaos, pain, and lack of fulfillment that so often accompany the codependent and obsessive-compulsive lifestyle? Check the statements below that apply to you:

_____ My life seems to be a long series of frustrations and unmet dreams. Somehow my most important goals or desires always seem to be out of reach.

_____ I wake up with a knot in the pit of my stomach. Everyday is a confrontation with the nameless fear that follows me like a dark cloud.

_____ I feel like a square peg in the round hole of the game of life. I never quite seem to belong or to fit in anywhere.

_____ I sometimes think life is a conspiracy and I am the object against whom it is conspiring.

_____ I feel that my life is a masquerade. I wear a mask on the outside that looks halfway okay, but I fear that if you saw beyond the mask to the inside of me, you'd be appalled.

_____ I sometimes wonder who's in charge of my life. It seems as if I don't have enough control of people and things around me, and yet others tell me I'm too controlling. Who's running the ship?

_____ I seem to be surrounded by people who are expressing concern about me. My children, my

spouse, my friends, my employer, everyone is upset about the direction in which my life is headed.

_____ I'm sick and tired of feeling sick and tired.

If you checked several of these statements, you may be
suffering from the symptoms of an addiction to people,
places, or things. At the clinic we frequently suggest that
patients who are suffering from any form of addiction join
Twelve-Step groups as they embark on their journey to
recovery. We've found that the Twelve Steps of Alcoholics
Anonymous and the techniques we use in counseling can
be a path to freedom from the addictive bondage. That's
why we've decided to write a book that walks the reader
down this same path.

What Are the Twelve Steps?

Many people who could not recite one of the Twelve
Steps know that this process forms the basis for the Alcoholics Anonymous (A.A.) program, which was founded
by Bill Wilson in the mid 1930s. A.A. modestly describes
their handbook, affectionately known as the *Big Book,* as
"the story of how many thousands of men and women
have recovered from alcoholism." Thousands may, by
now, be virtually millions. Although the organization has
no way to officially determine how many people have
overcome their alcoholic addiction through the Twelve-
Step program, today A.A. has over one million members
in the United States and another million outside our
country. And the *Big Book* has sold twelve million copies.
In the 1940s and '50s the Twelve Steps began to be
adopted by the spouses and children of alcoholics for use
in their Al-Anon meetings. In subsequent decades other
groups found that these steps were instrumental to their
recovery, Emotions Anonymous (EA), Overeaters Anonymous (OA), and Codependents Anonymous (CODA) to
name a few. Now rageaholics, codependents who are ad-

dicted to relationships, and the adult children of alcoholics have all adopted the Twelve-Step process as a path toward recovery from their obsessive-compulsive behavior.

The Twelve Steps we will use in our journey in this book are listed on pages 14–15, with the original Twelve Steps of Alcoholics Anonymous listed below. Our version only varies from the original steps in that we have broadened the addiction mentioned in Step One to include all dependencies, rather than just alcohol, and we have broadened those we reach in Step Twelve beyond alcoholics. We see Steps One through Three as the *surrender steps*—we surrender our addiction (and our efforts to control that addiction) and our lives to God. Steps Four and Five are *spiritual and moral inventory steps*—we assess the damage of our addiction to ourselves and to others, and we think back over our past, which may have laid the groundwork for that addiction.

Steps Six and Seven are the *miracle transformation steps*—we hand our character defects over to God's transforming touch. Then in Steps Eight and Nine, the *restitution steps,* we make amends, if we can, to those we have harmed and attempt to rebuild those critical, intimate relationships.

Steps Ten and Eleven are the *daily maintenance steps,* in which we continue to assess our lives—sorting through the distorted thinking and feeling patterns that impair our recovery—and seek a daily walk with God, through prayer and meditation, so we can continue to know "His will for us" and have "the power to carry that out."

Most people in recovery eventually talk about their journey as a life-long experience. Whereas they originally show up at the counseling office with the questions "What can I do to get beyond the pain? How quickly can I do it?" in mind, after a while they realize that the path to serenity is just that, a continuous process toward a destination.

As our patients walk through the counseling process, they ask us, "If God really loves me, why doesn't He help me overcome my eating problem (or my depression or my alcoholism) *right now?* Here I am in the hospital on my knees asking him to heal me, but nothing happens. Does that mean that God doesn't care what happens to me?"

We answer that question by saying that a slow gradual healing, not a quick cure, might be what God has in mind. "This can be a blessing in disguise," we say. "You may take three steps forward, then fall back two, but a refining process is taking place in your life. A slow, gradual, educational type of healing allows you to grow gradually. There may be hidden blessings in the fact that you are working through the recovery steps over months and even years."

That's why people in recovery go through the Twelve Steps over and over again, many for the rest of their lives. And it's the reason why recovering persons at Twelve Step meetings often introduce themselves as *grateful* recovering persons. They are not grateful for their addictive illnesses, but they are grateful for the relationship growth, the emotional healing, and the spiritual maturation that have been by-products of their recovery.

Finally Step Twelve is the *transcendence and evangelism step,* in which we realize that we have had—and will continue to have—a spiritual experience and wish to share that experience with others.

We call this step transcendent because now we have begun to transcend time and space. *Twenty-Four Hours a Day,* one of the first devotional books widely used by members of A.A., talks about living and growing beyond the three dimensional bondage of our physical and material world—height, depth, and width. Emancipation from our addictions requires that we go beyond the confines of three-dimensional reality and enter the special healing realm of the spiritual fourth dimension. Throughout the New Testament, for instance, we are constantly reminded that God calls us to an eternal perspective, which breaks beyond the dimensions of space and time.

Each of us is born with a natural spiritual longing for

this fourth dimension. As our patients walk through the Twelve Steps and continue to do so in recovery, they encounter another serendipitous surprise: "I can have a foretaste of eternity right now, here on earth. If I inventory my emotions, if I am in daily connection with God, I can experience a degree of peace and joy that I never before thought possible."

Yes, the car will break down. Yes, people will be irritating and undependable. Yes, some of the same problems will still be around. But now that I am aware of this fourth dimension, I will not respond to them with the same old patterns of anger and fear and relapse into my addiction as a means of coping. Instead of mere survival, I shall begin to experience what Bill W. talks about in the *Big Book*: "I was soon to be catapulted into what I like to call the fourth dimension of existence. I was to know happiness, peace, and usefulness, in a way of life that is incredibly more wonderful as time passes."[2]

THE TWELVE STEPS*

1. We admitted we were powerless over our dependencies—that our lives had become unmanageable.

2. Came to believe that a Power greater than ourselves could restore us to sanity.

3. Made a decision to turn our will and our lives over to the care of God *as we understood Him.*

4. Made a searching and fearless moral inventory of ourselves.

5. Admitted to God, to ourselves, and to another human being the exact nature of our wrongs.

6. Were entirely ready to have God remove all these defects of character.

7. Humbly asked Him to remove our shortcomings.

8. Made a list of all persons we had harmed, and became willing to make amends to them all.

9. Made direct amends to such people wherever possible, except when to do so would injure them or others.

10. Continued to take personal inventory and when we were wrong promptly admitted it.

11. Sought through prayer and meditation to improve our conscious contact wiht God *as we understood Him,* praying only for knowledge of His will for us and the power to carry that out.

12. Having had a spiritual awakening as the result of these steps, we tried to carry this message to others, and to practice these principles in all our affairs.

The Twelve Steps of Alcoholics Anonymous*

1. We admitted we were powerless over alcohol—that our lives had become unmanageable. 2. Came to believe that a Power greater than ourselves could restore us to sanity. 3. Made a decision to turn our will and our lives over to the care of God as we understood Him. 4. Made a searching and fearless moral inventory of ourselves. 5. Admitted to God, to ourselves and to another human being the exact nature of our wrongs. 6. Were entirely ready to have God remove all these defects of character. 7. Humbly asked Him to remove our shortcomings. 8. Made a list of all persons we had harmed and became willing to make amends to them all. 9. Made direct amends to such people wherever possible, except when to do so would injure them or others. 10. Continued to take personal inventory and when we were wrong, promptly admitted it. 11. Sought through prayer and meditation to improve our conscious contact with God, as we understood Him, praying only for knolwedge of His will for us and the power to carry that out. 12. Having had a spiritual awakening as the result of these steps, we tried to carry this message to alcoholics, and to practice these principles in all our affairs.

* The Twelve Steps are reprinted and adapted with permission of Alcoholics Anonymous World Services, Inc. Permission to reprint the Twelve Steps does not mean that AA has reviewed or approved the content of this publication, nor that AA agrees with the views expressed herein. AA is a program of recovery from alcoholism. Use of the Twelve Steps in connection with programs and activities which are patterned after AA but which address other problems does not imply otherwise.

The Twelve Steps, combined with the techniques we use at the clinic, worked for Andy Thomson and for many of our patients. In this book we will follow Andy, a workaholic, Martin Woodruff, an alcoholic, and Kathryn Markham, an obsessive-compulsive overeater, on their journey through each of the Twelve Steps. As we do so, we will show you exactly how each of these steps can work for you as they have worked for millions of people in the past fifty-five years.

Whether you are like Martin Woodruff, who was barely willing to admit the possibility of a Higher Power, or like Andy Thomson, in touch with the personal God of the Bible, this journey can be a road map to your own recovery.

We offer the unique approach of reuniting modern Twelve-Step recovery with its ancient, biblical roots. While all Twelve-Step programs emphasize spirituality, many Twelve-Step speakers are very vague about who God is. He doesn't have a name. He's just God "as we understand him." He doesn't have a face or a history of personal involvement with us. He's a nebulous entity who can be a tree or the first cause in the universe. He may be an abstract pantheistic god, rather than the personal and well-defined Judeo-Christian God of the Bible.

We've found that our patients have had difficulty walking through the Twelve-Step process into full recovery without the involvement of this God of the Old and New Testaments. "If the god in Step Two is just as lost as I am, how can he help me to take control of my life?" they wonder. The God of the Bible does have a name, a face, and a history of relating to His people from the beginning of time. That's the God who walks hand in hand with our patients through the Twelve-Step process and through eternity.

Some people question how biblical the Twelve-Step program really is. There is no doubt that the roots of Bill W.'s philosophy were firmly planted in mainstream Christianity. By his own admission the two most important influences on his thinking as he developed A.A. were the Oxford Group and the Reverend Sam Shoemaker, rector of Calvary Episcopal Church, New York City. The Oxford Group was an informal evangelistic movement dedicated to reclaiming "first-century Christianity," and Shoemaker was one of the most influential Christians of the twentieth century, author of over two dozen books and founder of Faith at Work.

Dr. Bob Smith, cofounder of Alcoholics Anonymous, was also emphatic about the Christian thrust of Twelve-Step recovery. He had a required reading list for everyone he worked with in A.A. On that list was the King James Bible, especially the Sermon on the Mount, the Lord's Prayer, the book of James, and 1 Corinthians 13. In addition, Smith strongly recommended the well-known daily devotional periodical, *The Upper Room.*

There is no denying Bill Wilson was something of a spiritual paradox. After an experience that he described as "finding the God of the preachers," Bill W. never took another drink. His wife reported that one of his favorite books, which he read daily, was *My Utmost for His Highest,* by Oswald Chambers. Yet, in other areas his life was inconsistent.

According to Bill Pittman, author of the authoritative and scholarly study of Alcoholics Anonymous, *A.A.: The Way It Began:* "One is also reminded that Bill W. did not wish to be known as a saint, a prophet, an author, or the inventor of a new religion, but just as another alcoholic trying to stay sober one day at a time."[3]

In Part One of this book we will give you the psychological and spiritual principles you need to walk through the Twelve-Step process. We will show you in careful detail a seven-point plan for working the often daunting Fourth Step, the inventory step, which is almost universally acclaimed as "the hardest thing I ever did" by those in recovery. And we will take you on to apply what you learn about yourself to the broad principles for living the path to serenity.

Part Two contains the autobiographical recovery stories of the listeners of our national radio talk show, "The Minirth-Meier Clinic" and the patients at our sixteen clinics throughout the country. We have divided these stories into three groups: those who are recovering from their own dependencies or addictions, their codependent spouses, and the adult children of dysfunctional families who still carry the after-effects of that emotional legacy. As you read through their stories, imagine you are sitting with them in a Twelve-Step group, for sharing our journeys with one another is an important part of the path to serenity and an important purpose of this book.

As you take each step down this path, you will come closer to a life of wholeness, a chosen life where:

- your dependency doesn't make poor choices for you,
- your own false identity doesn't make self-destructive choices,
- others don't force their choices on you,

- and you don't surrender your choices to any false gods.

Instead all of your choices are inspired by a new relationship with the one authentic God of the universe, and the gift of that newfound serenity is passed on to others through the fellowship of recovery.

PART TWO

The Twelve Steps

Step One

We admitted we were powerless over our dependencies—that our lives had become unmanageable.

Andy Thomson walked into the beige-walled meeting room and sat on a metal folding chair. What was he doing here? Okay, he had come to admit that his relationships with girls like Jennifer suffered because of his workaholism. He did too—maybe. But his father hadn't been an alcoholic. Why was he attending a Twelve-Step meeting for the adult children of alcoholics?

He'd only come to be able to respond to Dr. Hemfelt's repeated and insistent recommendation. Once he could say, "Sure, Doc, I tried. It didn't do anything for me—sorry," then he'd be off the hook. Andy sat down and looked to the front of the room as a small, dark-haired girl in jeans and a blue sweater stood at the podium with a bright, nervous, smile. He had to admit she looked like a model teenager—not like a loser.

"Hi, I'm Jo. I'm the adult child of an alcoholic."

"Hi, Jo," the twenty people sitting in the room responded.

"Hi," she repeated and smiled again. "Let's pause for a moment of silence and then repeat the Serenity Prayer."

Andy closed his eyes, then opened them part-way to peek at the prayer printed on a plaque on the wall: "God, grant me the serenity to accept the things I cannot

21

change, the courage to change the things I can, and the wisdom to know the difference."

As the prayer ended Andy was aware that the chair next to him had become occupied. He looked at the scuffed loafers and comfortable corduroys next to his own highly polished shoes and well-pressed slacks but didn't look any higher.

"Welcome to the meeting," Jo said. "I'd like to talk about Step One tonight, because I just have to keep coming back here. When things get to going good, and they have been lately, then I start thinking that my life never really was out of control and that all the spending I did to try to get my mother's attention wasn't really sick. I start thinking that I can handle things on my own just fine. Then I really have a lot of trouble getting myself to these meetings and working my steps." Jo paused to take a break and to organize her thoughts.

"But I've learned—*finally*—that as soon as I think I'm in control, that's when my insanity takes over and things really go berserk. So I just have to keep coming back to Step One. I have to start every day admitting I'm powerless over my compulsion. I have it taped to my mirror; I can't brush my teeth without being reminded." Jo smiled again and breathed a sigh of relief as she sat down. Andy knew it must have taken a lot of courage for a teenager to talk to a group composed almost entirely of people at least fifteen years older than she was.

Now the facilitator, a man whose grey hair and wrinkles made it hard to think of him as a child of any kind— even an adult child—stood up. *Why did these people think of themselves as children?* Andy wondered. *Why didn't they solve their problems as he had always done?*

Andy caught himself up short at that thought as he remembered his feelings of despair. No, he hadn't solved his problems himself. In fact, he had to admit that his life seemed entirely out of control, and he didn't even care what happened anymore.

The facilitator had been explaining that this was an

open meeting with no planned speaker, so anyone could speak. "The usual rules of preserving one another's anonymity and no cross-talk—no feedback from the group after someone has spoken—will prevail," the leader said. "We don't give each other advice, because we know that adult children don't take advice. Neither does anyone have to speak," he reminded them. "Just say, 'I pass.' Now, let's talk about Step One," he said, "as Jo suggested."

The grey-haired man invited the group to move their chairs into a circle and suggested that half the group go into another room. That left about ten people in Andy's circle. Now he looked at the latecomer who was still beside him, even though the chairs had been rearranged. His eyebrows shot up in alarm. *Oh, no. Someone from my counseling group at the clinic!* As Andy struggled to recall his name, the older man turned to exchange looks with him and Andy remembered—Martin. Martin Woodruff.

The discussion went around the circle. After each person spoke, the group responded with something like, "Thank you," but nothing more, in obedience to the "no cross-talk" rule. They worked their way around the circle until they came to Andy on the end. "Hi, I'm Andy. I pass," he muttered.

"Hi, Andy," the group responded, and then the meeting was over.

"Thank you for coming," the leader said. "Please remember that if this is your first time, we urge you to attend the same group at least six times in close succession before you make a final decision about whether or not to make this your home group. Now we'll close in our usual way."

Suddenly Andy found himself standing and holding hands around the circle. He was completely amazed, and pleased, as they began praying the Lord's Prayer—it was the one thing that had happened all evening that was comfortable for him. At the end of the prayer they pumped their linked hands up and down and said with religious fervor, "Keep coming back. It works!"

Andy dropped the hands on both sides of him and stood alone. He eyed the glossy brown beard of the man he had recognized earlier from a Minirth-Meier Clinic therapy group, wondering if he should speak.

Instead the other man took the initiative. "Well, what do you think?"

Andy shrugged. "I don't know. I'm not even sure why Dr. Hemfelt sent me here. My folks aren't alcoholics. There's been no alcohol at all in our family as far back as anyone can remember." He paused and shook his head. "Of course, Dad used to yell at us a lot, but I suppose we deserved it." Andy straightened his tie over the white cotton shirt that remained crisp and smooth even at the end of the day, a very challenging day at ALTEX Corporation. Andy had started the small computer business on his own, just five years ago, and had driven to some success by working on it "twenty-six hours" a day. "What did you think?"

"Oh, my dad was an alcoholic, no bones about it, but I don't know. I just enjoy a little beer during the day. And the way I see it, this Higher Power stuff is so much hocus-pocus. I doubt I'll come back. I've got a stack of essays on the Civil War that's brushing cobwebs off the ceiling in my office. I think I've got better uses for my time."

Both Andy Thomson and Martin Woodruff were reluctant participants in the Twelve-Step recovery process. They were both caught in the crosscurrents of opposing forces. On the one hand their denial mechanism (present in all addictions) told them, "Things are not that bad. You can handle this on your own. Just get a grip on your addiction and everything will be okay." On the other hand they were receiving not-so-gentle prodding from their therapists to open themselves to the Twelve-Step recovery process. And even more importantly they were being pushed, kicking and fighting, into recovery by that special motivating force called "hitting bottom."

Hitting Bottom

As terrible as "hitting bottom" sounds, the good news is that this realization is the first step in recovery.

Martin Woodruff hit bottom when his wife, Mary, "bottomed out," which often happens. At her wit's end, Mary heard Dr. Rick Fowler on the radio and called him and asked what she could do for her alcoholic husband. That had set in motion several weeks of planning an intervention, where people confront the alcoholic or obsessive-compulsive person under the careful direction of a trained therapist. Mary made lists of possible participants, called friends, and finally met with Dr. Fowler for a planning meeting on the Saturday morning before the intervention.

Then on Sunday morning at 9:15, right before Martin left for his ritualistic trip to the library to do research on his book, Dr. Fowler, Martin's department head, Gordon Thomas, their next-door neighbor, Ross, and their family physician, Dr. Ellis arrived at Martin's front door.

"We're here out of love and concern for you, Martin," Dr. Fowler had said, but the look on Martin's face showed he didn't believe it.

Dr. Fowler didn't let Martin's lack of receptivity stop him as he led the way to the living room and everyone sat down—just as if Martin had invited them to. "This is called an intervention, Martin. Let me explain the ground rules. We are not here to debate with you but simply to share our concerns and feelings. We're going to ask that for the next hour you simply listen . . ."

"Hour?" Martin had interrupted. "Half an hour maybe, but I've got to get to the library—my research . . ."

Dr. Fowler continued as if Martin hadn't spoken. "This is not a debate or a dialogue. We're simply sharing our concerns with you. And we're asking you to hear them."

Martin could see he was trapped. He sat back in his chair, his arms folded across his chest.

Gordon Thomas spoke first. "Martin, you're a brilliant professor and a good researcher, but I've been getting an increasing number of complaints from students about your irritability and your lack of availability. I checked the department log," he held out the book with its neat columns of careful entries, "and I find here an escalating pattern of missed lectures and missed faculty meetings."

Martin looked at the record of his work absences and shook his head. "There must be some mistake here. My student assistant probably forgot . . ."

But nobody was listening. It was Dr. Ellis's turn to talk. "When I gave you that physical last month for the renewal on your university medical insurance, you'll recall my mentioning that I noticed you had a significant weight gain, high blood pressure, and a slight enlargement of your liver. I even asked you about your drinking and I think your answer was something like, 'a couple of beers to relax on the weekend.' I told you that I felt there was more to it than that, but you wouldn't listen to me. Martin, your drinking has seriously damaged your physical condition and will shorten your life."

Martin glowered at him. Wasn't there something about doctor/patient communication being privileged? But before he could become angrier at the doctor, their neighbor Ross was talking. "You were a good neighbor when we first moved here five years ago, Martin. We even started becoming friends. But then you withdrew more and more. At first I regretted your isolation, but last summer when you came drunk to our neighborhood bar-b-que and talked to my wife in obscenities, I decided the less I saw you the better—although I missed the good visits we had when we tried to see who could come the closest to guessing the score of the Cowboys' games.

"And then there was last Halloween when Mary got me out of bed, knocking on the door at 2:00 A.M., because you'd passed out in the backyard and she couldn't carry you in."

Martin hit the arm of the chair with a bang. "What? You're making this up! That couldn't have happened without my knowing it!"

Mary confirmed it, and both Dr. Ellis and Dr. Fowler

agreed that it was entirely possible that he had drunk himself into unconsciousness.

"Okay, okay. I've heard enough." Martin ran his fingers through his shaggy beard. "Okay, maybe you've got a point. I'll cut down. Maybe I have been hitting it a little hard lately. I'll back off."

Mary looked at Dr. Fowler. He had told her this would be Martin's reaction, and they would have to hold the line. "I'm sorry, Martin," Dr. Fowler said. "We know you mean what you say right now, but we can't accept that. An addicted person simply cannot honor such promises. You must get professional in-patient treatment."

"But I'm *not* addicted . . ."

Mary didn't wait for him to finish. "I love you, Martin. I love you enough to say that if you will not agree to in-patient treatment I'm going to take the kids and separate from you. If I stay here, I'll simply be enabling the ongoing practice of your addiction."

Martin was too flabbergasted to protest. Dr. Ellis repeated the consequences of bad health and early death he had mentioned earlier, and Ross announced that if Martin ever again disturbed the neighborhood or passed out drunk he would call the police, rather than covering up for him.

Then Gordon Thomas said, "Martin, I'm on the verge of having to recommend that your contract not be renewed next year. I will delay that and see if your work performance turns around. If you refuse to go into treatment, I have no choice but to go ahead and make that decision."

Martin hunched behind his folded arms. "Okay, okay. I think you're all wrong. But I'll go pack a bag."

During that intervention Martin Woodruff hit bottom, but it was not in the way skid rowers hit bottom in the early days of Alcoholics Anonymous because we've now raised the bottom. It isn't necessary to be picked up dead drunk off an interstate highway or to lose your family and your job. Interventions are common. Some people even recognize their obsessive-compulsive behavior on their own. The bottom can be something as seemingly minor as a college student realizing his grades are slipping from too much partying, a housewife realizing she can't pay off her credit cards, or a man realizing that his romantic relationships are being damaged by his preoccupation with work. As soon as the person says, "Whoa, things are out of control, and I can't stop them. I need help!" he or she is ready to find that help.

It's important to recognize the warning signs. Early recognition that an abyss looms can help the person make the necessary changes early and avoid much worse disaster. Five types of bottoms are common: physical, emotional, spiritual, circumstantial (such as losing your job), and relational.

Warning signs that a *physical bottom* is approaching might be high blood pressure, sleeplessness, or chronic headaches. It might be your doctor saying, "You've got to slow down," or your body saying the same thing with a mild heart attack.

The approach of an *emotional bottom* may be signaled by depression, anxiety, panic attacks, or a nervous breakdown.

Recurring questions such as: "Is this all there is?" or "What's the purpose of it all?" or "Who am I?" or "Where am I going?" warn of an approaching *spiritual bottom*.

Being passed over for a promotion at work, excessive days off work, commissions falling off, constant overdraft notices from your bank, or collection calls from credit card companies are warning signs of a looming *circumstantial bottom*.

A *relational bottom* threatens if you are experiencing frequent fights with your spouse or significant other, broken relationships with your children, loss of friends, or a failing social life.

At Twelve-Step meetings you will often hear the phrase, "It takes what it takes." That means that everybody's bottom is different. Some people have to sink lower than others before they can start back up. Another phrase you will often hear is, "But for the grace of God," which is the way many people express their gratitude that they didn't have to hit the deepest bottom before they found their way to recovery.

To help our patients realize they need to make some changes, we ask them to check any of the statements below that reflect the way things are in their lives. We suggest that you also take this short quiz to see if you might be nearing a physical, emotional, spiritual, circumstantial, or relational bottom:

_____ I never seem to be at peace with money. No matter how much I have or don't have, financial insecurity haunts me continually.

_____ I feel like I am always on the outside looking in when it comes to the relationships in my life. Other people seem to have closeness, warmth, and trust in their family life. I don't.

_____ I have had a long series of bad luck. Life seems to work for other people but not for me.

_____ I always seem to be at war with someone or something in my life. If it's not my spouse, it's the I.R.S. or that unreasonable boss or that pushy neighbor or those demanding relatives.

_____ I know that there are some things and behaviors that are beginning to run out of bounds in my life, and I tell myself over and over again that I've got to buckle down and get back into control. But these New Years' resolutions never last.

_____ My life is an endless series of damage control maneuvers. I'm so busy patching leaks and steering around barriers that I never have a chance to set a meaningful course.

_____ I always feel vaguely guilty—guilty about things I'm doing and guilty about things I should be doing, but I'm not.

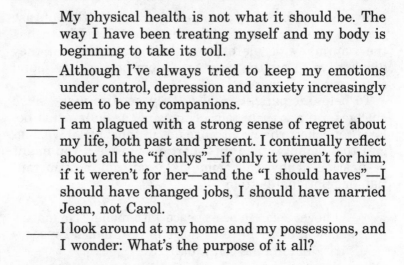

_____ My physical health is not what it should be. The way I have been treating myself and my body is beginning to take its toll.

_____ Although I've always tried to keep my emotions under control, depression and anxiety increasingly seem to be my companions.

_____ I am plagued with a strong sense of regret about my life, both past and present. I continually reflect about all the "if onlys"—if only it weren't for him, if it weren't for her—and the "I should haves"—I should have changed jobs, I should have married Jean, not Carol.

_____ I look around at my home and my possessions, and I wonder: What's the purpose of it all?

If you checked a few of these statements, you are paddling frantically to keep from slipping to the bottom. You may be suffering from an addiction to people, places, or things.

Taking Step One

Step One—admitting we are powerless over our dependencies and that our lives have become unmanageable—is a big one. The dependent person has been relying on his addiction, and ironically, the addiction may hold out the illusion that it's the one thing holding life together. Admitting powerlessness over that addiction removes all the props. Perhaps you, like Andy, have found your workaholism is killing you, but you still retain the illusion that if you work just a little harder, you'll get "it." You'll have that painful void inside filled, even if by working harder you lose the most important person in your life, as Andy lost Jennifer. This is called denial, and unfortunately, most of us deny our addictions.

Breaking out of denial, the universal enabler of all addictions, is the major psychological task of Step One. With our hospital and out-patient cases we use seven techniques to help them break out of denial. Andy found that these techniques brought major breakthroughs in this first step of his recovery.

1. Make a List of Things That Seem Unmanageable

In order to continue to break through Andy's denial, Dr. Hemfelt asked him to define addictive behavior as "bad luck," as Joe, one old-time A.A. speaker, used to do. Every time a newcomer would approach him at a meeting and say something like, "Well, I'm here; I'm attending the meetings, but I don't really know why. I'm not sure I'm an alcoholic," Joe would look the person straight in the eye and ask, "Are you having bad luck?"

A typical alcoholic, just as a typical rageaholic or compulsive spender, would look back over the past few weeks and say, "Boy, you'd better believe it. You've never heard of bad luck like mine. Let me tell you about the things that have gone wrong for me." A list of circumstantial blaming would follow.

Dr. Fowler told Dr. Martin Woodruff to make a list of the areas of his life that seemed to be haunted by "bad luck" as part of his hospital therapy. The intellectual professor, who had to know all the answers and be in perfect control of his class, sat in group therapy thinking, *If I had to show anyone the chaos in my life . . . I mean, I can write a treatise on history, but I can't balance my own checkbook and I can't carry on a conversation with my wife —people would look down on me until I'd disappear through a hole in the ground.*

Martin sat in silence, dwelling on the deepest, darkest bits of chaos that he worked the hardest to keep hidden:

- How he had begun to suffer memory lapses from his periodic drinking binges,
- How he had not been able to establish any consistent friendships with his fellow college professors,
- How he had to keep notes all over his office walls of

dates in history because they simply wouldn't stay
in his head,
- How he made his students sit in class according to
a seating chart because he could never remember
names.

These were all seemingly small, human things, but foibles he was sure would bring derision on his head if they
became known. Beyond these surface foibles there were
the even bigger issues: The fact that he and his wife had
not made love in months; the fact that a dark cloud of
anger seemed to hang between them; and the fact that
Martin feared that someday all of this personal chaos
would become transparent, bubble to the surface, and un-
dercut his professional status at the college.

We asked Andy to do the same thing. First on his list
was work. "People force me to overwork," he noted. "My
clients call me in at the last minute and then need a job
done yesterday. After all, if the computer's down, no one
can access customer records or input orders."

Next he listed relationships. "If women would just be
more tolerant, they would accommodate my needs," he
said as he put a question mark beside this area. "They're
just too demanding, too moody and irritable."

How about you?

How about you? List the unmanageable areas (like,
"My wife and I fight constantly" or "My checkbook never
seems to balance" or "There never seems to be enough
time to get done what I want to do") below. During the
next week add to that list as circumstances bring other
areas to your mind.

1. _____
2. _____
3. _____
4. _____

5. _____
6. _____
7. _____
8. _____
9. _____
10. _____

These areas of unmanageability are often the symptoms of your addiction, like Andy's workaholism and Martin's alcoholism.

2. Name Your Addiction

The first half of Step One asks us to name our addiction(s) by declaring that we are "powerless over _____."

We've found that once patients name their dependency —their slavery—they take an important stepping stone to moving out of it. One patient who had an alcoholic ex-husband had been going to Al-Anon and ACOA for years. Yet she knew something was missing; she felt stale in her recovery and seemed to be involved in difficult relationships with men.

Then her latest boyfriend crashed his car into his garage door one night after drinking heavily. "I'm not an alcoholic," he said when she confronted him about what had happened. "This is the only time I've had trouble with my drinking in the last year."

"But if you do this once every year, the potential is there," she argued. "It's like playing Russian roulette. Nine times out of ten you're okay, but the tenth time . . ."

As this middle-aged woman argued with her boyfriend, she realized that she was confronting herself more than him. She'd had quite a few bouts with excessive drinking over the past years. This drinking had seemed minimal in comparison to her husband, who had remained an alcoholic until his death, but she had to admit that she drank quite heavily herself.

The next week she walked into Dr. Meier's office and immediately pulled an A.A. silver desire chip out of her purse.

Dr. Meier was surprised to see the coin, since members of A.A. use these chips to signify that they have decided, "I'm going to commit to abstain from alcohol, one day at a time. I am going to commit to the program." As far as the doctor knew, this woman had never attended an A.A. meeting, just Al-Anon and ACOA.

"I've crossed over the hall," she quickly explained. "I now attend A.A. as well as Al-Anon and ACOA meetings. I've picked up my desire chip and I intend never to drink again.

"God works in strange ways," she continued. "The day I made that decision I opened up a meditational and read the statement for July 4: 'The price of personal freedom is to name my slavery.'

"I feel that freedom now."

Each of us has a choice. We can name our addiction or we can continue to dodge the issue as another patient of ours has. This sixty-year-old divorced businesswoman had already been to multiple counselors before she came to see Dr. Hemfelt. She had aborted counseling after the first few sessions because each of these counselors told her, "You suffer from codependency." After talking to her each counselor could see that she was overly controlling of her new husband and her subordinates at work.

The word *codependency* was abhorrent to this woman, since she associated it with words like *passive, submissive, a nonentity*.

Yet she made an appointment with Dr. Hemfelt after she read our book *We Are Driven*. "I can see myself as driven," she said during the first counseling session.

Dr. Hemfelt knew why. To this woman drivenness sounded strong, assertive, and consistent with the new image of womanhood she had fought to carve out for herself. She was unconsciously playing that old comedian's game, "You can call me John. You can call me son. But don't call me Johnson." Don't call me what I am.

We're not sure that we can help this woman, since she is so unwilling to confront the deep emotional dependency that underlies her apparent independence. Yet we know she's got to be willing to name her addiction. So must each of us. The following list identifies eighteen common addictions. Do any of the unmanageable areas of your life reflect one or more of these addictions to people, places, or things? Check the ones that do.

Common Addictive Agents

_____ Alcohol or drugs

_____ Work, achievement, and success

_____ Money addictions, such as overspending, gambling, hoarding

_____ Control addictions, especially if they surface in personal, sexual, family, and business relationships

_____ Food addictions

_____ Sexual addictions

_____ Approval dependency (the need to please people)

_____ Rescuing patterns toward other persons

_____ Dependency on toxic relationships (relationships that are damaging and hurtful)

_____ Addiction to physical illness (hypochondria)

_____ Excessive reliance on exercise and physical conditioning

_____ Preoccupation with cosmetics, clothes, cosmetic surgery, trying to look good on the outside

_____ Obsession with academic pursuits and relying on your mind and on an intellectual approach to life

> (rather than your mind being in harmony with,
> and balanced by, your emotions)
> _____ Religiosity or religious legalism (preoccupation
> with the form, the rules, the rituals, and the regu-
> lations of religion rather than the true spiritual
> essence of a religious faith)

Don't be surprised if you check more than one of these
addictions. Most of us are poly-addicted; more than one
obsessive-compulsive behavior holds us in its grips. Our
secondary addictions will show up months or years down
the line. Some of these more subtle or deeply buried compulsions will even emerge when we do our Step Four inventory.

Our patients will grudgingly say, "Well, I'm a little bit
of a workaholic." We've found that overcoming denial is a
continual process. We've chipped a crack in their armor of
denial, but it will take some reinforcements to break the
armor completely.

3. Look at the Losses.

Make a list of losses for each area of unmanageability
or possible addiction as you work on Step One of your
Twelve-Step journey. Andy noted his wacky sleep patterns. He remembered those nights when, after he finally
managed to fall asleep he would waken a few hours later
—unable to go back to sleep. He would simply lie there,
eyes wide awake with a lot of anxious thoughts spinning
through his head.

And his appetite loss. No matter how often he reminded
himself of the importance of a well-balanced diet to his
physical training program, he simply couldn't force himself to eat, and he was losing weight and muscle strength.

And his weakening faith. Although he was a devoted
Christian, his faith had seemed to deteriorate into a vast
maze of do's and don'ts with no real spiritual vitality. He
felt spiritually dead on the inside.

And then there was Jennifer. He couldn't deny the loss of that relationship.

Martin Woodruff also made a list of his losses. Once he identified his dependencies as true addictions and not merely "bad luck," he was able to think of quite a few losses: "I've been caught in a war with my department head for the last six months. Seems like he's down on me constantly and I don't know why. My wife's threatening to move out and I don't know why. Bad luck? Yeah, but more than bad luck. Things around me are out of control and I don't know how to fix them. I feel okay—I'm breathing, walking, eating—but my doctor isn't so pleased with me either. It's like nobody's happy with anything about me."

We often suggest that our patients solicit a list of losses from someone else—a spouse, a boss, a friend. Frequently these people will be able to confront us with losses we are unable to see or recognize.

How about you? List the losses from your addiction below.

1. _____
2. _____
3. _____
4. _____
5. _____

A list of losses often helps break a wider crack in that armor of denial. Sometimes, when our patients still refuse to name their addiction (some will say, for instance, "I have been told by my therapist, Dr. Fowler, that I'm a spendaholic or an overeater, but I still don't believe it."), we ask them to look for divine inspiration. We suggest that they say a simple prayer, like, "I can't see this issue on my own human power. I'm asking you, God, to remove the blinders from my eyes." Often that's exactly what happens in the next weeks or months.

4. Say It Out Loud

"I have discovered that I am powerless over people, places, and things" is often heard in recovery groups. We ask our patients to say statements that acknowledge the unmanageability in their lives and their need to surrender as they work on Step One. Dr. Hemfelt asked Andy to write, "My life is unmanageable. I am powerless over my addiction to workaholism. I cannot control my own workaholism. My workaholism has cost me significant losses." These negative affirmations could be thought of as a sort of confession.

This exercise should have three parts to it. First, write: "I acknowledge that I, by my individual human effort alone, am powerless over my dependence on _____." This is the formal naming of the addiction. In the second part of the exercise write: "As a consequence of this addiction to _____, my life has become painful and unmanageable."

Then in the third part, write your own statement of surrender and yielding. For example Andy wrote the following statement to surrender his workaholism and legalism: "I can't prove my right to exist or my worthiness through my own human endeavors. I surrender and let go of that compulsive need to prove my own worth."

In order to reinforce the reality of these acknowledgements, they should be spoken out loud to appropriate persons in your support network. Your spoken acknowledgement of your dependencies and the group's confirmation of them are important steps to keeping you out of further denial. Dr. Fowler suggested that Martin Woodruff take his list of losses and acknowledge them to his hospital therapy group. His job—in jeopardy. His wife—threatening to leave. The keen mind that had been so useful to him—floundering. Martin shuddered as he thought of his forgetfulness and the feeling that his mind was short-circuiting.

"Wow, it must be scary," Kathryn Markham, the middle-aged woman who had acknowledged her addiction to overeating, said, "not knowing why all this is happening to you."

Rafe, another group member, nodded. "Yeah, I know the sense of having the carpet pulled out from under you when your wife threatens to leave you. That's what got me here. Enid stood at the door with her bags packed and gave me the choice, sort of a one-woman intervention, I guess."

But it was Mavis, her voice as soft as her curly blond hair and pale pink jogging pants, who said, "Martin, I know this will be hard for you to hear, but it sounds to me like 90 percent of what you're describing is due to your alcoholism. I know—I was married to an alcoholic for fifteen years until he died of cirrhosis of the liver. I could have told Mary's story."

Rafe agreed. "Yeah, face it man—it sounds like alcoholism." The next day Martin came to admit his powerlessness over alcohol, but he still wanted to manage the people around him and the things going on around him. He finally came to see that "When I try to make the world rotate around me, things get bad. When I begin to surrender and let go—not try to be the director of the universe—things start going a little bit better."

The compulsive person needs confrontation because he will always look at his unmanageability through the glasses of denial. Always there will be the impulse to minimize, rationalize, justify, or downplay how unmanageable the addiction has been and what it has cost in terms of losses.

This is the value of a group session. The group can empathize and at the same time reflect back to the speaker what he's really saying and help him identify the core of his problem. For someone not in the hospital, a similar situation could be created in small bits and pieces in the broader fellowship of a group like Al-Anon, CODA, or ACOA with a program sponsor, or with a trusted friend.

Some Christians have become accountability partners to one another. They meet once a week—or even talk long distance over the phone—to discuss the events of that week and their struggle to maintain the Christian walk.

Each of us needs to have people around us who will keep prying open those blinders of denial. This process may span months and years of time. Our patients often report that at six months, twelve months, eighteen months, and twenty-four months they could look back down the road and see even more of the unmanageable areas of their lives. They can see more at each six-month interval; more at twelve months than at six, and more at twenty-four months than at eighteen months.

This is a very healthy process because if we received an instantaneous vision of the true weight of what our compulsive behavior has cost us and how unmanageable our lives have become, many of us would be so overwhelmed we would be paralyzed and couldn't work on our recovery. People in recovery often say, "God reveals to me just enough that I can deal with it at this point in time. He gives me just what I can handle."

The major breakthrough came for Andy when he realized that, "Yes, my life is unmanageable and the more I try to manage it with my old compulsive, perfectionistic workaholic techniques, the more unmanageable it becomes." He then took Step One: He admitted he was powerless over his dependencies—that his life had become unmanageable.

The spiritual principle of Step One is a paradox: We gain control by giving up control. Or you might say, We win by losing. This dynamic is expressed in Luke 9:23–25: "Then He said to them all, 'If anyone desires to come after Me, let him deny himself, and take up his cross daily, and follow Me. For whoever desires to save his life will lose it, but whoever loses his life for My sake will save it. For what advantage is it to a man if he gains the whole world, and is himself destroyed or lost?' "

Now that we are willing to let go, and admit that we

can't control our addiction, the armor around our denial
begins to fall away, but we must be careful or we will
unconsciously put it on again. Dealing with denial is a
continuous process, which goes back and forth, ebbing
with the tide. It's like building a sand castle on the shore
of the ocean. When the tide comes in, it can take away
much of what we've carved out for ourselves, a turret of
the castle, the drawbridge, or the entire fortification.

That's why every Twelve-Step group begins by the
members naming themselves. "Hi," they say. "I'm Joe. I'm
a compulsive gambler." Even though Joe realized his addiction five years ago, he needs to name and rename it to
keep the armor of denial from building back up again.

5. The Affirmation of Others

We need to feel affirmation from others that it's okay to
acknowledge our addictions, and this is the fifth of our
seven techniques for taking Step One. Researchers believe that one of the deep fears behind all addictions is the
feeling, "If I ever let go of my control addiction—my need
to make the world rotate around me—something cata-
strophic will happen. People will not like me if I don't
make them like me. I must manipulate others into liking
me or they will reject me." There is also a deep fear that if
I admit my unmanageability to another person that person will reject me. Fear of rejection and abandonment is
at the base of all addictions.

Andy believed that if he told people about the things
that weren't working in his life, people would judge him
as harshly as he judged himself, as harshly as his father
had judged him, and as harshly as he imagined God
judged him. Yet when Andy mentioned some of the ways
his life was unmanageable at an ACOA meeting, the response surprised him.

"Andy, I like you so much better when you admit your
weaknesses than when you try to hold on to your perfectionism," Kathryn Markham said to him.

"Yeah," another person added. "Now I can feel close to

you. I couldn't feel that I had anything in common with someone who never made any mistakes." The man paused and gave a big grin. "Of course, you still might try going for a wrinkle in your slacks or a hair out of place some-time." The group laughed, and remarkably, Andy laughed with them—but he wasn't ready to run his fingers through his carefully styled hair.

After the session Jo, the teenager who had talked about her spending addiction at Andy's first ACOA meeting, hugged him. "Thank you so much for sharing. I sort of had the idea that if I could just get as firm a grip on things as you had, people would like me. Now I see it wasn't work-ing for you either."

Andy went back home in a daze, hardly able to take in what he seemed to be learning; he was better liked, better accepted, when he wasn't perfect. His humanness, fallibil-ity, and vulnerability, which he had worked so hard to cover up, were attractive to other people.

Martin Woodruff was even more sure than Andy that no one would accept his foibles if they became known. In the hospital therapy group we asked him to sit in a chair in the center of the room, then we asked everyone in the group to walk away to the farthest corners of the room. "Martin," Dr. Fowler said, "this illustrates your fear, a fear that if you start to share yourself with these people, they'll pull away from you.

"Now I want everyone to come back and sit in a circle around you, and I want you to state your fears."

Reluctantly, Martin read his Step One statement. "I admit that I am powerless over my dependence on alco-hol. It has cost me the security I once had in my job, my ability to think straight, my self-respect, and my relation-ship with my wife." When he finished he was certain ev-eryone would walk away again, but to his amazement, they all stood up, moved closer to him, and put their arms around him.

"Now, Martin," Dr. Fowler said, as the group released him, leaving a pink glow under his beard, "this illustrates the true feelings of the group. As you take down the mask, take down the walls and the barriers, we move closer to you. You become a part of our family, and we can actually reach you, which we couldn't do before."

Once we've admitted to others that things are unmanageable, it's essential that we hear back from them that it's okay to admit this. This is why a Twelve-Step based group is important to recovery; the members have faced the unmanageability of their lives. Being accepted by a group to whom we've told the "awful" truth is a beautiful, grace-filled moment in the recovery process. Instead of feeling rejection, we feel people moving closer to us.

This can be done in nonverbal ways—a pat on the back or a quick hand-squeeze. Nodding encouragement to someone sharing his story, someone who had expected everyone to draw back, can be a light-filled moment. After-meeting hugs from someone who has been in the same place and feels your pain can be enormously important.

6. A Letter of Forgiveness

The sixth important step in the process is for the addicted person to write himself a letter of forgiveness and compassion about the unmanageability in his life. Throughout the recovery process, in addition to having to combat denial, we are also having to combat shame. Addictions bring shame upon us and they originate out of an old, archaic shame base. As we face our unmanageability in Step One, we can have feelings of deep shame and ask ourselves, "How could I?" "How dare I?" "I shouldn't have." "I'm such an awful person." "If I were any good, I couldn't have done this to myself or my loved ones." Facing unmanageability puts us at extremely high risk to start self-shaming and self-blaming. This letter is the antidote.

Three key elements are essential.

First, express understanding to yourself. Don't shame yourself about the losses, simply try to give yourself a chance to acknowledge and grieve the pain. Extend a loving hand to yourself, saying, "I know you hurt, I know about the pain."

Writing this letter was an enormous struggle for Andy. He made two or three failed attempts but each time he started, he only got one or two lines of compassion out to himself before he would begin to scold and chastize. He understood Dr. Hemfelt's instructions; he knew he was supposed to be expressing empathy and compassion for the pain of his losses. The lack of sleep, the weariness, the feeling that nothing was really worthwhile, the loneliness after Jennifer refused to see him anymore. But after a couple of lines his pen would go back into the legalistic, self-shaming preaching. "What you did was bad. You shouldn't have done this."

At last he went to Dr. Hemfelt. "Well, I haven't managed to write my letter, but I have learned something. I really see how deeply ingrained this legalism stuff is in me. I can tell myself I need to be tender and compassionate with myself and others, but my mind isn't buying it, thank you. I can really see how deeply ingrained my self-criticism is."

Dr. Hemfelt nodded. "Andy, you just stated at least three important insights you've gained. You've recognized your addiction. You've realized that your intellect won't solve your problem. And you've discovered a road map; you know you must be more compassionate with yourself or you will never overcome your self-criticism.

"Start your letter again," Dr. Hemfelt told Andy, "and begin by congratulating yourself on gaining these understandings. The letter doesn't have to be pages and pages. When you've said all the good you can say and feel yourself starting to criticize, just stop and go on to the next section of your letter."

If you have identified an addiction, why not take a piece of paper and begin to write your own letter. Start by congratulating yourself on breaking through denial and determining to walk through the Twelve Steps and the techniques in this book with us. Then remind yourself of the pain that this addiction (or addictions) has caused you and allow yourself to grieve over these losses. Tell the child inside you, "I know you hurt. I understand the pain. I'm sorry."

Then do as Dr. Hemfelt told Andy to do. Realize that you have tried to change your ways for a couple of years now. You have just used the wrong methods.

Second, express empathy about the pain and difficulty of failed past efforts at self-control. Most people who suffer from obsessive-compulsive behavior have made valiant efforts at trying to change certain patterns by their own willpower, as we mentioned earlier. Instead of shaming yourself over these failed attempts, it's very important to extend empathy and compassion to yourself about the pain of those previous failed efforts at self-control. This helps set the stage for self-surrender because we see how our own efforts have failed.

Andy mentally went down the list of his previous efforts: willpower, intellect, shaming himself. None of them had worked. "I know I've tried to curb this addiction myself," he wrote. "Yet nothing worked. It was painful to learn that, but now I'm convinced that I can't do it alone. It takes 'willpower plus.'"

In your letter be sure to express the same kind of empathy to yourself. You tried to change. It didn't work, but you did try.

Finally, recognize that in the practice of all your dependencies and addictions—as destructive as they might have been—at the time you were doing the very best you knew how, considering your resources and your background.

This doesn't excuse or defend the addiction, but it's a powerful statement of acceptance and compassion. Often our addiction originates out of painful emotional patterns that were established early in our childhood experiences. The addictive and compulsive coping mechanisms that we gravitated toward in adolescence or adulthood were our own best efforts to address that pain and to try to make sense out of the nonsense of a dysfunctional family. It's not that we seek to blame that original family, but that we must avoid self shame.

Andy found expressing compassion to himself very difficult. His parents hadn't been accepting, and he had never let others see any need for them to respond to him with compassion so he'd never received acceptance. At least it was an improvement for him to stop blaming himself for not working harder, even if he couldn't say too much that was glowing and laudatory about himself.

When you write your letter, remind yourself that you did the best you knew how—considering your situation and your experience.

When Andy's letter was finally done, he read it to the group at Dr. Hemfelt's request. Robert Hemfelt commented, "Andy, you've come a long way in that letter." Kathryn Markham added, "I think you're a lot better person than you give yourself credit for, Andy. Talk about compassion. You claim to dislike animals, but yesterday I saw you chase a cat away from the bird nest in the tree outside the clinic."

Andy grinned. "Thanks, Kathryn. What worries me is that now that I've seen how harshly I was judging myself, I'm afraid I was judging others just as harshly. Maybe I can start working on that too."

Dr. Hemfelt held up his hand, "Whoa, Andy, as usual you're running way ahead of us. Accepting yourself will lead to accepting others, but for the moment, stay focused on yourself. Let's avoid that phrase, 'work on.' All we need to do in this step is let go."

And that's what it's all about. To let go. To admit that our lives have become unmanageable and we are powerless over our dependencies.

Step Two

Came to believe that a Power greater than ourselves could restore us to sanity.

M om, *go*. I'm fine." Jason picked up his fork and dived into the hot beef sandwich Kathryn Markham had just set before him.

". . . And there's a plate in the refrigerator for your dad. If he comes home all he has to do is put it in the microwave for two or three minutes." Kathryn looked around uncertainly. "You're sure you have everything you need? Do you want a red apple or green apple to go with that?"

"Mom! I said go on. I'll get what I want." The sixteen-year-old boy held up his hand when his mom started to open her mouth. "No, I don't need any more milk."

"Right." Kathryn smiled and went out to her car. What would she do when he left for college in two years? When her oldest, Steve, joined the army it wasn't too bad, because she still had Polly and Jason at home. But Polly got married two years ago, and that just left Jason and he was growing fast. And Henry. Kathryn shook her head as she braked for a red light. She'd finally given up trying to get her husband to A.A. With an empty nest looming nearer, she had finally realized that she would just have to concentrate on getting her own life together. She had been going to Al-Anon for two years now and Overeaters

48

Anonymous for almost a year. She put her hand to her stomach under her seat belt. Hmm. Well, she'd never be a fashion model, but there was definitely progress there.

Then just three months ago she and Dr. Meier had been exploring her family of origin in greater depth, and he shocked her by suggesting she go to ACOA as well. "But, Doctor, my parents weren't alcoholic. At least, I don't think so. They were awful quiet ones if they were. They were just sort of 'there,' in their separate bedrooms, going their separate ways. They didn't see much of each other, and I didn't see much of them. I was really raised by my grandmother. And *she* didn't drink!"

Even alone in the car, Kathryn gave a bitter little laugh at the thought of her grandmother touching alcohol—even for communion. "Grandma had the Bible. She didn't need anything else," she had explained to Dr. Meier. "She got all her pleasure terrorizing my sister and me about the devil, sin, and hell. 'God's watching you,' she'd always say, and the clear implication was, 'with a lightning bolt poised right at you.' Every time I messed anything up I remember looking over my shoulder and wondering, 'Was this the sin God was going to get me for?'"

Kathryn put her thoughts on hold as she pulled into the parking lot of the old grocery store, which an A.A. group had remodeled for their meetings and had offered rooms to Al-Anon, Al-Ateen, and ACOA groups as well. Just as well she had done a bit of reviewing, because she had agreed to tell her story tonight, and she hadn't really prepared in much detail.

Dr. Meier would probably approve of that, she thought; he always told her she worried too much, about being in control of everything. Well, she hoped someone, her Higher Power maybe, was in control of this talk, because she sure wasn't.

After the usual preliminaries, Kathryn found herself in front of the group, telling her story. "I'd like to talk about Step Two, 'Came to believe that a Power greater than ourselves could restore us to sanity' today.

"When I first began my Twelve-Step journey, I had some trouble accepting the notion that my life apart from God was a life of insanity as Step Two suggests. Sure I knew I had a food problem. I knew I couldn't manage my marriage. But insane? Needing to be restored to sanity? That was tough to buy.

"An early sponsor offered two helpful tips. First, she said being restored to sanity simply means being made whole or complete. Second, she told me that the insanity we speak of in recovery does not have much to do with lunacy or asylums. Instead she defined insanity as doing the same thing over and over again but somehow expecting different results. I knew that I was repeating the old patterns of addictive control and magically expecting that this time I wouldn't bump into the painful consequences. That was a definition of insanity I could understand and relate to.

"For me the Power greater than myself was God. I guess I believed in Him when I was a kid. At least I believed in Grandma—I'm not sure I realized there was a difference. I joined the church real young because she wanted me to. No one ever asked me if I wanted to. And then at Vacation Bible School they always had these checklists whether you read your Bible, prayed, brought an offering, all that stuff. Bringing visitors was a real big thing; they really wanted you to bring them, and I wanted to please. I hadn't brought any visitors, so I lied. 'I brought twelve,' I said. When they asked me where they were, I said, 'Well, in other classes.' So at the assembly at the end of the day they marched me down front and pinned an orchid on me for bringing twelve visitors.

"You know, I should have realized right then that God was a forgiving God, because I wasn't struck with lightning and the teacher didn't even ask my visitors to stand up!" Several of her listeners laughed at that, and Kathryn paused for a sip of water. "Well, when I was in high school, Grandma wasn't around quite so much—I think she had gone to live with my uncle or something—so I told

my mother I wasn't going back to church. I believed there
was a God, but I couldn't cope with Him. I wasn't at all
sure Grandma wasn't right—God probably *was* dangling
me over the fiery pit on a string as thin as a spider's web,
but I just decided to have fun until the string broke.

"But you know what? It wasn't a whole lot of fun. It's
like so many people tell marriage counselors—we can't
live with each other, and we can't live without each other.
I couldn't live with God, and I couldn't live without Him."

Often our patients find themselves in Kathryn's predicament. They've rejected God, but they feel an emptiness
inside, a hole in their soul. At some deep, perhaps inex-
pressible, level, they know that they need God to restore
wholeness (sanity) to their badly fragmented lives.

Losing God

Taking Step One brought us face to face with the truth
that we are powerless. This leads naturally to Step Two.
There has to be something or someone out there with
power. I'm not holding this universe together. Something
else must be. This discovery is not unique to obsessive-
compulsive persons. It is common to all people: All humanity has lost God, all humanity has tried to substitute
other gods for Him, and all humanity must again find the
authentic God.

Most of our patients lost their relationship with God in
one of four ways:

The Addictions Themselves Became False Gods or Idols, Which Were Pursued and Worshipped

These addictions expanded to preoccupy progressively
larger portions of our time, attention, and energy until
they replaced God as the center of our lives. The energy
we invest in our addictions gradually pushes aside our
receptivity to God, even if we retain our spiritual convictions.

The problem is that, because of our fallen nature, we have often reached too low in our quest for God so we put little powerless gods in His place: our intellects, our material possessions, a spouse or dating partner, a chemical substance. Andy Thomson is an example of a Christian who does not trust God. He had spiritual convictions galore. Yet, in the day-to-day struggle to feel whole (to be "sane"), Andy relied on the false gods of his computer business, his exploitation of a series of dating relationships, his physical conditioning, and his ritualistic practice of the rules of his religion. Andy affirmed one Higher Power with his statements of faith. Yet Andy's addictive actions betrayed his emotional allegiance to a radically different set of gods.

Pascal, the 17th century mathematician and philosopher for whom a modern computer language has been named, said, "People, in trying to avoid God, create diversions. These diversions then are created so they do not have to confront God."

That's just what Kathryn Markham was also doing. She had tried her grandmother's faith in God and it seemingly didn't work. In her confusion she used her family and food to fill her spiritual void. For a while such a substitute will work. When Kathryn's children were small and before her overeating really got out of control, she was simply too busy to worry much about her spiritual condition or the emptiness of her marriage. Now she must face these things or spiral further into her addictions.

Kathryn, as with all addicted persons, is like someone who has broken through the ice as they are walking across a frozen river. They are sinking into the black, icy waters because of their own weight and because of the swirling of the current beneath them and the weight of their own saturated clothing. Everything seems to be against them. Kathryn has struck out twice, and she fears that one more strike out will put her out of the game permanently.

Yet Bill Wilson, founder of Alcoholics Anonymous, was

in an even more desperate situation before he overcame his alcoholism. His wife, his friends, and his doctors had all given up on him, and he, like Kathryn, had long ago given up on a personal God.

"When they [ministers and world's religions] talked of a God personal to me, who was love, superhuman strength and direction, I became irritated and my mind snapped shut against such a theory.

"I had always believed in a Power greater than myself," he says in the *Big Book*. "I had often pondered these things. I was not an atheist. Few people really are, for that means blind faith in the strange proposition that this universe originated in a cipher and aimlessly rushes nowhere. My intellectual heroes, the chemists, the astronomers, even the evolutionists, suggested vast laws and forces at work. Despite contrary indications, I had little doubt that a mighty purpose and rhythm underlay all. . . ."[1]

Martin Woodruff, the history professor and student of the human predicament, had also been baffled by the prospect of a Higher Power. Intellectually Martin had always known there must be a higher order of life responsible for the intricacy of all creation. Yet, in his academic circles, it was not fashionable to talk about God and unthinkable to claim a personal, intimate relationship with Him. For Martin, the intellectual barriers were formidable.

How about you? Do you worship intellectualism, as Martin did? Or the false gods of money, success, alcohol or drugs?

How About You?

Check the statements below that apply to you:

_____ I believe that vast laws and forces are at work in the universe, but I don't see the hand of a personal God.

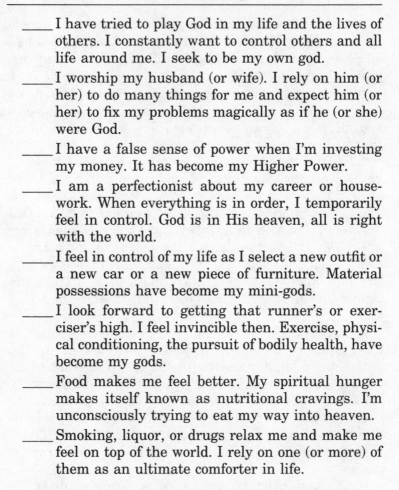

_____ I have tried to play God in my life and the lives of others. I constantly want to control others and all life around me. I seek to be my own god.

_____ I worship my husband (or wife). I rely on him (or her) to do many things for me and expect him (or her) to fix my problems magically as if he (or she) were God.

_____ I have a false sense of power when I'm investing my money. It has become my Higher Power.

_____ I am a perfectionist about my career or housework. When everything is in order, I temporarily feel in control. God is in His heaven, all is right with the world.

_____ I feel in control of my life as I select a new outfit or a new car or a new piece of furniture. Material possessions have become my mini-gods.

_____ I look forward to getting that runner's or exerciser's high. I feel invincible then. Exercise, physical conditioning, the pursuit of bodily health, have become my gods.

_____ Food makes me feel better. My spiritual hunger makes itself known as nutritional cravings. I'm unconsciously trying to eat my way into heaven.

_____ Smoking, liquor, or drugs relax me and make me feel on top of the world. I rely on one (or more) of them as an ultimate comforter in life.

If you checked more than one of the statements above, don't feel bad. You are not alone. All of us tend to worship the false gods of money and success. The loss of the true God and His replacement with substitute gods results in the loss of our true identity and its replacement with a false or "survival self," which we try to maintain by the practice of our addiction.

In recovery terms we could call this, "how we came _not_ to believe" in the real God. Instead we began to worship

false gods, our addictions. We admitted we were powerless over these addictions in Step One. Now we need to
renounce the addictive misuse of these people, places, and
things.

Abusive Relationships with Our Earthly Parents Have Distorted the Emotional Pictures We Hold of the Heavenly Father

Some of our patients have also lost their relationship
with God because their image of God has been distorted
by painful encounters with their human parents. This is
the second way people lose their relationship with God.
Andy Thomson was one of those patients. He realized this
after a confrontation with his father one Thursday night.

Thursday night at the Thomsons' was family night. Although Andy had lived on his own for more than ten
years, he still tried to get home every Thursday night. He
knew how much it meant to his mom. Melinda Thomson
always cooked a big dinner, real old-fashioned, homestyle
cooking—fried chicken, gravy and mashed potatoes,
homemade bread, salad, vegetables, and her specialty, apple pie. There were times when Andy wasn't very hungry
or would rather have done something else, but he felt a
special responsibility as an only child. If he didn't go
home, Mom and Dad wouldn't have anyone.

Tonight, however, he did wish he could bring the conversation to a wrap-up so he could get to his Twelve-Step
meeting. But his father, Garrick, was on one of his favorite topics—loss of standards in the church. "Do you know
why our people are living so loose these days? Because the
preachers don't lay down the law enough, that's why.
Take tithing, for example . . ."

Andy shook his head when his mother offered another
piece of pie, and as soon as his dad paused for breath he
jumped to his feet. "Great dinner, Mom! Sorry to inter-
rupt, Dad, but I've really got to go. I don't want to miss
that meeting tonight; we're having a special speaker."

"Andy," Melinda put her hand out to him. "Why do you

go to those meetings all the time? I don't see the sense in them. You're not sick like those people. You're not addicted to anything, you just got too tired. You work too hard."

Andy opened his mouth to try—for the hundredth time —to explain to his mother, but Garrick jumped in with a crash of his fist on the table. "I've had enough of this tomfoolery! You've been brainwashed! That doctor is just bleeding you for your money. No son of mine is sick; they just keep you going to those meetings to make you think you are. All you have to do is stand on your own two feet. Work hard and obey God's laws—that's all anybody needs to get through life just fine." His voice and his color rose as he continued. Andy began backing quietly away, as he had done all his life when his father got into one of his rages. When he was little he'd hidden under the table, but he was too big for that now. He said a quick good-bye and headed for the front door.

Andy told Dr. Hemfelt about that confrontation at his next counseling session. The doctor listened intently and then said, "How was the little boy in you feeling as you walked out of the house that night?"

"Mad," Andy replied immediately. "I'm tired of my dad's rages. I'm tired of him telling me what to do. I felt that way when I was twelve, so you can imagine how it makes me feel now."

"I imagine you must have felt as humiliated as you did when you were a little boy and crawled under the table to hide."

"Just about. At least he didn't ridicule me as he used to." Andy let out a sigh of relief.

"It probably wasn't a good idea for you to confront your dad at that moment, when you were so angry. But I'd like you to do that now in this moment of therapy, Andy," Dr. Hemfelt suggested. "Go ahead and tell me what you as an adult want to tell your dad. Then maybe next time you'll be able to set some appropriate boundaries with him."

"It's no use, Doc. My dad would never hear me. Believe

me, I've tried a couple of times." Andy put his hands out in a gesture of uselessness.

"But I'll hear you, Andy. God will hear you. And most importantly of all, the little boy inside of you will have the opportunity to hear the adult Andy stand up to his dad. Once those internal boundaries are set, it isn't as important for your dad to hear you because you'll naturally react to him in a different way."

In the next ten minutes Andy carried on a therapeutic monologue with the imaginary presence of his dad in Dr. Hemfelt's office. Andy mentioned several times when he had felt he had suffered from his dad's rage and unfair ultimatums, like the time he had qualified to compete in the state track finals and his dad had refused to let him go because the meet conflicted with a young people's retreat at church. "I'm tired of your always running over me. I was never allowed to be my own person. I have my own beliefs and thoughts and convictions now, and I want you to understand how important my recovery journey is to me. I know you disagree with that, but I want you to know that this is the single most important thing that's going on in my life now. It's life changing and I will continue it, whether you like it or not. I'm my own person now."

Finally, Andy sat straight up in his chair and said, "Dad, you've been a guide to me most of my life. I've always looked up to you, even though I've been frightened of you most of the time. I have to let go of you as my god.

"In the past I've never questioned either you or God— I've been too paralyzed by fear. But now I'm coming to believe in a God who allows me to ask questions. I'm going to try to find that God and understand Him better."

In counseling sessions after that Dr. Hemfelt and Andy began to look at his image of God. Andy feared that if he ever stepped out of bounds, God would explode as his father did. The little boy who hid under the table from his dad was also hiding from the wrath of God. And as Andy grew older his fear of his dad and God translated into his working harder and harder at his religion. More prayer, more church attendance, more adherence to superficial rules. And the more religious works he crammed into his life, the less room there was for a loving, compassionate God. Andy's image of God had been distorted by his relationship with his father.

Since parents are our earliest representations of God, we see God through their actions toward us. It's almost as if we are seeing Him through a distorted set of glasses. In fact, a major recovery writer, Chuck C., wrote a book called *A New Pair of Glasses,* in which he said his own spiritual conversion and rebirth was like taking off one old pair of glasses through which he had been seeing God, and putting on a different set.[2] God was not the one who changed. This man's perspective of God changed during his Twelve-Step recovery process.

What pair of glasses are you using to see God? Think about your mother and father or another person who raised you. Put that person's name in the blanks below:

1. I question whether or not _____ genuinely loves me and accepts me.
2. I see _____ as a harsh, stern disciplinarian, and I fear his or her disapproval, punishment, and wrath.
3. I am angry and bitter at _____ about my past failures, illnesses, and disappointments. I wonder why _____ has not spared me from these?
4. _____ seems distant and remote from me.
5. I imagine _____'s agenda is filled with people and things far more important than I. Surely _____ doesn't notice me.
6. Some part of me feels so unworthy. I question if I could ever win _____'s love and approval.

Now go back and read each of the above statements out loud, inserting God's name in the ones that apply to your image of Him. In each of these descriptions you are seeing your heavenly Father through the filter of your old experiences with an earthly father or mother.

The Escalating Unmanageability of Your Obsessive-Compulsive Lifestyle Has Convinced You That "There Is No God Whom I Can Trust"

The third way our patients become disillusioned is because God doesn't seem to rescue them from their addictions. Andy Thomson had drifted away from God. Subconsciously he was blaming God, and himself, for not being able to deal with his workaholism. The tapes that played within him went something like this: "If my faith were real I'd be able to deal with this problem. If God was really there for me, He and I could do it together. Either God doesn't care or I don't really have a meaningful relationship with Him."

As we mentioned in chapter one, God doesn't always perform instant miracles in someone's life. The *Big Book* makes this very clear. Many alcoholics have concluded, it says, "that in order to recover they must acquire an immediate and overwhelming 'God-consciousness' followed at once by a vast change in feeling and outlook. Among our rapidly growing membership of thousands of alcoholics such transformations, though frequent, are by no means the rule. Most of our experiences are what the psychologist William James calls the 'educational variety' because they develop slowly over a period of time."[3] The sanity and emotional integrity that God restores to us may come through small progressive steps, spanning over weeks, months, or even years of recovery. We must be patient and compassionate with ourselves as we allow this restoration miracle to unfold in God's timing.

All Addictions Are Founded On, to Some Extent, a Belief in Magic

The prescription drug addict believes that the right pill or combination of pills will magically transform his mood —help him to deal with a problem or the pain of a problem—better. As we buy into the illusion of this magic, the fourth way we become disillusioned with God, we limit God's ability to work in our lives because we are relying on the addiction, rather than on God.

Once we realize why we have lost our relationship with God, we are at a critical crossroad. Our old dependencies and false gods still beckon to us. Yet we have begun to see the falseness of those promises and have caught a glimmer of the true Light. We may be like the young man at an A.A. meeting who told an old-timer of all his struggles to find a Higher Power in the group or in his program sponsor or in the Twelve Steps themselves or even in the congregation of his local church. "I hear you going to all the branch offices," the old-timer said. "Why don't you just go to the main office?"

We Came to Believe

Bill Wilson, the founder of A.A., found himself at this crossroad in 1934. A stock broker by trade he had endured the pain of October of 1929, the beginning of the Great Depression, when the stock market fell to an all-time low. Some of his friends jumped out of windows. Bill went to a local bar, a habit he had begun in college and leaned on ever more steadily in his years as a stockbroker.

In the next five years alcohol became more and more of an escape for him. By 1934 doctors told his wife that he would either develop a wet brain from the effects of his alcoholism, perhaps in less than a year, or die of heart failure during delirium tremens.

Fear kept him sober for a while, but by November of 1934 he resumed drinking and was back in the addiction cycle again, doomed, most thought, to remain there until his death.

Then in the end of November an old school friend and drinking buddy, Ebby Thatcher, who had been facing involuntary commitment for alcoholic insanity, called Bill W. He was sober, he told Bill. He wanted to come visit him.

Bill agreed, foreseeing an evening of drinking like old times, regardless of what Thatcher claimed.

Yet Bill noticed something different about Ebby when he came to the apartment that afternoon. The gray pallor of Ebby's skin was gone. His eyes were unusually alive.

Bill pushed a drink across the kitchen table to test Ebby's resolution. He refused. "I've got religion," Ebby said simply.

Bill W. expected Thatcher to rave on. Instead he simply told him his story. Two men had appeared in court and asked the judge to suspend Ebby's commitment. Then they told him of a simple religious idea and a practical program of action. In the next couple of weeks Ebby Thatcher began to attend meetings of an Evangelical Christian organization, the Oxford Group, at Calvary Episcopal Church in New York City.

That had been two months earlier. The result was evident. His friend sat before him, and he said that God had done for him what he could not do for himself. His human will had failed. Doctors had pronounced him incurable. He had admitted defeat. Then he had been "raised from the dead," as Bill W. says in the *Big Book,* "suddenly taken from the scrap heap to a level of life better than the best he had ever known."[4]

In the next days Bill Wilson began a spiritual search that ended one night after he had been admitted to the hospital for delirium tremens. He tells of this experience in the *Big Book:* "There I humbly offered myself to God, as I then understood Him, to do with me as He would. I placed myself unreservedly under His care and direction. I admitted for the first time that of myself I was nothing;

that without Him I was lost. I ruthlessly faced my sins and became willing to have my new-found Friend take them away, root and branch. I have not had a drink since."[5]

Progression of Faith

In the more than fifty-five years since then, millions of other men and women have made that same decision as they have recovered from all types of addictions, ranging from drug dependence to relationship codependency to workaholism. The phrase, "We came to believe" in Step Two suggests a progression of faith that evolves over time. Members of A.A. say it this way:

First, we came. We physically showed up at an A.A. meeting and we stumbled through the door.

As we often hear in Twelve-Step groups, "Bring the body and the mind will follow," or as Woody Allen is quoted as saying, "Ninety percent of life is showing up."

Second, we came to. We sobered up and came to our senses. We began to experience emotional sobriety.

Although our dependencies cannot be overcome entirely by willpower and making right choices, this part of the step must be made by force of will. We must choose to place our addictions in a sufficient state of surrender so that we can begin to make rational choices. Only a small percentage of the brain is under conscious control. We are responsible for this part of our thought processes. The vast majority of brain function is subconscious. This large domain of subconscious functioning we can choose to reprogram through our Twelve-Step recovery program.

If we are intoxicated on any of the false gods of money, sex, power, or chemicals, these must be put into proper perspective or at least controlled enough to allow the recovery process to take root. Dr. Fowler tells of the man who came into his office and offered him a "deal." "Doctor, I'll give you six months. In that time if you can show me why I should quit drinking, I'll do it." Dr. Fowler declined.

"Unless you can abstain, at least temporarily, my reasoning won't reach you."

The addicted person will use the cop-out, "I *have* to do this; I'm addicted." The person whose walk through Step Two is genuine will say, "I choose to deal with this and ask God to empower me to abstain from addiction, one day at a time. I am responsible." The sincerity we bring to this effort to "come to" in Step Two is emphasized in the A.A. preface to the steps, which cautions, "With all the earnestness at our command, we beg of you to be fearless and thorough from the very start. Some of us have tried to hold on to our old ideas and the result was nil until we let go absolutely. Remember that we deal with alcohol—cunning, baffling, powerful! Without help it is too much for us."[6]

Third, we came to believe. We found the Higher Power who was there waiting for us all along. The warning about alcohol in the A.A. preface ends with the promise, "But there is One who has all power—that One is God. May you find Him now."[7]

How about you? Can you lay aside your distorted picture of a god who is harsh or rejecting? Can you embrace a new, authentic image of the God who loves you profoundly? Over fifty-five years ago when Bill Wilson took this step, Ebby Thatcher suggested, "Why don't you choose your own conception of God?"

That statement hit him hard, he says. "It melted the icy intellectual mountain in whose shadow I had lived and shivered many years. . . . It was only a matter of being willing to believe in a Power greater than myself. Nothing more was required of me to make my beginning. I saw that growth could start from that point. Upon a foundation of complete willingness I might build what I saw in my friend. Would I have it? Of course I would!

"Thus was I convinced that God is concerned with us humans when we want Him enough. At long last I saw, I felt, I believed. Scales of pride and prejudice fell from my eyes. A new world came into view."[8]

We often give a challenge similar to Ebby Thatcher's to our patients as they are taking this second step. "If you are not at peace with God, describe the god you would like to believe in," we say.

Their descriptions are often alike:

- "I want a god who will love me no matter what I do. I know that doesn't sound reasonable, but that's what I want."
- "I want to know a god who cares about me personally. He will hear my deepest needs and concerns and respond to them."

It's no coincidence that the God they describe is the God of the Bible who loved people just like us, in all our brokenness.

A God who loves us no matter what

Most people think of King David as the young boy with a slingshot whose faith in God helped him to kill the giant Goliath and as the great Hebrew king who overcame all the heathen empires around the Mediterranean Sea and united them to form a kingdom dedicated to God's principles. David is known in the Bible as "a man after God's own heart."

Yet David had another side to him, just as we all do, and the Bible does not remain silent about David's baser nature. In 2 Samuel, chapter eleven, we read about his adultery with Bathsheba, the beautiful wife of Uriah the Hittite. In the next chapters we watch David send Uriah into the forefront of the battle so that he is doomed to death. David broke two of God's commandments: You shall not commit adultery and you shall not kill.

Yet God forgave him, because he was truly repentant. That's the history of God's interaction with people like you and me. And David's not the only man who was forgiven in this way. The apostle Paul was responsible for the death of early Christians before he became a Christian himself. Yet God forgave him. Talk about a god who loves us no matter what!

We told one of our patients, whom we'll call Ann, about David and God's love for him, no matter what, and her response was typical of many others: "I never had any trouble saying there is a God. But I was afraid of not being good enough for Him, afraid I just couldn't work hard enough to earn my way into his graces."

We showed Ann Ephesians 2:8–9, where the apostle Paul taught us that we are saved by grace (unmerited favor) by merely trusting Christ's death and resurrection to save us, not by any good works that we could ever do. We must depend on Christ to save us just like we depend on a chair to hold us up off the ground. We depend on Him to save us from the eternal penalty for our sins, and we also depend on Him to salvage our lives from lives of addiction to lives of usefulness and meaning.

In the next weeks Ann had to abandon everything she thought she knew about God and become childlike in her faith. When one of us would ask her, "Ann, what does God mean to you?" she'd just cry.

She explained her reaction to us by saying, "The only real love I've ever known was from God. My father is a rageaholic, and trying to earn his love and approval made me crazy. Prescription drugs, sex—I've tried it all and nothing worked. Now I've learned that even though I can't earn my earthly father's approval, I don't even have to try to earn my heavenly Father's. The most freeing thing in the world is realizing that I *couldn't* be good enough, *couldn't* earn my way, but that I don't have to.

"Sometimes I'm still a little bit afraid of Him, though. I feel like a three-year-old girl who sidles up to someone and wants to sit in his lap but is afraid to. But He's always there, always wanting me to sit in *His* lap."

A God who hears and responds

As we turn toward our emotional and spiritual goal of sanity, it's important to understand that by insanity we are referring to a sense of brokenness, incompleteness, or alienation from God, not a severe mental illness, as Kathryn's sponsor explained to her. Restoration to sanity is a return to a whole, complete relationship with God and a whole, complete sense of our identity, which is the goal of the next several steps—the spiritual and moral inventory steps (Steps Four and Five) and the miracle transformation steps (Steps Six and Seven), not just this one.

We begin now to submit our insanity to Him and as we do so we look forward to the process that will transform our addiction. God does walk with patients, like Kathryn, through this process, just as He did with people in the Bible. In fact, a major part of the Psalms is David's dialogue with God. Over and over again David testifies to God's great care for him. David says in Psalm 34:15, 17: "The eyes of the Lord are on the righteous, And His ears are open to their cry. . . . The righteous cry out, and the Lord hears, And delivers them out of all their troubles."

If the God you want to believe in is similar to David's God, why not take Step Two right now. As the *Big Book* says, ". . . there is One who has all power—that One is God. May you find Him now!"[9]

Come

Come to

Come to believe.

Step Three

Made a decision to turn our will and our lives over to the care of God as we understood Him.

A few months after Martin Woodruff attended his first ACOA meeting, he parked his car in the garage and walked slowly into his house. If he was quiet maybe Mary wouldn't hear him. Maybe she'd be putting the kids to sleep and he could get busy on the article he wanted to submit to *The American Journal of History.* He had to prove he was still a good historian. And Mary? He had thought everything would be all right when he stopped drinking. Then he'd realized that the tensions and conflicts between them he had escaped with a drink or two were even worse when he was sober.

He closed the door quietly behind him and stepped softly down the carpeted hall. The door to his office didn't squeak when he pushed it open, but it didn't need to. Mary was sitting in the office, waiting for him. His first thought was, *What have I done wrong now? Did I miss Derek's ball game or Dana's piano recital?* But for once Mary didn't speak to him in an accusatory way; she just looked up from her chair and said quietly, "I wanted to hear about the A.A. meeting."

Martin sank into his desk chair and ran his hand through his hair as he always did when he was disturbed. How did she always manage it? The one thing he wanted to avoid talking about, above all else, and she went straight to the heart of the matter. He shrugged, "Oh, we talked about the usual stuff, I guess. Turning our lives over to a Higher Power, a lot of stuff from the *Big Book* about how our troubles arise out of our own self-centeredness and our compulsions to be the stage manager of every detail of our lives—to be director, producer, playwright, and star. Then the show flops." He sat silent for some time. Dr. Fowler had been so sure A.A. would help but things seemed more depressing than ever now that his sponsor had thrown him this curve about the best way to do Step Three.

Martin decided to tell Mary about it since she was being so open and accepting—like in the old days before his drinking got between them. Now he wondered if her nagging drove him to drink or his drinking drove her to be a shrew, or how much they really hinged on each other. But that wasn't the point at the moment.

"Well, my sponsor, Alan, sort of gave me this assignment—homework, like—for taking Step Three. He said in the old days they used to take it publicly, pray a written prayer in front of the whole group. Well, now they aren't quite so public about it, but they suggest taking Step Three with another person, someone close to you. . . ."

"I think I get it," Mary said. "What am I supposed to do?"

"Well, we're supposed to pray . . . together. Er, on our knees . . . er, out loud, I'm afraid."

Without hesitation Mary slipped to her knees beside her chair. "I always liked to kneel in church when I was a kid," she explained as she saw Martin's astonished look. "And I always knelt by my bed to pray until I was thirteen."

For the first time Martin wondered about his wife: Did she still pray? Did she believe in God? He had a vague idea that maybe she had gone to church when he met her, but she gave it up when he ridiculed religion in that supercilious manner that had always provided such a solid shield for him. Did she miss her childhood faith, or at least her old friends at church? What had he done in tearing her away from all that? But he felt too ashamed to ask.

Martin tipped forward on his desk chair until he could just sort of slip to a sitting position on the floor.

"I think kneeling means 'on your knees,' " Mary said softly.

"I've never felt such a fool in my life." He looked up to see if the mini-blinds were closed. Thankfully, he saw they were.

"Have you ever done this before—prayed—out loud?" Mary asked.

"Well, we say the Lord's Prayer and the Serenity Prayer . . . together at all the meetings, usually holding hands. But this . . ." He started to deny any such experience, then realized how hard it was to lie when you were on your knees. Was that what his sponsor had in mind when suggesting this?

"Yeah, when I was a kid. When my mother wasn't too busy protecting Dad from anyone finding out his awful secret, so he could go on being a city councilman and pillar of the community, she'd pray with me." Once Martin started, the memories seemed to roll back. Things he hadn't actively recalled for thirty years. "I always liked it when she would come in to tuck me into bed, and we'd talk and pray together."

Suddenly his voice took on the old biting edge he normally used. "No wonder I gave it up. I always asked God to make Dad quit drinking and help Mom not be scared and make Dad quit yelling at me and hitting me. But He never did. It didn't take me long to figure out that either God didn't exist, or He didn't care, or He couldn't do anything for me. So I quit praying. And you know what? Things got better. My life was worse when I was praying and going to Sunday School."

A wave of embarrassment washed over Martin. Why had he been so stupid as to ask God for anything? And groveling on the floor in front of Mary, too. He started to get up, but Mary held out her hand. It was the first time she had voluntarily touched him in months. "Martin, let's just try. Now that we're here, it seems a shame not to. What is that prayer you're supposed to say?"

From his knees Martin could reach the *Big Book* on his desk. He glanced over the brief paragraph. "Oh, I hate all those phony-sounding 'thees' and 'thous'—I don't have to say it that way, do I?"

Mary shrugged. "I shouldn't think so. I expect that's just a guide."

"Right. Here goes." Martin closed his eyes, then realized he'd have to open them to read the prayer, even if he was going to change some of the words: "God, I offer myself to you—to build with me and to do with me as you want. Relieve me of the bondage of self, so that I can do your will better. Take away my difficulties, so that my victory over them can be a witness to others of your Power, your Love, and your Way of Life. Help me always to do your will." He closed the book. "Amen."[1]

Mary, who had edged closer to him during the prayer, whispered, "Amen," and reached out and squeezed his hand. Martin was overwhelmed by the bond of closeness he suddenly felt with his wife. He helped her to her feet.

"Well, how do you feel?" she asked.

He considered that for a minute. "Relieved—because it's over, and because I think I've done the right thing. No big thing you could really call a 'spiritual experience' though." Then, he realized he was still holding his wife's hand. "Er, Mary, um, thank you."

Mary stretched up on her tiptoes and very lightly kissed him on the cheek above his shaggy beard.

Although Martin had very little understanding of what he had done, this simple act of obedient surrender was the first tiny step toward a whole new direction in his life. Driven to it in desperation and performing it more in obedience to his sponsor and the urging of his wife than by any conscious desire or obedience to God, he had spoken the words of the Third Step prayer. For now it was enough.

Turning Over Control to God

One reason Step Three looks so hard is the fact that it is an external step, not just an internal decision as Steps One and Two were. This step requires action toward another person. And that person is God. The *Twelve Steps and Twelve Traditions,* a publication of Alcoholics Anonymous, which is often fondly referred to as *The 12 × 12,* says, "It is only by action that we can cut away the self-will which has always blocked the entry of God into our lives."[2] Only when we submit our will to the will of God can we begin to use our willpower in the proper way. The addict's problem is not a lack of willpower, as so many believe, but a misuse of willpower, as we mentioned before. It is not necessary to bombard our problems with our willpower but rather to bring our will into agreement with the will of God. For this reason, the successful working of this step is absolutely essential to the success of all the rest of the Twelve Steps.

Our first act in taking Step Three is submitting to God.

We Submit Our Powerlessness to Him

When Dr. Hemfelt helps his patients to admit their powerlessness he often mentions an experience he once had. "One day when I was driving to the hospital, I heard the weatherman on the radio trying to explain why it was windy in north Texas. He traced it to some kind of a front that was moving across the United States and extended into Canada. It had to do with some other weather phenomenon in Alaska and the fact that it was snowing in Tokyo—and it never snowed in Tokyo at that time of the year! All that just reminded me of the vast interplay of forces that God has control of. If we think we're controlling much of anything, we're sadly mistaken."

Realizing our real powerlessness makes it easier to submit our lives to God.

We Give the Universe Back to Him

When faced with the realization that we are powerless over much that surrounds us, like the weather, the elements, or the laws of physics, we realize that the last thing we really want to do is to control the universe. Most of us are exhausted from simply trying to run our own lives. Once we realize that we really want to turn our lives over to God, the process is much easier. Then we realize that, as large and all-encompassing as this step sounds, it must be played out in daily, tiny acts of submission. Allowing God to run the universe translates moment by moment into learning to say:

- "I will let the governor run the state."
- "I will let the boss run the company."
- "I will let my spouse see to his or her responsibilities."
- "I will let my kids be responsible for their homework."

And we learn to submit to circumstances as well as to people. We learn to say:

- "I am not responsible for the fact that it's raining today."
- "I am not responsible for the fact that the garbage collector changed his route."
- "I am not responsible for the fact that the Bears lost the football game."
- "I am not responsible for the war on the other side of the world."

Submission is simply coming to understand that it's God's world, and He can run it. Submission is also a way of coming to understand that we do not always have to have our own way. Our happiness is not exclusively dependent upon getting what we want.

As our patients submit their lives to God they naturally search for a clearer idea of who He is. "Who will be running this show if I don't?" they want to know. "Can I trust Him?" Often we recommend that they consider a couple of the following six suggestions as they struggle to find a personal God whom they can trust with their lives.

If You Don't Have a God Who's Working for You, Borrow Ours

Sponsors in Twelve-Step groups often make this suggestion to sponsorees. New members are caught in a dilemma: They can't fully move through recovery until they find a god to turn their lives over to, and they can't find God until they have experienced some recovery. "I can't recover until I find God," they realize, "and I can't find God until I'm in recovery from the false god of my addiction."

So the sponsor will suggest, "Simply borrow my faith. Lean on me for a while. But as you do so, realize that you are not really leaning on me, you're leaning on the God I've found."

That's just what Martin's sponsor Alan suggested to him. When a student complained to Dr. Gordon Thomas, Martin's department head, that Martin was unavailable during office hours (and Martin had only been tied up after class, talking to another student) Martin Woodruff was angry at the student, at Gordon Thomas, who sent the memo to him about the incident, and at God. After all, he'd been trying so hard to reform. He couldn't seem to shake off this resentment, so he called Alan. "I'm really tempted to fire off a terse memo, explaining what happened," Martin said. "But it may seem to be just another excuse." Alan suggested another alternative. "We need to turn this over to God," he said. "If you can't trust your old notion of God, borrow mine. Let's turn this over to Him. Pray about it; then if you still feel you need to talk to your department head, do so."

Martin mentioned this problem to God for several nights, and the answer always seemed to be the same. So he scheduled an appointment to talk to Gordon.

After a few opening comments about the weather, Martin told Gordon how hard he had been trying—about the counseling, about the ACOA meetings—and how he had missed seeing the one student. "He didn't wait more than ten minutes," Martin said. "I was there by 4:15."

To Martin's surprise, Gordon listened intently and then apologized. "I'm sorry, Martin. Sounds as if you might be making some progress after all."

When Martin told Alan what had happened, he replied, "That's why my God is called the 'God of the second chance.'"

We also approach patients, like Martin, very pragmatically, seeing as they are still searching more with their minds than their hearts. To do so we borrow a familiar Twelve-Step slogan: "Stick with the winners."

Give Yourself Permission to Believe in a God Who Is Bigger Than Life

Often non-Christians and Christians themselves limit God. The person who's skeptical, like Martin Woodruff, usually makes God smaller than He is by making Him fit into a scientific box. God must adhere to principles man can understand. God may be scientifically reduced to the notion of an impersonal first cause of the universe or to a mathematical equation for nuclear physics or to the "Big Bang" of creation who has now forgotten His creatures.

Legalistic Christians, like Andy Thomson, may see God in a different, but equally narrow way. They try to so thoroughly and precisely define God by legalistic rules and descriptions that God's image is compromised. Once

we helped Andy realize this, he said, "I see now. I'm trying to paint God by numbers. I'm trying so hard to get all
the right colors in the right numbers and not smear across
the lines, I'm actually defacing God. I'm limiting Him by
making Him conform to my legalistic grid of what I think
God should be like."

Andy further recognized that his spiritual legalism had
almost become a form of magic. He believed that if he
could somehow get all the rules about God right, then this
perfectionism would magically buy or win God's approval.
Andy commented, "My religion had become as supersti-
tious as the old childhood rhyme, 'Step on a crack, break
your mother's back.'" For Andy that childhood magic now
translated into "Step out of line, and God will reject you."

When we box in God in either of these ways, we hamper
our recovery. Remember the caution to the alcoholic in
the *Big Book:* "We deal with alcohol—cunning, baffling,
powerful! Without help it is too much for us. But there is
One who has all power—that One is God."[3] The all-powerful God is a God who is bigger than life. We warn our
patients, "If your God is too small, He will never have the
power to help you overcome your addiction."

We challenge our patients to remember they are on a
healing journey, and we suggest that they open the Bible
to the first book in the New Testament, the book of Matthew. "Can the Jesus who is portrayed there heal your
addiction?" we ask them. "Don't you want to choose the
God who can perform the miracle that is needed?"

Choose a God Who Can Perform a Miracle

During one counseling session, Martin Woodruff confessed to Dr. Fowler, "I really have trouble understanding
and believing this whole concept of miracles. At A.A.
meetings I see the slogan, 'Expect a miracle,' and I'm
enough of an historical student of the Bible to know the
record of God's miraculous interventions in the history of

mankind. But I have trouble believing God would inter-vene with *me*, personally, in a supernatural manner."

Dr. Fowler, half-jokingly, half-seriously, responded, "Martin, the fact that you, the hard-nosed intellectual cynic, are sitting in my office sober and talking to me about God—all of that is nothing short of a miracle. There must be a God who performs miracles."

On a more serious note, Dr. Fowler continued. "Martin, there is a God, Jesus Christ, who cares personally for you and who is capable of working miracles in your life. The problem is, the road toward a personal encounter with this God must be a journey of the heart, rather than a journey of the mind. You and I can debate intellectual aspects of God for hours on end, and that probably will not move your recovery one step forward. Instead, I invite you to explore the miraculous side of God from the van-tage point of your heart. You've told me yourself about the warm feelings you have when you hear people at A.A. meetings talk about how their lives have been trans-formed. Trust and believe those feelings. The miracles are real, Martin. The miracle of eternal salvation and the miracle of recovery are yours for the asking."

A triangle, with A.A. in the center and bounded by a circle, with the words *recovery, service,* and *unity,* is the symbol of Alcoholics Anonymous. In the Dallas area a lot of the A.A. groups write above the circle: "Expect a Mira-cle."

If we are going to break out of our addictions, we need to expect a miracle, and this is the fourth suggestion we make. The God of miracles is Jesus. The New Testament is a journalistic account of His healing the sick in body, mind, and spirit.

"Christ could be considered a biblical Marcus Welby," Dr. Fowler told Martin Woodruff. "If your body is racked with pain, if your mind is weighed down by depression, do you not want to have a God who will administer His heal-ing touch? The God you have borrowed from us, Jesus Christ, can do just that."

Yet Martin still hesitated. Many of our patients have a natural longing for a God who will also understand their guilt and shame.

Look for a God Who Understands Your Guilt and Shame

The big obstacles to recovery are guilt, shame and resentment. We may carry an old sense of false shame from our childhood about situations over which we had no control, such as childhood sexual abuse. We carry additional shame and guilt about the damage our addictions have inflicted on others. Further, we may be riddled with deep resentments about how others have hurt us, real or imagined. The Christian God, the God of atonement and redemption, is the only God who offers an antidote to this dual package of shame and resentment. God's gift of salvation to us provides the ultimate spiritual answer to our deep feelings of shame and guilt.

One of our patients, a thirty-five-year-old woman, was a sexual addict who had purposely broken up three marriages and knowingly infected several men with herpes. She just couldn't imagine that God would forgive her for consciously causing such pain.

So we told her, "We know a God who can and does forgive you for your sins. In fact, the God we know is a God who fully empathizes with your pain and unconditionally extends His gift of love to you." We showed her passages in the Bible that said just that: "God demonstrates His own love toward us, in that while we were still sinners, Christ died for us."[4]

And we turned to other passages that vividly showed her sins being forgiven. God told the Hebrew people who were riddled with moral and spiritual disease, "Though your sins are like scarlet, They shall be as white as snow; Though they are red like crimson, They shall be as wool."[5]

The woman who had purposely destroyed three marriages understood all we were saying, yet she still hesitated.

Finally we realized that she had such incredible guilt about what she had done that she had to be assured that God would allow her to become a totally new creation under His transforming touch. When we read her 2 Corinthians 5:17—"Therefore, if anyone is in Christ, he is a new creation; old things have passed away; behold, all things have become new"—she could feel God's acceptance of her. And she could accept Jesus Christ as her Redeemer, depending only on Him to save her from the penalty of her sins and also depending on Him to salvage her life.

Look for a God Who Will Redeem You

If we don't accept the Savior, we will constantly try to become our own codependent redeemer. Many of our addictions are crude efforts at self-sacrifice and self-redemption. We will overeat, in an attempt to eat ourselves to death. Or we will try to starve ourselves, become anorexic. Or we will use our workaholism or alcoholism to try to pay for our sins or to satisfy the emptiness inside us. (The workaholic will often joke, "This job is killing me." There's more truth, than jest, to this statement.) Or we will try to do something grandiose—like being the perfect homemaker or making a million dollars or putting our name on a building that will last for fifty years or more—to redeem ourselves. "Here is our money offering," we unconsciously think, "to place on the altar. Please, God, allow the compulsive behavior to fill the emptiness in us and accept the pain of the addiction as payment for the shame we feel."

All these redemption roles violate the fundamental spiritual principle that we cannot function as our own redeemer. There is only one true Redeemer who can pay the price for our sins and that is Jesus Christ. Redemption comes only through accepting His sacrifice. Through this we can be freed from our false shame and find the true personality God created for us.

Step Out in Faith

The sixth, and final, suggestion we make to our patients who are searching for a clearer picture of God as they understand Him is to step out in faith.

Our desire to save ourselves from our addictions must be so great that we will step out in faith. We can reason and question and hesitate all we want, but finally we must step out and embrace the God of the Bible.

Theodore was one of our patients who took the healthy risk of faith. We want to share his experience with you in his own words. First, Ted had to make the choice to get help for his alcoholism. Then taking Step Three really set him on the road to recovery. Here is how he tells it:

October 22, 1990

Dr. Robert Hemfelt
Minirth-Meier Clinic, P.A.
2100 North Collins Boulevard
Richardson, TX 75080

Dr. Hemfelt:

It is with great joy that I write you this letter. I was in your group at the clinic. I was diagnosed as being severely clinically depressed. Before I left, you told me I needed to join Alcoholics Anonymous. You told me I had a disease and that it was a life and death matter. You gave me information on A.A. and told me about the Twelve Steps. I heard you, but I didn't hear you.

I told my wife that I would quit drinking myself and that I didn't need to go near an A.A. meeting and I didn't need your advice or anyone else's advice. I did manage to quit drinking for about four months and my depression was less severe, but I was still miserable.

In the later part of October I drank two or three beers on a hunting trip. I knew I shouldn't have done it, but I did. After that my drinking became more frequent until it became as serious a situation as it was prior to my trip to Texas. I ruined Christmas for my family. My wife and three children were scared to death. I knew I was dying and was resigned to let it happen. Still, I refused to heed your advice and I couldn't stop drinking.

On March 2, 1990, I took my last drink about 7 A.M., prior to my law firm's monthly meeting. During the meeting my partners put me on a mandatory leave of absence and told me I had to "get help." I then remembered your advice. I spent thirty days in a local Alcohol Treatment Center. On March 17, while in treatment, at about 5 A.M. I surrendered my life to Christ. I wrote twenty-three pages, outlining my shame, guilt, and fears. I told the Lord that I couldn't handle life any longer doing it my way. I then took the third step of A.A.

From that point on my life has just gotten better every day. I left my old law firm and started my own practice. It is flourishing.

My youngest son will join me next year in the practice. I attend three–six A.A. meetings a week and really enjoy them. I now understand what my minister says and what the Good Book says. I am able to help others personally and professionally better than I ever have. I try to do a lot of Twelve-Step work with other alcoholics. My marriage is stronger than ever. My wife is beginning to heal from all the abuse she received from me. My oldest son graduated from law school and got married this May and has a good job. I am able to enjoy all these wonderful events. As they say in the *Big Book* of A.A.. . . . I'm happy, joyous and free.

God granted me the miracle of sobriety and recovery, and I believe that I can continue to stay healthy one day at a time, as long as I take Step Three every day.

An amazing thing happens to patients like Ted. A year later or two years later or three years later, they will return (or write us as Ted did) and tell us, "If I had to make a list of what I hoped would happen to me after the moment I accepted Christ as Savior, it would have fallen far, far short of what Jesus actually delivered."

We are not surprised. That's what we expected from the God we lent them at the beginning of Step Three.

The *Big Book* describes this working of the Holy Spirit and the transformation God's Spirit brings to our lives: "We will comprehend the word serenity and we will know peace. . . . That feeling of uselessness and self-pity will disappear. We will lose interest in selfish things and gain interest in our fellows. Self-seeking will slip away. Our whole attitude and outlook upon life will change. Fear of people and of economic insecurity will leave us. We will intuitively know how to handle situations which used to baffle us. We will suddenly realize that God is doing for us what we could not do for ourselves."[6]

Twelve-Steppers call these "the promises." Christians call them the fruits of the spirit: love, joy, peace, patience, kindness, goodness, faith, gentleness, and self-control. They are ours if we make a decision to turn our will and our lives over to God as we understand Him, our Savior, Jesus Christ.

Step Four

Made a searching and fearless moral inventory of ourselves.

I can't for the life of me see how doing this inventory is going to make the dean renew my contract." Martin Woodruff shook his head at Dr. Fowler. "My job's in jeopardy because I drank too much. I'm sober now, but I still don't know if I'll have a job next year. I think I should be spending my time with an Equal Opportunity Employment officer, not an Alcoholics Anonymous group."

Martin spoke with a wry sense of humor that made Dr. Fowler smile, but his reply was serious. "Martin, you won't be doing this inventory to find a job; you'll be doing it to find yourself—and God—in that order. Because of the pain and loss of self-esteem in your childhood, you never had a chance to find the real Martin when you were growing up."

Martin opened his mouth to disagree, then his rigorous training to academic honesty took over and he leaned into the highbacked leather chair with a wave of his hand to indicate that he was listening.

Why Should I Take a Moral Inventory of Myself?

Most people approach Step Four—"Made a searching and fearless moral inventory of ourselves"—with a desire to change their circumstances, not a desire to change themselves. For instance, Andy Thomson couldn't see how taking Step Four would give him more time to get his work done—just the opposite, it would take time away from work. And he was certain it wouldn't improve his relationship with Jennifer. Likewise, Kathryn Markham really resented having to do something that was so much work when, really, Henry was the one who should be doing it. After all, he was the alcoholic. It is only when most people are well into the recovery process that they fully realize that changing themselves also changes their circumstances.

The first step toward any kind of change, however, must be to know yourself as you are and to know where you are now. And understanding the now comes through understanding the past. Almost all dependent persons have lost their true identity because they grew up in dysfunctional families where they were forced to assume false survival roles. These roles, such as being the model child or the problem child, may actually have been essential for emotional survival, even physical survival, at the time, but the roles became habitual and even self-destructive in adulthood.

For example, a child who experienced sexual violation at the hands of a trusted adult may learn to put up a barrier against any and all physical intimacy. That barrier serves a protective purpose in childhood. That same self-protective stance may become a permanent adult barrier against any possibility of intimacy with the opposite sex.

Worse, the dysfunctions that first occurred in the family of origin may now be repeated, and so "the sins of the fathers are visited on the children unto the third and fourth generations."[1]

A tragic example of the results of a dysfunctional family was seen recently in the news when another of Bing Crosby's sons committed suicide. Although Bing Crosby the singer and actor was beloved by millions, Bing Crosby the father was hated and feared by his four sons. Robert Slatzer, a family friend and coauthor of *Bing Crosby—The Hollow Man* said, "Bing was so abusive to his boys that they learned to hate him. They also learned from him that they were worthless nobodies.

"Dennis [the son who most recently committed suicide] told me, 'When I was a teenager, my dad used to work me until I'd drop—and when he didn't like what I did he slapped me around. He told me I'd never amount to anything and it looks like he was right.' "[2]

Dennis turned to alcohol, his second marriage failed, a trust fund that supported him ran out, and he suffered several heart attacks. The final straw was when his favorite brother, Lindsay, killed himself. The pain Dennis Crosby carried from childhood was too heavy to cope with so he took his own life with a 12-gauge shotgun. A major purpose in walking through Steps Four and Five is to identify and release this pain from the past so that we do not remain in self-destructive lifestyles.

But How Do I Do This Inventory?

"Now don't panic." Kathryn's sponsor, Helena, looked at her with level green eyes. "Everyone says the Step Four inventory is the hardest thing they've ever done in their life. Words like *grueling* and *brutal* pale in comparison to the actual experience. But the good news is that we all live through it—and we'll all tell you it was more than worth the pain. It's really the only way."

Kathryn groaned and looked at the empty paper in front of her, her whole life flashing in confusion through her mind.

"Think of it this way," Helena continued. "A business that doesn't take inventory will go broke. A dependent person who doesn't take inventory will stay broken. This inventory is a major step in getting your life back together again."

"But I don't know where to start. My whole life has

been a mess—people who've hurt me, people I've hurt—
I'll never get it all down. This looks like a huge mountain
to climb, a real Mount Everest."

Helena nodded. "I won't tell you it isn't, but let me show
you how to lay it out to get started." She started listing
inventory items on the paper, then paused. "This will
help, but the most important thing to remember is *just
tell the truth.*"

Unlike Kathryn, who found the inventory so daunting,
Martin, the trained teacher, was delighted with our list of
questions, which gave the assignment real structure. "You
know," he said, "Most people don't understand. They see
specific directions like this and think they're going to be
tied down. Really giving someone a road map to follow
opens the world up for them. Take my students. If I say,
'Go write an essay,' they're terrified—paralyzed. If I give
them rules for writing a good essay, an outline of the
structure, some solid literary examples, and a list of appropriate topics, they're delighted. They can't wait to get
out of class to start writing down their own creative ideas.
But you have to show people how to do it."

We suggest that our patients take a more complete inventory than the one displayed in the *Big Book.* The extensive inventory explained there can best be understood
as a model of how *all* areas of one's life should be explored. The inventory you will take in Step Four and
share in Step Five (when you will express deep feelings of
guilt and resentments) will help you to diagnose yourself
as we would in several counseling sessions. For this reason you might wish to take one area each day for a week,
rather than trying to accomplish the entire inventory in a
day or so. And you might want to look back at the inventory weeks later to add other memories that begin to appear as you walk through later steps.

Prepare with Prayer

The *12 × 12* says, "There is direct linkage among self-examination, meditation, and prayer. Taken separately, these practices can bring much relief and benefit. But when they are logically related and interwoven, the result is an unshakable foundation for life."[3]

The deep, soul-searching experience of taking an in-depth inventory of one's life should not be undertaken without a strong underpinning of prayer. The arrangement of the Twelve Steps is not haphazard. They must be taken in order. A belief in a Higher Power to whom we have surrendered our will and our lives is absolutely essential before Step Four can be taken. Without this undergirding of divine security the trauma of looking back over all the old pains, anger, and resentments can be devastating. We know one young man who attempted this without faith in a Higher Power and was so overcome with depression from what he learned that he committed suicide before his inventory was complete. Surround yourself with prayer and lean on the support of God's guidance as you embark on this critical step.

Take Psalm 139: 23, 24 as your theme prayer as you work through Step Four: "Search me, O God, and know my heart; Try me, and know my anxieties: And see if there is any wicked way in me, And lead me in the way everlasting."

Here's how you do it.

1. Tell Your Story

Helena told Kathryn, "I want you to take this a step further and begin to write a brief summary of your life story."

Kathryn protested, "My whole life story! Who wants to hear that, and besides it would fill volumes and most of it is trivial."

Helena teased back. "Maybe no one would buy your life

story as a bestseller, but the point is that the telling of your story, at least the highlights of it, is an excellent way to begin your overall inventory. You're writing about your life to benefit yourself. Not anyone else. This doesn't have to be the great American novel. It simply needs to be an outline of the major events and experiences that have taken place in your life, told in roughly chronological order from the beginning to the present. Remember, a great deal of our Twelve-Step recovery involves honest disclosure of who we are. My own sponsor reminded me that every time we go to a meeting and share about our life, we are 'telling our story.' Please, commit the highlights of your story to paper. It's an excellent way to open the door to the rest of your inventory."

From the beginnings of Alcoholics Anonymous, and before that in the Oxford Group, storytelling has been the basis of the program. There is nothing else you can tell that will make such a unique contribution as your own story. No one can tell it but you, and it's the one thing you can tell that no one can argue with—it is *yours*.

Writing and then telling your life story is a very healing thing to do. Many people never had the chance to tell the story of their lives until they came to a Twelve-Step group. Perhaps no one cared enough about them to listen. You will learn surprising things about yourself in your own telling. An example of how healing this can be is the New Testament account of the woman at the well. Although the woman tried to cover up some of the facts of her life, Christ revealed them to her. He told her that He knew all about her, the full story of her life, and He loved her and accepted her. This transformed her life.

Take time now to write your story on separate paper. (Parts Three, Four, and Five of this book are collections of stories from our patients and those who listen to our national radio talk show, "The Minirth-Meier Clinic." You might want to read a few of these before you write your own story.)

When you are ready to share your story be sure you choose a safe place with a non-critical audience such as a Twelve-Step group, a counselor, a therapist, a sponsor, or a pastor. You may not be comfortable sharing some aspects of your story in public. That's fine. Write them out anyway, share them with yourself first, and then perhaps you can share them with one person whom you feel you can trust. Also, you may not choose to tell all your story at once. Sharing your life a piece at a time, or continuing to share as it unfolds on a daily basis after your initial sharing, is what most Twelve-Step groups do at their discussion meetings. Remember, the unfolding of your life story is a survey of the broad "lay of the land" to prepare you for the other major elements of your Step Four inventory.

Dr. Meier encouraged Kathryn in the Fourth Step work she had begun with her sponsor. After Kathryn read her life story to Dr. Meier, he suggested a second major component for her inventory. "Kathryn, I want you to take that summary of your life and try to identify just how much of a role addiction and codependency have played in your life. For example, you've known for a long time that compulsive eating is a primary addiction."

Dr. Meier paused and chuckled. "In fact, you and I both share in recovery from that dependency. I've lost twenty-five pounds myself in the last year."

A Complete Step Four Inventory

1. Tell your story:
   a. Choose a safe place.
   b. Journal to yourself about the central parts of your life story.

2. List all your dependencies, codependencies, and addictions:
   a. Review the list of addictive agents on pages 14–15.

b. Identify primary and secondary addictions.

3. Go back and look for the roots of your addictions—look for family of origin dysfunctions, which may have laid the foundation for your addictive hunger:

   a. Active abuse
   b. Passive abuse
   c. Emotional incest
   d. Negative messages

4. Inventory your major life relationships:
   a. List major people in your life—past and present.
   b. Describe the relationship from the perspective of your feelings.
   c. Look for repeating styles of dysfunctional relationships and painful patterns in the relationships.

5. Look for guilt feelings related to people in the above list:
   a. Write down guilt feelings.
   b. Distinguish between authentic and false guilt.

6. Look for the good:
   a. List positive legacies brought from childhood.
   b. List positive survival mechanisms learned.
   c. List skills, talents, abilities.
   d. List positive permissions granted self.
   e. List positive recovery steps currently being implemented.
   f. List positive contributions to relationships.

7. Inventory resentments:
   a. List resentments.
   b. List the anger underlying resentments.
   c. List the hurt underlying anger.
   d. List the fears producing anger.
   e. List unmet needs that produced fear.

2. Acknowledge the Full Extent of Your Dependencies, Codependencies, and Addictions

"You first faced your dependencies in Step One," Dr. Meier reminded Kathryn. "Now in this part of your Step Four inventory, be certain you have recognized *all* of your dependencies."

Kathryn responded, "I think I understand. My two biggies are my compulsive eating and my codependent rescuing of others. Those would be what you call primary addictions. In addition, I'm just now coming to appreciate that playing the martyr role in our marriage is what you call a secondary addiction."

Most people are poly-addicted, although many have been so consumed by their primary addiction they do not recognize the lesser addictions until the primary one is in control. Go through the list of fifteen primary addictive agents on pages 14–15 again, using this as a checklist to identify your dependencies. Number them in order of the extent of their control over you. (For instance, Andy Thomson listed work as number one, perfectionism and control addictions as number two, and religious legalism as number three; Martin Woodruff listed alcohol number one, academic pursuits and relying on his mind as number two, and control addictions as number three).

None of the addictive agents is either good or bad by itself. The question to ask yourself is, "Am I in charge or have these things taken charge of me?" God's Word cautions us to exercise moderation in the fulfillment of our human needs. If our emotional or spiritual neediness is too great, then we cross the line into addictive dependency on a person, substance, or behavior.

3. Discover the Roots of Your Addictions

Once the dependencies have been identified, we need to go beyond the fact of their existence to understand their roots. In most cases this means going back to our child-hood. The *Big Book* talks about the inventory as being similar to a business inventory, where the owner must go in and identify good and damaged merchandise, then pol-ish and display the good and jettison the bad. As we come to understand the importance of our family of origin in shaping our adult personalities, we see that it's impossi-ble to do a thorough moral inventory without going back and understanding some of that damaged merchandise from childhood. Any childhood situation that blocked or limited our receiving love from one or both parents consti-tutes a form of abuse.

Types of Abuse

You need to consider briefly the types of family of origin dysfunctions, which most commonly generate a later ad-diction. Consider which of the following describe your family.

Active Abuse

Active abuse is the type Dennis Crosby described in his home. In this case the parent is projecting his or her pain onto the child. Most physically abusive parents were physically abused themselves. Did you grow up with ex-cessive discipline? Slapping? Other physical abuse such as forced overwork? Sexual abuse? Verbal abuse?

The vast majority of abuse occurs under the pretense of discipline, so it is easy to see how these people may deny they were ever abused. Yet even people who were overtly battered are often in denial about the experience. In their denial, they may reason: "All children are treated this way; all parents at one point or other lose control like this." These men and women have a clouded perception of the physical abuse to which they were subjected. For ex-ample, clients often tell us during counseling: "My father cut a switch off the tree and beat me severely, but I'm sure I deserved it." While these adults might veer away from using the actual term *abuse* to describe their punishment, the harsh realities of the treatment have nevertheless done damage.

There is nothing wrong with punishment; in fact, the physical reinforcement of boundaries is actually reassuring to a small child. But corporal punishment in excess or in conjunction with public humiliation (being physically disciplined in the middle of a shopping mall) very likely went beyond discipline and into the realm of abuse.

At first Kathryn Markham resisted the notion that anyone had actively abused her. Then, with Dr. Meier's guidance, she recognized that her grandmother's angry voice and rather violent picture of God were forms of emotional and spiritual violence; they were active abuses.

The following checklist will help you identify specific active abuses that occurred in your childhood. Place a check by each abuse that played a significant role in your life, then identify which family member was responsible for that abuse.

Abuse	**Abuser**
_____ Abusive anger or rage	_____
_____ Physical violence	_____
_____ Excessive punishment	_____
_____ Profanity	_____
_____ Sarcasm	_____
_____ Derogatory "pet" names	_____
_____ Inappropriate touching	_____
_____ Overt sexual molestation	_____
_____ Rape	_____
_____ Parental alcoholism	_____

_____ Parental drug abuse   _____
_____ Parent overcontrol of
         a child   _____

If you think you might have experienced sexual abuse, we feel you should consult a counselor as soon as possible. You could call your local church for a referral or ask your family doctor.

Passive Abuse

Passive abuse is harder to identify, but it is equally destructive. It is made up of the things that aren't there; any failure to meet a child's needs is passive abusive. Were there things missing in your family? Love? Attention? Caring? An opportunity to express yourself? Passive abuse can occur because of parental abandonment or parental preoccupation with their own pain or their own addictive illness. For example, Kathryn recognized that her parents had been so preoccupied with her dad's compulsive affairs and their continuous fighting that they had essentially abandoned her to the care of her live-in grandmother. Check the passive abuses you might have experienced from the list below:

Passive Abuse through
Abandonment   Abuser
_____ Parental divorce   _____
_____ Premature death of a parent   _____
_____ Separation   _____

Passive Abuse through Parental Preoccupation
with Obsessive-Compulsive Behavior
_____ A parent who was a:
      _____ perfectionist   _____
      _____ shopaholic   _____
      _____ workaholic   _____
      _____ foodaholic   _____

Emotional Incest

Emotional incest is the abuse that occurs when the parent is emotionally "married" to the child and the child is required to provide emotional companionship that should be supplied by the spouse. Did you have to listen to confidences that should only have occurred between adults? Did your parents expect that you "parent" them? Were you required to provide emotional support or even take on physical or financial responsibility that your parent should have been providing for you?

As you look back on your time in your family of origin, were there any "parental" roles that you began to assume prematurely? Check as many of the following activities that apply:

_____ Disproportionate responsibility for housekeeping

_____ Functioning as a parent to my siblings

_____ Inappropriate support and emotional stability (having to be a parent or spouse to my own parent)

_____ Functioning as a confidant to a parent

_____ Functioning as a confessor for a parent

_____ A sense of "being on my own" at any early age

_____ Financial responsibility for the support of the family

Negative Messages

Negative messages, which were repeatedly heard, sensed, seen, or experienced in childhood, may still be dictating one's life in adulthood. Many negative messages are never spoken out loud. One of our patients, a middle-aged woman, told us that she had had two abortions in young adulthood from a sexual relationship with the same man. She was the fifth daughter in her family, and as we talked to her about her childhood she realized that the unspoken message she had received was: "You are not supposed to be here. Dad wanted a boy." She was symbolically reliving that message each time she generated life and then terminated it. Part of this woman's healing was to talk to her mother about this message so she could openly deal with it.

What negative messages about yourself do you carry inside you?

Negative messages about myself (like "You never do anything right" or "You're so fat and awkward no one would be attracted to you."):

_____

_____

_____

Negative messages about other people (like "Don't trust people" or "All men will abandon you."):

_____

_____

_____

4. Inventory the History of Your Major Life Relationships

As Kathryn continued her inventory, Dr. Meier urged her to inventory all of the major relationships in her life. He reminded her, "So often our addictions to things, such as food, have more to do with the people relationships in our life than with the thing itself."

Begin this part of the inventory by simply thinking about the major people in your life—past and present. In order to be complete, be sure you give thought to all the major categories or life relationships:

Family of origin

During my growing-up years, my relationship with my biological parents was:

_____ Loving and tender.

_____ Cold and distant.

_____ I felt a strong push to conform to their values.

_____ I was given permission to have my own identity.

_____ I felt their encouragement. A can-do spirit of encouragement was always part of our relationship.

_____ Our relationship was always clouded by negativity and pessimism.

_____ I always felt I had to earn their love.

_____ My parents were so involved with their problems, they seemed to give me too much freedom.

_____ My parents seemed to be overcontrolling.

_____ My parents consistently balanced their control over me with my age and the responsibility I could accept.

_____ I'm angry at my parent(s) for what they did to me.

_____ I always felt I was the wrong gender in sibling mix. My dad (mom) wanted a boy (girl) instead of who and what God made me to be.

Opposite sex

During my junior high years, three of my close friends of the opposite sex were:

_____

_____

_____

These relationships were enjoyable in the following ways *(I felt safe and secure.)*:

_____

_____

_____

These relationships were painful in the following ways *(I caught on very early that somehow I had to barter my sexuality in order to prove it.):*

_____

_____

_____

During my high school years, three of my close friends of the opposite sex were:

_____

_____

_____

These relationships were enjoyable in the following ways *(I felt comfortable to say either yes or no to the control boundaries and sexual boundaries in this relationship.):*

_____

_____

_____

These relationships were painful in the following ways *(As a girl I had to have intercourse with my boyfriend or as a boy I had to score with a girl to prove my maleness):*

_____

_____

_____

During my college and later years, four of my close friends of the opposite sex were:

_____

_____

_____

_____

These relationships were enjoyable in the following ways *(I felt that my identity was respected by these persons. I did not have to prove myself by being the superscholar or the athletic champion.):*

_____

_____

_____

These relationships were painful in the following ways *(I was never sure of my own identity, and I found myself always trying to fit into a group to prove myself to the opposite sex. For example, as a girl in college in the '60s I became a hippie and practiced free love to win the approval of males.):*

_____

_____

_____

As Kathryn began the next part of her relationship inventory, she realized that every time Henry went on a binge, she went on a binge. If her favorite sweets and junk food weren't in the house, she hurried to the grocery store to satisfy her hunger. In truth, she was on as much of a roller coaster as Henry was. Somehow she had to keep herself from being so intertwined with his illness.

Now think about your relationship to your current family if you are married. Could your relationship with your spouse have anything to do with your addiction? Or is it a shelter in the storm?

My Spouse

This relationship is enjoyable in the following ways *(We seem to have good skills in sharing money and authority in the marriage. Both of our needs are reasonably well met.):*

_____

_____

_____

This relationship is painful in the following ways *(I am terrified that I will not be able to control my wife. Therefore, I maintain almost dictatorial control over all spending and investing and dole out an embarrassingly small allowance to her.)*:

_____

_____

_____

One patient of ours was amazed to see his own pattern regarding women. "Look at that!" He pointed to his survey. "In the past seven years I've walked out on every woman I cared for when I feared losing her. I walked out on her before she had a chance to walk out on me." Although the event had occurred at least five times, R. T. had no idea of the pattern until he saw it in black and white, in his own handwriting.

Michelle was another example of someone for whom this step was life changing. She was struggling to understand why she seemed to be addicted to abusive men. Early childhood aspects of her survey showed that apparently she was a happy, open child. But in her teen years she was the victim of incest. She experienced date rape in college. Her first husband, whom she married in her early twenties, was abusive. From then on the pattern seemed to be set as she subconsciously sought to punish herself for the false shame she carried over being an incest and rape victim.

Remember, the key is finding the pattern—the experiences that repeat.

The pattern I've repeated over and over again in these relationships is *(I have never felt able to establish boundaries with the opposite sex.* **Or,** *I have always feared abandonment by the opposite sex, and I have unknowingly pushed them away, rather than risk possible intimacy and subsequent abandonment.)*:

_____

_____

_____

Once Kathryn had inventoried her intimate relationships, Dr. Meier asked her to think about the authority
figures in her life. "How did you feel about the teachers in
school?" he asked her.

"Well, I have to admit that every time I got a bad grade
on a test in high school, I'd go on an eating binge," she
admitted. "I'd think, 'Grandma's right. I'll never be able to
please anyone. I'll never be special.' "

How about you? Could your addictions have anything to
do with these relationships?

Once Kathryn understood how her relationships with
her parents, her husband, and her teachers had influenced her compulsive overeating, Dr. Meier suggested
that she think about her relationship with herself.

Her sponsor, Helena, and Dr. Meier had confronted her
enough in this area, and she immediately laughed out
loud. Then she said, "Uh, oh. Now I'm really in trouble."

And sure enough she was.

Dr. Meier suggested, "Imagine that you are telling
someone who you are. Can you do so without talking
about your children or Henry or where you live or what
you own?"

Kathryn remained silent for quite a while. Then she
began, "Well, I . . . Er, I'm a . . ." Finally she looked up
at him with a blank look on her face.

"We ask you to do this so you can begin to look for your
authentic self," Dr. Meier said, "the person you are deep
down inside, beyond the identity you try to borrow from
people and things around you."

Dr. Meier also asked her to work through the following
statements to take a careful look at her relationship with
herself.

My Relationship with Myself
(Try to find your authentic self.)

One of the most important relationships that we form in our lifetime is a relationship with ourself. As a way to begin an inventory of how you may be estranged from yourself, check the statements below that describe you:

_____ I don't feel as if I live in my own skin. I'm almost an alien in my own body.

_____ I am constantly trying to borrow and mimic other people's values.

_____ I'd like to start over now, in mid-life—change everything I'm doing and begin again.

_____ I want to be liked by those around me. I often try to please them, even when it means doing something I'm not comfortable with.

_____ Every decision and action that I initiate is clouded by fear, doubt, and shame.

_____ I question whether I even have a right to my own feelings and thoughts.

_____ I sometimes question whether or not I was supposed to be born. Whether or not I have a right to exist.

As a means of assessing the authenticity of your relationship with you, check the statements below that describe you:

_____ I know my own values and attitudes.

_____ I am a child of God. I accept me the way I am, and I accept God's love for me.

_____ I judge myself by how He sees me, rather than how other human beings see me.

_____ I try to be forthright in expressing my honest feelings.

Unfortunately Kathryn felt more comfortable checking the first statements than the last four, which Dr. Meier said reflected a knowledge of who she really was. He told her, "You will never be able to develop your authentic self until you learn to become a good friend to yourself."

People, like Kathryn, who are married to spouses who are addicted to alcohol or other dependencies, and people who are single parents are least likely, we find, to be good friends to themselves. For instance, one of our patients was a single mother who would overeat and isolate herself when her daughter was away during the summer, living with her father, as if the mother meant to inflict punishment on herself during this time. "Plan to be a good friend to yourself this summer," we advised her. "Treat yourself to some good times. Attend your Twelve-Step meetings. Invite a friend out to dinner. Do something for yourself."

That's the advice we gave to Kathryn Markham. She would never be able to develop her authentic self until she became a good friend to herself.

Think about the kind of friend you might be to yourself. Check the statements below that reflect your attitude toward yourself:

_____ I am my own best friend.

_____ I enjoy being with myself.

_____ I would invite myself to a party.

_____ I am forgiving and compassionate toward myself. (For instance, if I don't close that business deal, can I reassure myself that it's okay, and I'll have a chance at another sale this afternoon? Or do I berate myself for not getting the sale?)

_____ I give myself miniature pep talks and words of encouragement in every area of my life.

_____ I do nice things for myself and to myself.

If you only checked one or two of the above statements, you are not being a good friend to yourself. We suggest that you think of treating yourself in the future as you would treat someone else. We also suggest that you pick a few role models to copy, people who treat you well or whom you see treating each other well. We often suggest that single people, for instance, visit a couples' class at church, rather than only the singles group. "Watch how these couples nurture each other and learn to treat yourself in the same way," we tell our patients. "Also gather some pointers to apply to your own relationships with people of the opposite sex."

Finally Dr. Meier suggested that Kathryn consider her relationship to God. "You will never be able to say, 'I am a child of God. I accept me the way I am, and I accept God's love for me' until you have a personal relationship with Him," Dr. Meier told her.

Consider your relationship to God, the single most important relationship of a lifetime. Complete the following exercise as a means of inventorying your relationship with Him:

God

My family _____ did _____ did not attend church
Instead I:

____ Went by myself.

____ Did not attend church.

____ Went to church with one parent.

At Sunday school I was taught that God was:

____ Watching over me in a loving way.

____ Watching me to harshly judge what I did.

I feel as if:

____ God is out to get me.

____ God doesn't care what happens to me.

_____ God is a puzzle that I can never quite find the key to.

_____ God is a close and trusted presence in my life.

I became disillusioned about God (for instance, when He didn't answer my prayers to help me stop my addiction)

I might be able to trust God better if I knew for sure that *(He had a direct and personal involvement in my recovery, that He was walking side by side with me through these Twelve Steps.):*

If I live according to God's principles—focusing on God rather than on myself and on reaching out to other people—my one fear is that *(God will disappoint me and I'll have to fall back to that old superhuman self-reliance.):*

It might help to discuss these doubts with someone; one person who might have some answers would be *(my Twelve-Step sponsor, my pastor, a good friend from church, my therapist):*

Once Kathryn had looked at her relationships, Dr. Meier suggested that she look for any guilt feelings that she felt about those relationships.

5. Identify Your Guilt Feelings

Look over your list from part four of your inventory to discover what relationships and events make you feel ashamed or guilty. It's important to spread this out, not attempt it all at one sitting. Also be sure to do it when you're relaxed, and suspend censorship over your writing. You will discover that much of the guilt you have imposed on yourself is false shame or unnecessary guilt, guilt you feel when you're not at fault. Guilt is one of the most powerful and potentially toxic emotions we can feel.

Authentic (true) guilt is good when it reminds you that you have sinned against God, others, or yourself. True guilt is good when it reminds you to ask God to forgive you and motivates you to forgive yourself. True guilt is also good when it motivates you to make a tactful and appropriate confession to a person you have harmed.

The release of your true and false guilt through inventory in Step Four and confession in Step Five may be one of the most freeing experiences of your entire recovery journey.

Again as Kathryn looked back over these relationships, she realized that some of the guilty feelings she felt were authentic. Yes, she had broken some of God's commandments, and she knew that her conscience accurately made her feel guilty about that. But she also knew that those scary messages that God would punish her for every negative thought were her grandmother's voice in disguise. Those were messages of false guilt.

Authentic Guilt

As an adult and a sinner, an imperfect human being, each of us has probably hurt many people in our lifetime. We will carry the items of our authentic guilt into Step Five with us, where we must acknowledge and confess our guilt over anyone we have really hurt. Because our re-

sponse to authentic guilt and false guilt will be so different, it is important that we understand the difference and
sort them carefully.

For example, you may feel guilty about your wife's depression. But her condition really stems from her parents'
bad marriage and from the fact that she doesn't take care
of herself, not from any mistreatment from you. Accusing
yourself for this would be false shame. Also be certain
that you don't accept shame for your parents' problems,
such as a father's alcoholism, or as Andy did for his father's rageaholism. If, however, you have been contribut-
ing to your wife's depression by running around with
other women, or if Andy had, as a teenager, decided to get
back at his father for his rages and purposely provoked
him, these would be elements of authentic guilt for which
restitution to God, and perhaps to that person, must be
made in Step Five and again in Steps Eight and Nine.

By now Kathryn Markham was truly depressed about
what had happened to her. This often happens as a patient takes a Step Four inventory. We always tell them to
stop a minute and look for the good.

6. "Look for the Good"

This is a slogan of Emotions Anonymous that all of us
can adopt for our lives. People doing their inventories
often need to be reminded that this is not an *immoral*
inventory. The purpose of this exercise is not to make a
"list of bad things about me." Melody Beattie, author of
Codependent No More, says that treating ourselves badly
is as much a moral issue as treating others badly. Not
allowing ourselves to enjoy life is a moral issue, a nega-
tion of all the good things God has created.

For this part of your inventory "accentuate the positive"
as the song says. Come to appreciate the special worth
and beauty in the creation God has made you to be. See
even the value of certain survival skills you acquired,
growing up in a dysfunctional family.

As you continue to "look for the good," realize that we are not meaning to minimize your losses or trying to justify the abuses that were inflicted on you. That pain must be recognized and grieved in Step Five. We just want you to realize that what happened to you may serve you in some way. The Apostle Paul says it this way: "And we know that all things work together for good to those who love God, to those who are the called according to His purpose."[4]

Think about:

1. The positive legacies you have acquired from your childhood *(Even though Dad was a workaholic, he demonstrated to me the values of commitment, perseverance, and loyalty. That was a positive legacy.):*

_____

_____

_____

2. The positive survival mechanisms I have learned from my struggles to cope are *(Andy Thomson discovered that he had excellent skills in conflict resolution, learned from coping with his rageaholic father. When his customers became agitated, he was able to be a good mediator.):*

_____

_____

_____

3. The skills, talents, and abilities you possess *(your natural ability to figure out math problems or to communicate your ideas to others or to influence people):*

_____

_____

_____

See how long a list you can make of "Things to Celebrate About Me."

Then think about your recovery process so far. What

positive recovery steps have you already undertaken by completing the first four steps? Check the ones below that apply to your present journey:

_____ I have broken out of denial and have begun to face my addictions. And I continue to do so.

_____ I have begun to turn my addictions over to God and to trust Him to walk with me through this process.

_____ I have broken out of isolation by talking to my counselor and/or attending Twelve-Step meetings. This isolation was causing a lot of my pain and dysfunction. I am making progress.

_____ I have begun to feel a personal relationship with Jesus Christ. He is my personal and intimate Higher Power.

_____ I have begun an emotional sharing and grieving process. I didn't understand how to do this when I first started, yet at my first Twelve-Step meeting tears came down my cheeks when others told their stories.

_____ I have committed to undertake this difficult, but healing, inventory process. I am excited about my commitment to long-term recovery.

_____ Other_____

An excellent Scripture to guide you here is Philippians 4:8. "Finally, brethren, whatever things are true, whatever things are noble, whatever things are just, whatever things are pure, whatever things are lovely, whatever things are of good report, if there is any virtue and if there is anything praiseworthy—meditate on these things."

7. Make an Inventory of Your Resentments

This is the part of the inventory that most people do first, and the only part that many people do, because it is outlined in detail in the *Big Book*. Emphasis on this aspect of the inventory is wise, because it is one of the most important parts.

Resentment can be defined as "simmering anger"; it is only the thinnest surface layer of the emotions we are feeling. We like to use the analogy of a geologist digging through the layers of geothermal activity to get to bedrock. *Resentment* comes from a Latin word which means "to feel over and over again." So resentment is anger that we're stuck in, feeling it over and over again with only little bits of steam escaping and the pressure building below. Resentment is the crust; turn a shovel and you'll find beneath, not the simmer of resentment, but a full, rolling boil of anger—anger that our needs have not been and are not being met.

With another shovelful of digging we find hurt from unmet needs. And when we go deeper yet—at the very deepest core—there is fear, fear that our needs will never be met. So we go from *resentment to anger to hurt to fear*. That's a very important inventory process because it is essential to know our deepest fears and insecurities. This knowledge gives us the key to move beyond our most deeply held resentments.

Until we inventory these resentments and know the deep fears that underlie them, those resentments will fester like emotional cancers. We like the metaphor of toxic waste. You can put toxic waste in drums and bury it deep in the ground, but over months and years it will bleed through and begin to poison the environment. The same thing will happen with deep resentments. If I resent that my spouse doesn't love me enough, deep down is probably a fear that no one will ever love me enough. Mom and Dad didn't really love me; God may not even love me. Unless I can inventory that fear and know what it is and find a way to meet it, it will eat away like toxic waste to poison my emotional and relational environment.

The Big Book says, "It is plain that a life which includes deep resentment leads only to futility and unhappiness."

Resentment is fatal. "For when harboring such feelings, we shut ourselves off from the sunlight of the Spirit. The insanity of alcohol returns, and we drink again."[5]

In inventorying your resentments, remember that you will need to work down through all the layers of your feelings from resentment to anger to hurt to fear to the unfulfilled need at the core. It is essential that you dig to this deepest level because needs and fears can be dealt with. On the other hand, resentment is paralyzing, and too many people have been frozen in this simmering anger for years, trapped and unable to escape.

Let's begin by looking at our relationship with our spouses or dating partners.

My Spouse or Dating Partner

Do I feel resentment toward:

____ My spouse or dating partner?

What happened to cause me to feel this way (One patient told us, "My spouse never listens to me. He doesn't hear what I'm saying. He doesn't honor my requests."):

_____

_____

_____

_____

I was angry because (As we talked to this patient, she told us that she often argued with her husband about how they spent money. "My husband wants to lavish large amounts of money on our adult children, and I keep warning him that we should be saving some of that money for our retirement."):

_____

_____

_____

_____

I was hurt because (This woman was hurt because her request wasn't being honored. "My husband's doing the exact opposite of what I'm asking him to do."):

_____

_____

_____

_____

My hurt may have stemmed from the fear that (This woman was afraid of two things. First, she naturally feared for their financial security in old age. Second, she was afraid that her husband was more connected to their children than to her. Unconsciously she was thinking, "He loves them more than he does me. He can't or won't hear me."):

_____

_____

_____

_____

The need that is unfulfilled in my life is (In this woman's case she needed to be loved, honored, and respected in her marriage relationship.):

_____

_____

_____

_____

We urge our patients to get beneath their resentments so they can understand their unmet needs. Some of this woman's strong resentment of her husband's giving money to their adult children was justified. However, some of her resentment stemmed from her childhood, echoing an unmet need from long ago. We realized this as we talked to her about this situation.

"My father died of a heart attack when I was eight years old," she told us. "In the next years my family went

through a painful period of financial insecurity." That was
the core of this woman's resentment. She was hounded by
insecurity. We helped this woman to see that these old
unmet needs from her childhood were a part of her strong
resentment of her husband's actions. "A key to confronting your husband successfully is to separate these
old needs from this current situation," we told her. "If you
don't, you and your husband will continue to attack each
other. You will continue to accuse him of not really caring
about you. And he will continue to ignore your concerns.

"However, if you admit your fear of needing this money
for your retirement, and the old fears from your childhood, both of you will understand the current situation
better and be better able to deal with it. You will be able
to confront your husband about this issue without super-
imposing the life-and-death emotional intensity you've
felt from thirty years of financial insecurity."

Our primary reason for inventorying our resentments
is to grieve out old unmet needs, like this woman's, but a
second reason is very practical. Two people who are trying
to work through an issue, as this husband and wife are,
cannot resolve it as long as anger and barbed statements
are part of the discussion. This woman is likely to attack
her husband with statements like, "You never managed
our money well. You've always given too much to the kids.
You're just trying to buy their love." And the husband will
respond to her in like manner.

But when she says, "I fear where we are headed once
we retire. I have certain needs for security and structure.
I have always felt insecure since my dad died. I need to
talk about that and I need you to hear my fears and my
needs." Now the atmosphere in this discussion changes.
The husband and wife are not attacking one another or
putting each other down. Instead the underlying perception is, "I'm not the enemy; you're not the enemy. Maybe I
have overresponded to this situation, but please talk to
me about it." The couple switches out of the anger mode
and starts to talk about their own fears and unmet needs.

Try to do this in the situation you inventoried with your own spouse or dating partner. It takes practice, but we've found that this approach resolves a lot of problems in any marriage or relationship, even our own.

Other People in Your Life

Now consider other people in your life—your friends or family members, employer or church pastor—and take the same kind of inventory. Also consider your resentment of certain institutions. For instance, some patients harbor a resentment toward the college that kicked them out or their church. One woman told us that her pastor never came to see her when she was in the hospital for cancer surgery. For years afterward she resented the church and didn't go regularly because of that.

Unless you inventory resentments like these, you will spend a disproportionate amount of emotional energy on the little things of life. As Dr. Chris Thurman says in *The Lies We Believe,* you will turn nickel events into four-hundred-dollar events and suffer unnecessarily.

Name three persons or situations about which you have experienced resentment:

1. _____
2. _____
3. _____

What offenses to yourself have these resentments led you to commit? What needs have you ignored? Complete the following statements about each of the three resentments named above:

1. I have resented _____
   I was angry because _____
   I was hurt because _____
   My hurt may have stemmed from the fear that __

_____

The need that was unmet was _____
_____

2. I have resented _____
   I was angry because _____
   I was hurt because _____
   My hurt may have stemmed from the fear that _
   _____
   _____

   The need that was unmet was _____
   _____

3. I have resented _____
   I was angry because _____
   I was hurt because _____
   My hurt may have stemmed from the fear that _
   _____
   _____

   The need that was unmet was _____
   _____

Take Your Time

It may take you weeks to do a thorough job of Step
Four. Don't rush. Dr. Meier warned Kathryn to take her
time. "You are looking at a four-hour movie of your life,"
he reminded her. "Even movies become tiring when they
run that long. So take your time."

Pam, whose life was transformed through working the
Twelve Steps said, "I worry that most people don't do Step
Four rigorously enough. It's so important. Making a list of
a few things you resent and a few people you've offended
isn't enough. You have to dig. And you have to hurt."

We agree with Pam, but we also say to you, "Don't
worry. Remember, these are steps. Take them one at a
time. Baby steps are quite sufficient." You can rely on God

and your own subconscious to bring answers—it's your job to ask the questions. It's your job to make a searching and fearless moral inventory of yourself. God will give you the answers as you walk through the next steps.

Step Five

Admitted to God, to ourselves, and to another human being the exact nature of our wrongs.

Kathryn sat at the small desk in her room looking over her inventory. It had taken quite a while to complete the entire thing; she thought she knew how Tolstoy must have felt when he finished *War and Peace*. And the slight smugness in her smile wasn't just from the satisfaction of having completed a tough job. Looking back over her life, she had found lots of good things to celebrate about herself and the items on the list that were less than celebratory—like overprotecting her children, or worrying too much about Henry—weren't such terrible defects. And when she looked at her list of resentments and what those people, like her parents and her grandmother and her husband, had done to her, she had good reason to resent them. Yes, she really felt quite justified for the self-pity she was inclined to slip into. Life *had* dealt her a bad hand.

Well, Step Five wouldn't be so bad. She didn't have anything really deep, dark, and horrible to confess to God or to herself. And never mind confessing to another person. She had no intention of telling all this to another person. They might laugh at her, or use it against her, or worse, criticize her. She really didn't know anyone she could go to with all this anyway. But that was okay, she and God could handle it alone. She was doing very well.

The jangling of the telephone interrupted her thoughts. "Is this Mrs. Markham?" The official ring to the voice was an added jar.

"Yes."

"This is Sergeant Mackey of the city police. We're holding your son Jason here. He was picked up about an hour ago with three of his friends engaged in shoplifting."

The sergeant's voice continued, but Kathryn couldn't take it in. "Just a minute, officer," she stammered when there was a pause on the line. "I'll be right down. Oh, no— I can't. I don't have a car." She couldn't think what to do. And Henry would be no help. It was an hour after the office closed; he'd be on his third drink by now.

"That's all right, ma'am. We'll bring him home."

By the time the conversation was over Kathryn's hand was shaking so she could hardly replace the receiver. She needed help—but who? A lawyer? Yes, they would need one, maybe the one who wrote their wills a few years ago, if she could remember his name. A preacher? The idea was comforting. She'd been meaning to get started in a church ever since Steps Two and Three had led her back to a beginning faith in God. A friend? Suddenly Kathryn realized the vacuum she lived in. She couldn't think of one friend. Neighbors, acquaintances, people she did business with—but a *friend*. Even in Al-Anon—there were lots of friendly people there, people she really liked, but she had held aloof from them just as she had held aloof from her husband and everyone she knew except her children.

Her children! It wasn't fair! She had given her whole life to her kids. She'd put everything she had into being a good mom. And this was how Jason repaid her. *Shoplifting?* What had he ever wanted that she hadn't supplied— usually before he asked? Why would he need to steal? She glanced at her inventory notebook, which now lay in a heap on the floor. See how unfair life was to her!

When the phone rang again she was afraid to pick it up.

The police again? The storeowner? Realizing how unlikely that was gave her the courage to answer. She couldn't believe it when the warm, caring voice came over the wire. "Helena!" she said. "How did you know I needed you? I would never have thought of calling my sponsor!" She hadn't seen Helena since she'd launched her Step Four inventory.

Helena laughed. "A lot stranger things than this happen when you turn your life over to God. What can I do for you? I just called to ask how you're doing on your steps, but it sounds like you've got trouble. I'll come right over—shall I?"

By the time Helena got there Kathryn had found their lawyer's telephone number and called him and had dug out all the money from three of her hiding places to pay the storeowner and lawyer.

But Helena didn't want to talk about lawyers or money or Jason's needs. Kathryn couldn't believe her sponsor could be so impractical. Here was a major crisis and Helena wanted Kathryn to talk about *herself.* "Yeah, I finished the inventory. Actually I was sort of doing Step Five when the police called, but really . . ." The sound of the timer on her stove interrupted. "Just a minute, Helena. I popped some cookies in the oven. The police will be bringing Jason home soon, and I know he'll be upset. I thought some warm chocolate chip . . ."

"Kathryn!" Helena gripped her by the shoulders and spun her around. "The answer to this problem is not chocolate chip cookies, not even good legal advice. The solution has to start inside *you*—the way you smother Jason, the way you take responsibility for everyone's lives, the way you're so busy taking care of everyone else that you don't take care of yourself!"

"The cookies will burn," Kathryn protested. She tore herself away to the kitchen.

But later that night when Jason was in his room with orders to do his homework, and Henry was slumped in front of the television, Kathryn returned to thinking about her work on Step Five. Why was she so suspicious of other people and unwilling to let anyone into her life? Was it possible that all—or at least some of—the faults she'd seen in other people really came from defects in herself? Was she unwilling to admit her wrongs to another person because she was afraid to see herself through another's eyes?

Kathryn suddenly began to suspect that, just as she had been unable to run the lives of her family all by herself, so she couldn't handle the job of her recovery all by herself.

Admitted the Exact Nature of Our Wrongs

All of the Twelve Steps go contrary to our natural inclinations because they are all ego-deflating; they all challenge that false grandiosity that covers our true insecurity. But few steps are more humbling than Step Five: Admitted to God, to ourselves, and to another human being the exact nature of our wrongs. At the same time, no step is more necessary to long-term recovery and peace of mind than the confession step.

You may be like our patients who balk when they are told they must confess to God. "Wait a minute! Doesn't God already *know?*" they ask.

"Yes," we tell them. "God knows what you've done and God knows how you feel about it, immensely better than you know. But confession is for your growth, not for God's. Confession helps the person who's confessing, not the person who's listening."

In the course of being human all of us have inflicted damage on those around us, either intentionally or unintentionally. If we have an addictive personality and are living out that lifestyle, we have probably contributed more than our fair share to the pain of those around us. It's a natural part of God's plan for us to feel guilt about this. We may try to minimize or bury or deny that guilt, but the guilt is still there. And we are usually burdened by our guilt. The feelings of remorse are bottled up inside us and confession is the only way to release the pain of our authentic guilt and the anger and resentment from our false guilt. We suggested that Kathryn begin her Fifth Step by confessing her authentic guilt, the wrongs she had actually committed.

Authentic Guilt

If you read the story of the prodigal son in the fifteenth chapter of Luke, you will notice in verses 18 and 19 the son practiced his confession: "I will arise and go to my father, and will say to him. . . ." So in preparing to do your formal Fifth Step, it is a good idea to make some specific preparation beyond your Step Four inventory.

Step Five says we admitted "the exact nature of our wrongs," so we begin our Fifth Step by examining the ways in which our addictions have harmed ourselves and others.

Acknowledge the Wrongs in Your Own Life: Your Addictions

Obviously one of the things you have done against God is to replace Him with your addiction. Acknowledge that as part of Step Five.

I acknowledge my primary addiction to (In Kathryn's case the answer was obvious: food. It will probably be obvious in yours also.) _____.

Next acknowledge the other addictions you listed on page 90 (For instance, Kathryn acknowledged codependency—rescuing, overprotecting, and overcontrolling others.):

1. _____

2. _____

3. _____

4. _____

5. _____

We also need to acknowledge the specific ways in which we have wronged others by the practice of our addictions. For example, the workaholic may at first try to minimize the impact of his lifestyle on his family, but through honest confession he will probably develop a long list of how he has hurt his family as he invested more and more in his work and neglected his family.

My addictions have harmed the following people in the following ways:

Who I Harmed	How I Harmed Them
1._____	_____
2._____	_____
3._____	_____

Acknowledge the Wrongs that Have Occurred in the Major Relationships of Your Life.

"Think back about the major relationships you reviewed in your inventory," we said to Kathryn. "Which relationships have been harmed by things you have done?"

How about you? Think back to the relationships you inventoried in your Fourth Step, beginning with your relationship with your parents.

I contributed to the problems in my relationship with my parents because I *(Never told them the truth about what I was doing, so we couldn't have any honest relationship.)*:

_____

_____

_____

I contributed to the problems in my relationships with the opposite sex because I (For example, Kathryn recognized that she always anticipated being a victim in relationships with men and so she set herself up to live out that role.):

———————————————————————

———————————————————————

———————————————————————

I contributed to the problems in my relationships with my spouse because I *(even though Kathryn didn't cause her husband to be an alcoholic, her efforts to fix and rescue him enabled his alcoholism. And her nagging for him to get on the straight and narrow drove him farther away from her.)*:

———————————————————————

———————————————————————

———————————————————————

Kathryn also had to consider her relationship with her children. As she thought about this relationship she finally acknowledged that she had been overprotective and overcontrolling. Some of that was natural, she knew. Henry certainly didn't have time for the children. One of Jason's friends had even said to him one day, "Your dad loves beer more than he loves you." Jason had denied that to his friend, but inside he knew his friend was right, as he later told his mother. Yet now she had to acknowledge the damage she had done and grieve about it. Her children were not as close to her as they would have been if she had not smothered them so. And as Helena had pointed out, Jason's stealing was related to her overprotectiveness.

We also pointed this out to her in counseling. Oftentimes a child Jason's age cannot put what he feels into words. Yet he instinctively knows that his boundaries are being invaded. At some deep level he feels overpowered,

so he kicks back and creates some breathing room by re-
belling. Stealing. Taking drugs. Trying promiscuous sex.
Running away from home. Joining a cult. Kids have so
many options to choose from these days.

Look carefully at your relationship with your children
as you fill in the blanks below:

I contributed to the problems in my relationships
with my children because I have:

_____

_____

_____

_____

And your relationship with yourself:

I contributed to my own problems by not being a
friend to myself in the following ways ("By always
thinking of others first and denying myself," Kathryn
wrote. "Inwardly I resented this and was always angry
about it, which made me very depressed."):

_____

_____

_____

_____

Finally your relationship with God:

I contributed to the problems in my relationship with
God because I *(Didn't try to find the real God earlier in
my life,* Kathryn wrote.):

_____

_____

_____

_____

Now Kathryn needed to admit any ways she had violated moral and legal standards.

Acknowledge the Ways You Have Violated Other Moral, Legal, Ethical, or Financial Standards or Boundaries

As Kathryn thought about this, she realized that at times she felt so powerless over her life that she purposely took something without paying for it, just to prove she could do what she wanted to do. If she was in a candy store, for instance, she just picked up a small box of chocolates and walked out. She also knew that her sexual promiscuity was outside of Christian standards. Andy Thomson also had to realize that he was tempted by sexual fantasies. Sometimes he would look at a beautiful young woman and wonder what it would be like to make love to her. And the professor, Martin Woodruff, had to admit that he sometimes fudged on his income tax return.

How about you? Is there some area in which you are out of bounds morally or legally or financially? If so, mention it here:

1. _____
2. _____
3. _____

After Kathryn had thought about these three areas, she took stock of the exact nature of her wrongs. She felt extreme remorse for the damage her overprotective parenting had imposed on her children. She was also overcome with guilt about all she had done in the years she had rebelled against God and her grandmother. She came to appreciate the absolute necessity of having some means to spiritually release her guilt. Those of us with addictive personalities either find a means to purge this guilt from our minds and hearts or the guilt accumulates as a vast toxic residue. Unless we release this guilt in Step Five through confessing the exact nature of our wrongs to God, the pain of that remorse may bring us back into the active practice of our addictions.

Admitted the Exact Nature of Our
Wrongs to God

Kathryn told Dr. Meier, "I really want to see the sin in my life. I know I've hurt and damaged others. Yet every time I think about what I've done and try to confess it to God I suddenly hear Grandma's voice reciting the Old Testament injunction, 'An eye for an eye, a tooth for a tooth.' I'm scared to death about what God might do to me."

"Kathryn, I know you realize that's a poor picture of God. You're just having trouble believing that in your heart," Dr. Meier replied. "Instead of seeing God trying to squash you with His thumb, let me give you another definition for sin, which will show you that God's not going to zap you for committing a sin. The word *sin* comes from a Greek word which means 'missing the mark.' God has set up certain natural laws for us. They are there for our good, and if we step outside them, we end up hurting ourselves and others. Every sin listed in the Bible hurts either ourselves, others, or God—and sometimes all three. One of the natural consequences of our sin is authentic guilt. It is a warning, much like a burglar alarm that tells us we are moving out of bounds. Confessing the exact nature of our wrongs to God releases us from our feelings of guilt."

We had to help Kathryn see that she was always going to be imperfect and fall short of God's expectation for her. The apostle Paul tells the Roman Christians this in Romans 3:23: "For all have sinned and fall short of the glory of God." Then he goes on to add that we are, however, justified by God's grace through the redemption of His Son, Jesus Christ.

"God only expects you to try to be all you can be," Dr. Meier told Kathryn. "He knows you're human. He will forgive you."

Once our patients finish an examination of the exact nature of their wrongs, we suggest that they make a general confession of those wrongs to God. The guidelines given to Christians years ago by St. Alphonsus Liguori are also applicable today. He said, "For a good confession three things are necessary: *An examination of conscience, sorrow, and a determination to avoid sin.*"[1]

Richard Foster examines the three elements of a good confession in *Celebration of Discipline*. First, *an examination of conscience*. Foster says that, "We must be prepared to deal with definite sins. A generalized confession may save us from humiliation and shame, but it will not ignite inner healing."[2] So the first rule in how to confess is to be specific (which we have just done).

Next, *sorrow* is necessary to a good confession. By sorrow, Foster means, "not primarily an emotion . . . but an abhorrence at having committed the sin, a deep regret at having offended the heart of the Father."[3] Sorrow is not just easy tears, which might actually be a cover-up of deeper emotions. True sorrow begins with the will, with making a choice to experience true regret and deal with it.

St. Alphonsus' third element *"determination to avoid sin"* may not come so easily. Recognizing and admitting to a dysfunctional pattern in our life is not the same thing as determining never to do it again. It is enough in the beginning if we are simply willing to ask God to give us the desire to change and for an abhorrence of our old way of life.

Richard Foster in *Celebration of Discipline* points out the advantages of a formalized confession: "It does not allow for any excuses or extenuating circumstances. We must confess that we have sinned by our own fault, our own most grievous fault. Our sins cannot be called errors in judgment, nor is there any room to blame them on others."[4]

Read through an historic general confession, which Christians have used since the Reformation, with us and put the specific wrongs you have identified before God:

Most merciful God, I confess that I have sinned against you in thought, word, and deed, by what I have done _____, and by what I have left undone _____. I have not loved you with my whole heart; I have not loved my neighbor as myself. I am truly sorry and I humbly repent. For the sake of your Son Jesus Christ, have mercy on me and forgive me; that I may delight in your will, and walk in your ways, to the glory of your Name. Amen.[5] [Paraphrased to change the word *we* to the word *I.*]

Remember a general confession like this is a guideline for the confession of authentic guilt, not false guilt. Making a general confession like this about areas of false guilt merely results in a destructive compounding of our addiction shame base. Some of our patients are more comfortable with just talking to God directly, as they do to us. That's fine, we say. "You can use this general confession as a model or just strike out on your own."

Admitted the Exact Nature of Our Wrongs to Ourselves

One of the most beneficial aspects of confessing to God is that it leads us to be absolutely honest with ourselves. It's easier to lie to ourselves than to lie to God because we'll believe our own lies. God won't. In fact, it's hard to lie on your knees as Martin realized when he made Step Three.

In order to take the Fifth Step we must lower our psychological defenses and become emotionally vulnerable. The idea of pouring out old memories, which are accompanied by deep feelings of shame, or disclosing experiences that you have kept hidden for a lifetime—even from yourself—may fill you with fear. Do you fear your own condemnation? Many of our patients do.

The antidote to this fear is compassion. You must extend compassion to yourself. Do this by giving yourself permission to give and accept forgiveness. We often suggest that our patients make a litany of absolution a part of their confession to themselves. Begin by saying:

"I forgive myself so that I can heal." God has given you this permission. Christ gave his followers the authority to receive confessions of sin and to grant forgiveness in His name. "If you forgive the sins of any, they are forgiven," He said.[6] This is a grace we must not refuse to extend to ourselves.

Kathryn said those words out loud as she sat one afternoon at that same desk in her room, making her confession to God and to herself. "I forgive myself, Lord, so that I can heal," she said and felt as if those words had been spoken by God Himself.

The second part of your litany to yourself should be: *"I accept myself as a human being with character defects."* We have probably all seen the bumper stickers that say, "Christians aren't perfect; they're just forgiven." Taking Step Five will not make you a perfect person, but it can make you a forgiven person—forgiven by God and by yourself.

Kathryn decided to write the words, *"I accept myself as a human being with character defects,"* beside Step Five in the *Big Book,* as well as saying them aloud to herself. Every time she read from that book, she would be reminded of that underlying acceptance of herself.

Now she was ready to deal with the second part of this step—the false guilt she carried from her childhood.

False Guilt

Most people who take Step Five only deal with their authentic guilt. However, we give equal weight to grieving through all of the relationships and life situations that have instilled a sense of false guilt in us. Unresolved guilt is emotionally corrosive, and false guilt carries the same power to damage us emotionally as authen-

tic guilt does. Unfortunately children are highly vulnerable to picking up unnecessary guilt, especially those
growing up in pain-filled homes. No matter what the dysfunction, the child will blame himself. "If I were prettier,
Daddy wouldn't yell at Mama." "If I were smarter,
Mama wouldn't drink so much." "If I hadn't been born,
Daddy wouldn't be so depressed." That's false guilt.

Kathryn is coming to realize, for instance, that all of
her life she has carried false guilt because her mom and
dad did not have a harmonious marriage. She blamed herself. She took on that false guilt. Now she resents the pain
she had suffered from that guilt.

When we feel any significant pain, we must go through
a series of predictable stages so we can process our pain
and let go of it. If we have grown up in a dysfunctional
family, we probably have not seen how people deal with
pain in a healthy way, so we will need to learn how to go
through the five emotional stages of the grieving process:

- Denial,
- Anger,
- Depression,
- True grief or sadness,
- And acceptance, forgiveness, and resolution

—in order to truly put aside our false guilt and the shame
and resentment that comes from it. We must begin by
grieving through the wrongs in our families of origin.
These are things over which we had no control. We were
wronged by what went on around us. Yet these abuses are
the seeds of false guilt.

Acknowledge the Wrongs in Your Family of Origin

If a child in a family sees pain, unhappiness, or conflict
on the faces of Mom and Dad, the child intuitively asks,
"What's wrong with me?" Since the child thinks magically
("I have a magical influence over the events in my world")

and is egocentric ("The world revolves around me"), the child naturally thinks that he or she has caused the pain or chaos. "If Dad disappears, I must have something to do with it." "If Mom and Dad divorce, it's my fault."

That causes false guilt. And the parents' problems also cause the child to feel unloved. The parents are so caught up in their pain, they are not available to meet the child's needs. And the pain of listening to their fighting about their problems will even wash out any love the child is receiving from them. The parents' unhappiness is a toxin that poisons whatever positive love they do try to express.

Yet a hunger for love is an inborn part of every person that is as basic as the physical need for food. Hospital nurseries learned this graphically after World War II. When trying to cope with large numbers of war orphans, they placed the babies on strict feeding, changing, and turning schedules. The formulas were scientifically calculated, the environments were clean, comfortable, and healthy. And yet the babies sickened and died. Almost by accident nurses began to discover that babies that were not just turned, but were also patted and played with, and babies that were not just fed, but also held and talked to, flourished. Babies could die from love hunger just as readily as from physical malnutrition.

And yet many adult children are as near emotional death from love hunger as those war orphans. Our love hunger left us susceptible to pick up an addiction as a way to fill this hunger and to medicate the pain of our emptiness. We are trying to satisfy our love hunger with drugs, sex, work, or some such addiction.

Check the abuses below that you experienced in your family of origin and listed in your Step Four inventory. (Remember, denial is the first stage of the grieving process so you will be tempted to deny a family member's addiction. Yet denying this can be as serious as failing to admit to your own addiction.)

_____ Active abuse

_____ Passive abuse

_____ Emotional incest

_____ Negative messages

Often our patients feel very angry as they think about the ways they have been abused. "I was terrified as a child," they realize, "and I'm furious that I had to live that way." They walk through the second phase of the grieving process—anger—when they acknowledge the wrongs in their family of origin.

As therapists we had to get Kathryn Markham to let all those buried feelings come to the surface so she could be free of them. She didn't realize how angry she was at her grandmother until she thought about the negative messages her grandmother had given her. When grandma said, "God's watching you," Kathryn had always seen a policeman with a billy club, ready to discipline her for any misbehavior. Now she admitted to us, "I'm flat out angry at Grandma. She gave me a distorted picture of God, which led me to fear Him and reject Him. And even worse, Grandma's picture of God led me to believe that I never could be acceptable to God."

Kathryn was also sad. She had to grieve through the loss of all those years when she could have had a close relationship with her Father in heaven. "God only expects you to try to be all you can be," we told Kathryn. "He knows you're human. He will forgive you."

False guilt also comes from experiences in our present families. Kathryn Markham had heaped a lot of indirect guilt upon herself from all her years of living with Henry. Even though Henry did not say things to her like, "If you were only a better lover" or "If you were only a better housekeeper, I wouldn't drink so much," Kathryn unconsciously thought them to herself. "If only I were better," she thought, "Henry would be better." She carried an inordinate amount of responsibility for Henry's dysfunction.

Once we have grieved out the pain that our false guilt has caused us, we are ready to hand it back. "It is not my fault that Dad sexually abused me. It had nothing to do with me, in fact. That was Dad's problem, Dad's addiction. I hand it back to him and no longer take responsibility for it."

How about you? Think about the things you feel guilty about. Are you carrying any false guilt? If so, decide to hand those feelings back to the person who should be carrying them. Say, "I realize that the following feelings are really false guilt, not authentic guilt. If someone else should deal with this issue, I hand it back to him or her." Do so by filling in the blanks below:

1. I realize that *(I feel a deep sense of shame and embarrassment about our childhood financial poverty. In fact, if someone gave me a ride home from school I would ask them to drop me off several blocks from our house so that they would not see where we lived)* _____ is false guilt.

I hand it back to *(my parents; they were the financial providers for my family of origin):* _____
2. I realize that *(I have always felt dirty about my own sexuality, even when I have kept it within God-given boundaries)* _____ is false guilt.

I hand it back to *(my mom. I realize that this shame largely comes from her deep sense of shame about her own sexuality. It was Mom who was pregnant out of wedlock. Not me. I don't have to carry that shame for her.)*

3. I realize that *(Kathryn wrote, "My feeling that I can never please God and that I don't deserve His salvation.")* _____ is false guilt.

I hand it back to *(Kathryn wrote, "My grandmother. I realize that she was afraid of God and she*

*handed that fear down to me. Now I hand it back to
her."*)

Once Kathryn handed her false guilt back, she also had
to release her resentment toward her grandmother and
others who had hurt her.

Resentment

False guilt always causes resentment because deep
within us we realize that we were not really responsible;
this shame and guilt was imposed upon us by others. We
have suffered the harmful emotions that resulted from
this guilt unnecessarily. A final part of our litany of absolution to ourselves is to say, *"I release my resentments so
that I can grow."*

Yes, abuses have occurred in our childhood, and we became aware of that when we did our Step Four inventory.
Yes, abuses have occurred in our relationships today. Yes,
our personalities have been distorted as we attempted to
cope with what happened and to medicate the pain
through our addictions.

We often remind our patients of the popular recovery
slogan, "No one is to blame, but everyone is responsible."
Yes, your parents were responsible for some of the things
that shaped your personality. Yes, your spouse may be
responsible. But they are not to blame. Neither are you.

Check off the resentments that you identified in your
Step Four inventory and are now ready to release:

I release my resentments toward:

_____ My spouse or dating partner

_____ Dad and/or Mom

_____ My sibling(s)

_____ My friend(s)_____

_____ My employer

_____ My children

Now you are responsible for making the changes in your personality. In Steps One, Two and Three we laid down our addictions and surrendered our lives to a power greater than ourselves, to our Savior, Jesus Christ. In Step Four, the inventory step, we attempted to understand how our addictions got started and the full weight of the damage they created. In Step Five we accept responsibility for who we are: our character defects, our narcissism, our addictions. We take a step beyond identifying what happened to us and take adult responsibility for who we are today, regardless of what happened in our past.

Admitted to Another Human Being

Kathryn was ready to take the final part of Step Five: to talk to another person about her authentic guilt and her false guilt. In doing so, she would take full adult responsibility for who she was today.

"As you confess the exact nature of your wrongs to this other human being, you will walk through a major stage of the grieving process, true grief or sadness," we told her. "At this stage it is very healthful and cleansing if the tears flow, washing away the hurts and all that has built up around them, cleansing the soul."

That's why Step Five is an addendum to Step Four. We call these steps, "couplet steps," because one leads to the other. In Step Four we inventory what has happened to us. In Step Five we take action, we move beyond what has happened to us. True healing will only come from confession and grieving and both of these processes, by their very natures, can best be done person to person. That's where emotions can be released. And that's how we enter into the final stage of the grieving process: acceptance, forgiveness, and resolution.

We talked earlier about forgiving ourselves, but the key here is forgiving others. The written work in Step Four and the first part of Step Five took you only part of the way. Now there needs to be the interaction between you and another human being. The caution at this point is that there must be genuine grief in order for the forgiveness to have integrity. A slick, "I forgive. It's over with and forgotten," without taking the intermediate steps of anger, depression, and sorrow is really just denial in different words.

The 12 × 12 says, "Often it was while working on this Step with our sponsors or spiritual advisers that we first felt truly able to forgive others, no matter how deeply we felt they had wronged us. Our moral inventory had persuaded us that all-around forgiveness was desirable, but it was only when we resolutely tackled Step Five that we inwardly *knew* we'd be able to receive forgiveness and give it, too."[7]

We told Kathryn Markham that this part of Step Five has three major benefits. By talking to another person:

- We choose to live a life based on honesty in our relationships, now and in the future.
- We move out of loneliness and isolation.
- We connect with another person on an intimate sharing level.

We Choose to Live a Life Based on Honesty in Our Relationships

Years of living the addictive lifestyle have taught us to be masters of deceit and cover-ups, but now, in our new lives, we choose to live honestly. The introduction to the Twelve Steps cautions that the single greatest barrier to recovery is the inability to be honest. "We soon realized that we'd have to have outside help if we were surely to know and admit the truth about ourselves—the help of God and another human being. Only by discussing ourselves, holding back nothing, only by being willing to take advice and accept direction could we set foot on the road to straight thinking, solid honesty, and genuine humility."[8]

Fifth Step sharing with another person is an extraordinary step of trust and truth. For once in our lives we're going to open the deepest, darkest secrets and reveal the most sensitive pains to another human being. A solitary, self-appraisal and admission of our defects alone aren't nearly enough.

The 12 × 12 says: "Somehow, being alone with God doesn't seem as embarrassing as facing up to another person. Until we actually sit down and talk aloud about what we have so long hidden, our willingness to clean house is still largely theoretical. When we are honest with another person, it confirms that we have been honest with ourselves and with God."[9]

This advice is also consistent with the advice the apostle Paul gives to the Corinthian Christians: "Therefore, . . . as we have received mercy, we do not lose heart. But we have renounced the hidden things of shame, not walking in craftiness, nor handling the Word of God deceitfully; but by manifestation of the truth commending ourselves to every man's conscience in the sight of God."[10]

We Move Out of Loneliness and Isolation

Another purpose of admitting the exact nature of our wrongs to another human being is to break out of the loneliness Kathryn felt at the beginning of this chapter. She couldn't think of a friend to turn to. Only neighbors. Acquaintances.

All addicts are tortured by loneliness—a disease symptom most often described as "suffering from terminal uniqueness." We always felt we were different from other people, always on the outside looking in. Confessing to another human being breaks down this isolation and the fear that, "If you really knew me, if you saw behind my mask, you wouldn't love me—you'd reject me and abandon me."

Members of Recovery, Inc., talk about "averageness vs. exceptionality." They know that most addicts consider themselves uniquely bad when in fact, we all make mistakes. Members tell newcomers, "We've walked in your shoes. Many of us have had those same experiences. You're really remarkably average."[11]

Sometimes this assurance is nonverbal. We look into the eyes of the person we are confessing to and instead of seeing astonishment and rejection, we see warmth and compassion, which pulls us back into community with other people. We find this compassion deeply reassuring because so much shame is superimposed on top of the wrong we have committed. Yet once we break out of secrecy, once we break out of our isolation and tell another person about our mistakes, this layer of shame dissolves. We find that people's hair does not turn green when they hear what we have done. Yes, we've done things that we should feel guilty about. But so has everyone else. Welcome to the human race!

As we tell the exact nature of our wrongs to another person we also realize that we've magnified those experiences over the years. Each year they've remained hidden in our brains, the experiences have grown worse in our minds. Now those experiences shrink back down to size. They were wrong, but they were not as monstrous as we have led ourselves to believe.

We Connect with Another Person on an Intimate Sharing Level

Finally, making the Step Five confession to another person also teaches us how to connect with another person on an intimate, sharing level—an experience which most dependent people have not experienced. This connectedness opens us to a new energy and greater capacity to change our lives. Our confession strengthens our commitment to recovery because we now have companions—both earthly, like Helena, Kathryn's sponsor, and heavenly, our Savior, Jesus Christ—interceding in prayer for us, encouraging us, and sharing with us.

We often mention to our patients the comforting picture that the apostle Paul painted for the Roman Christians. He saw Christ at the right hand of God, making intercessions for us. As people often say, "I can't think of a better attorney than Jesus, pleading to God, the Father, to forgive my foibles."

These three benefits are available to any of us who are willing to admit the exact nature of our wrongs. One woman whose recovery has hinged on breaking out of the isolation and secrecy of her addictions is Kitty Dukakis, wife of presidential nominee Michael Dukakis. Kitty had been addicted to diet pills for twenty-six years. She went through three recovery programs in the space of eighteen months. During that time she drank rubbing alcohol, inhaled hair spray, and ingested nail polish remover. She is a compulsive smoker. She has been diagnosed as manic-depressive and takes lithium to control her severe mood swings.

Kitty wrote her book, *Now You Know,* as part of her recovery therapy—telling her story in written form. "One of the things I'm learning is that secrets are devastating for someone with my disease," she told a reporter for the *Dallas Times Herald.*[12] So Kitty Dukakis has told her story nationwide in print and on talk shows. It's such an essential part of her prescription for recovery that some observers feel that had Michael Dukakis been elected president, his wife's chances for recovery would have been slim. And Kitty agreed that the pressures of being First Lady would probably have prevented her from seeking treatment.

Kitty Dukakis was suffering from depression, the third stage of the grief process, which is really our anger turned inward. Because confession to another person is an outward act this can help us break out of depression and redirect the resentments that have been eating us like a cancer.

Choosing Your Confessor

Most of us do both a formal and an informal Fifth Step. The formal step occurs when we say to ourselves, "I'm going to go see a minister in a town faraway, a person I don't know so well so I will feel free to confess all my faults." Or our patients sometimes come to us and say, "Since we've been working through some of these issues together, I'd like to stop and take three or four therapy sessions to devote to doing the Fifth Step."

The informal Fifth Step is ongoing. Every time we attend a Twelve-Step meeting and talk about our past mistakes and present errors we take a miniature Fifth Step. And every time we talk to our sponsor or a friend and are candid about our problems and the way we deal with them, we take another informal Fifth Step. As you can see, we will have many miniature Step Five encounters throughout our lives.

The Formal Fifth Step

To take the formal Fifth Step a person usually tells their sponsor or therapist or minister, "I want to do a Fifth Step." They schedule a time for it and may take written notes to the meeting, compiled from the exercises in this chapter or their Fourth Step inventory.

Once you realize why you must confess to another person, the next step is deciding who that person will be. This is a major decision and should not be taken lightly. When Kathryn decided she needed to reach beyond herself, Helena counseled her, "Now, you're going to feel a lot of fear about choosing the right person. But when you're careful and ask God's help, the right person will be there."

Three practical considerations are important in choosing this person:

First, choose someone with some degree of detachment. Usually a spouse or immediate family member would not be a good choice. They are too close. Many people choose to do this part of the Fifth Step with a complete stranger, such as a pastor in another town. A therapist or counselor by their very professional role may also offer the needed detachment.

Second, choose someone who is absolutely trustworthy. It is important to choose someone who will not use the information against you. In warning Kathryn about this, Helena shared a story from her early days in a recovery program. "I had a friend who was making remarkable recovery in A.A. She stayed sober. She finished her nursing degree. She got a new job. She had new friends. But her husband, who was not in recovery, was jealous of Patti's success. Now, she didn't do her Fifth Step with him, but this shows how careful you have to be—he got hold of the page of her inventory in her own handwriting where she listed all her sexual misconduct, and he photocopied it, and put it on the windows of all the cars in the doctors' parking lot at the clinic where she worked. Fortunately the director of the clinic found them and burned the pages before many people saw them. Patti didn't lose her job, but it was an awful trauma for her. So be *sure* your confessions only get to people who are absolutely trustworthy."

Third, choose someone who is experienced. The person to hear your Fifth Step might be someone experienced in dealing with problems like your own, such as your Twelve-Step sponsor, or someone experienced in receiving confessions, like a therapist or clergyman. But either way, it needs to be someone who will be understanding and compassionate and will not shame or condemn you for what you're confessing.

In the end, however, your own instincts will guide you. You will choose someone in whom you have confidence, someone in whom you are willing to confide, someone to whom you feel comfortable talking.

Achieving the Chosen Life

In taking Step Five we make great strides toward our new chosen lifestyle as we get rid of the false shame we've carried, grieve out old angers and hurts, and take a bold stride toward honesty and connectedness. Proverbs 28:13 says, "He who covers his sins will not prosper, But whoever confesses and forsakes them will have mercy." Now we can say:

"I choose to admit to God, to myself, and to another human being the exact nature of my wrongs."
"I choose forgiveness."
"I choose mercy."
"I choose freedom."

Step Six

*Were entirely ready to have God remove
all these defects of character.*

Andy pulled on his black and red running tights and
shirt and called through his open bedroom door to Gene,
his sponsor, who was sitting in the living room. "Hey, it's
great of you to go running with me—I know it's not really
your thing, but I can't miss training if I'm going to compete in that triathalon next month."

Gene stretched his lanky frame, clad in an old grey jogging suit, and laughed. "You never stay still long enough
for me to talk to you. Only thing that worries me is how
we'll get any talking done this way. I'll do well if I can
keep your back in sight, let alone your ear within range."

Andy came into the living room and sat down to put on
his running shoes. "No problem. I did three miles for
speed this morning. This evening I'm running for endur-
ance—nine miles, I hope. We'll trot along together and
talk, then you can drop out when you get tired."

As Gene shook his head, a few strands of grey-brown
hair fell onto his high forehead. "After about a block or
two, you mean? Well, we'll give it a try. I know a certain
amount of this fitness stuff is supposed to be good for you,
but are you sure you aren't overdoing it?"

Andy began doing some bending and stretching exercises. "You better do these with me—warm your muscles
up." From a wide-legged position he lunged first to the

right, then to the left. "No, I'm not overdoing it—this is
what it takes to get to the top. I want to be one of the
finalists in the triathalon. I bike to and from work and get
in about forty miles on the weekends. Everyday at lunch
time I swim five miles of laps at the 'Y.' I figure I'll be just
about peak for the competition."

The warm-ups over, Gene followed Andy out of the yard
at a jog, hoping that his longer legs might help him keep
up. "I've got to admire your commitment," he said as they
started down the street. "You look as if your muscles are
in great shape. But what about the rest of you?"

Andy turned a corner and headed toward the edge of
town. "Oh, great! Business has never been better. I sold
five of my top computer systems in the last three weeks. If
I could keep up that pace I'd break a million before I'm
thirty."

"Great—money and muscles." Gene was quiet for a few
strides. "What about people? How are your relationships?" He felt the first beads of sweat form on his forehead.

"Oh, lots better. Dr. Hemfelt told me to set boundaries
with my folks, so I'm spending less time with them and
enjoying it more. My dad still goes into a rage now and
then, but instead of sticking around to listen I just leave.
Actually, things have never been better."

"Sounds good. What about romance? Or friends?

"Hey, you really know how to push a guy, don't you?
You want me to increase our pace here?" They both
laughed, but then Andy got serious. "Well, there are only
24 hours in a day, and only one of me. I can only do so
much."

"That means no Jennifer."

"No Jennifer. I did sort of hope she'd come to see me
compete in the triathalon but I don't know . . . I invited
her to go running with me, but she didn't seem too interested."

"Did you ever consider asking her to *walk*—like in the
park, maybe?"

"You can't get your heart rate up strolling in the park."

"Oh, I don't know—there might be more than one way to get your heart rate up." Gene was breathing heavily now, but he noticed Andy was barely warmed up. "Seriously, Andy, I wanted to talk to you about taking Step Six. Where are you on that? Do you feel ready to let God start working on what you confessed to me back at Step Five—the things that cause your workaholism, your perfectionism, and your tendency to be pretty legalistic at times?"

"Of course I'm ready to be rid of my defects. Who wouldn't be?" Andy no longer turned to look at Gene as he jogged but kept his eyes straight ahead. "Trouble is, I don't know how I could do any more. I give everything in my life 300 percent and I still mess up." He held up his hand. "Wait. Don't talk to me about just having faith in Jesus. I do. I always have. It seems to me that what I'm supposed to do next is literally change my personality, but I'm just not sure how to go at it . . ."

They jogged on in silence for a few minutes with Andy's unfinished words hanging in the air. Then he picked up his thoughts and continued, "Besides, I think I *need* some of what you and Dr. Hemfelt call 'defects of character.' For example, if I let go of working hard, I lose business. If I let go of training hard, I'll do lousy in the triathalon. Besides, what's the matter with setting high goals? I don't want to be sloppy and just get by—I want to do my best. What's so wrong with that?"

"Andy," Gene was laboring now. "I've got to drop out here, but let me give you a verse to meditate on for the next eight miles or so, okay?"

Andy nodded and with his last bit of wind, Gene gasped, "Remember what Christ said; 'For what is a man profited, if he gains the whole world, and loses his own soul?' "[1]

Gene limped to the side of the road and slumped on a big boulder, his sides heaving. Andy sped on down the road, wondering how he could lose his soul when he'd been a Christian since childhood. That he had missed Gene's point—and the real purpose of Step Six—never occurred to him.

Where Are the "Stuck" Places?

The key to Step Six is being *willing* to have God remove *all* character defects that underlie your addictive behavior. The single task of Step Six is distilling down all that you discovered, inventoried, and confessed back in Steps Four and Five. You ask the basic question, "What needs to be changed inside of me?" Then, in Step Seven you will work on how to make the necessary changes that will remove the defects you have pinpointed in Step Six.

The way our counselors explain it is that now the patient must distill down "what it is in me that needs to be transformed." In other words, "What is it in me that is *stuck?*"

Taking Step Six is not simply repeating Step Four, when you did an inventory of what is wrong. Now you will be honing in and looking especially for those areas of feelings or behavior that do not seem to yield to logic or willpower. These are what you want to work on as you do Step Six and Step Seven, which are a couplet. Here's where you become willing to turn to God and admit, "Even though logically I know I shouldn't be doing this, and even though I've tried to exercise willpower over it, I can't break out of this in my own power. I need YOUR help."

In a real sense, that was Andy's problem. He thought he had taken some important steps in dealing with his workaholism by cutting down on the number of hours he was putting in at the office. He couldn't see that he had done very little about letting go of his perfectionism. In fact, he told Gene as they ran down the road that he couldn't see what was wrong with trying to be as perfect as possible. Andy was kidding himself with an idea that a lot of people keep hanging on to: "More is better." Ironically, Andy thought that if he could just try harder, somehow his workaholism would go away. In truth, he hadn't given up his workaholism at all. He was simply "trying harder" while putting in fewer hours per week!

Why It's Hard to Release Our Shortcomings

After the progress you made in Step One (admitting that you had a problem you couldn't handle alone) and Step Four (taking a moral inventory of your life), you might think Step Six would be easy. Not so. As soon as you start thinking about being *entirely ready* to have God remove all your character defects, fear starts to make you question the process. "Wait a minute," you think. "If I start letting go of all my old ways of doing things—what will be left? Maybe some of them are shortcomings, but when they're gone, will I still be *me?*"

Several days after Andy and Gene went jogging, Andy went in for his weekly therapy session with Dr. Hemfelt. The first question he asked centered on his fear of letting go of so much that there wouldn't be anything left. Didn't he need to work hard if he wanted to succeed? And what was wrong with trying to do things perfectly? It wasn't as if he literally wanted to be perfect. But what about having high goals and standards?

"Trying harder is what I'm all about," Andy sighed. "If I don't, I won't be me."

"Andy," Dr. Hemfelt said kindly, "if you truly become willing to let God remove your character defects, He will take nothing away that you really need. And what He does take away will be replaced by something better. The result will be that you will be more *you* than you ever were before." And for the next hour Dr. Hemfelt explained why Andy found the idea of surrendering his defects of character a frightening prospect. Here is what Andy learned.

First, no matter how much trouble negative behavior patterns (character defects) may get you into, *they are at least familiar.* Like an old pair of shoes that may be worn out, smelly, and unable to protect your feet from sharp stones or hot pavement, your character defects are still comfortable because they are what you are used to.

Second, many dysfunctional patterns are hard to give up because in some way, *usually early in childhood, they served as survival mechanisms* that helped you cope emotionally and physically with the dysfunctionalism in your family. In Andy's case, he developed his patterns of workaholism and perfectionism in order to survive a family where his parents were critical perfectionists who showed him very little love and affection. Instead they always seemed to be raising their standards a little higher, and he felt he had to continually do more and more to earn their love. In addition, his father was a rageaholic, and Andy was continually trying to pacify him by making special efforts to please and achieve.

Third, the compulsions we practice usually *offer some kind of payoff,* if only for a short time. In Andy's case, running anywhere from three to ten miles several days a week gave him much more than just the typical runner's high. By reaching difficult physical goals and doing well in preparation for triathalon competition, Andy was actually satisfying the love hunger he had developed as a child, when his needs for love, acceptance, and security were not met. His love hunger drove him into becoming a workaholic and a perfectionist who could never be satisfied, who was always biting off more than he could chew and who was always telling himself, "It's all or nothing."

When explaining love hunger to a client, Dr. Hemfelt often uses the analogy that for a love hungry person the addictive agent—whether it be alcohol, work, sex, or drugs—is like giving salt water to someone dying of thirst. You can never get enough. Your addiction creates the illusion that it will satisfy, but it *can't* and *won't.*

Fourth, when patients start to deal with the question of being ready to let God remove *all* defects of character, they are *often confronted by internal blackmail messages.*

These messages tell them, "This won't work. You don't *dare* get rid of me. If you do, you will self-destruct."

Dr. Hemfelt told Andy, "Your compulsions are ticking away inside of you, something like a terrorist bomb. They're telling you, 'If you disengage us, terrible things will happen. If you quit working so hard, no one will like you . . . no one will see you . . . you'll cease to exist!' "

Because of the barriers cited above, character defects are often highly resistant to change. Fortunately, Step Six does not demand that you be ready to remove all of your defects of character *through your own strength*. Step Six asks that you be entirely ready *to have God remove them*. You rely on God to help you release your defects of character. Then the burden is not entirely on you. As Jesus said, "Come to Me, all you who labor and are heavy laden, and I will give you rest. Take My yoke upon you and learn from Me."[2]

Kill the Defects, Not Your Personality

When Dr. Hemfelt finished describing the barriers that arise when anyone gets serious about trying to get rid of character defects, Andy was silent for almost a minute. Finally he said, "What you seem to be telling me is that part of me, the defective part, practically has to die or wither away and something else has to take its place."

"That's a good observation," replied Dr. Hemfelt. "Here at the clinic we often speak of Step Six as dying to the old and Step Seven as being reborn into the new."

"Now you're starting to sound like Bible lessons I've heard at church all my life. We are to see ourselves as dead to sin and alive to God in Christ."[3]

"It's a very similar process," Dr. Hemfelt agreed. "Andy, I'd like to give you this sheet to study between now and our next appointment. It lists personality flaws, cracks, and weaknesses that often show up in people with addictions, compulsions, and obsessions. I'd like you to read these over and identify which of these areas might apply to you and your workaholism. Then, next time we'll go over some of the questions that are included to help you zero in on going further with Step Six."

The reason Dr. Hemfelt wanted Andy to look at the list of personality flaws and weaknesses was to help him understand just what character defects really are and how to become willing to let God remove them. At the very base of any character defect is that huge unresolved love hunger that drives a person to an addiction in the first place as he or she tries to fill that hunger in inappropriate and extreme ways. Love hunger occurs in people who come out of dysfunctional families where their basic needs for love, security, acceptance, and trust, to name just a few, are not met. Growing up in this kind of family almost always causes some kind of personality flaw or twist.

Six Major Personality Defect Patterns

Following are six of the major personality defect patterns that we see in our patients. This is not an exhaustive list, and you may not see yourself pictured perfectly in any one of these basic patterns, but you should be able to pick up pieces and parts that will help give you a better picture of your own personality and where you may have snags and kinks of some kind. Keep in mind that in working through all six of the following personality defect patterns, your only goal is to identify defects. You will work on removing them when you reach Step Seven.

1. *Chronic depression (low self-esteem).* The vast majority of addicts we work with are people who have suffered from chronic low-grade, simmering depression, probably from early childhood on. In fact, this chronic depression has been such an integral part of their personality and outlook on life that even after entering recovery they still don't recognize it as depression. To them, their feelings of apathy, mild listlessness, pessimism, and what might almost be called a weary lack of enthusiasm about living, are normal.

They may be able to speak of certain points in their

lives when they were "really depressed," or they may even tell us they are deeply depressed at the moment. What they are talking about, however, is moving from their low-grade depression, which has always seemed normal to them, into an acute, debilitating depression, which is much more severe.

Even though Bill Wilson had a dramatic spiritual experience that ended his drinking forever, he continued to struggle with periods of deep debilitating depression. For a time he worked with a psychiatrist to receive help for this ongoing problem.

For patients with low-grade, chronic depression, the good news is that, as they go through recovery and work on Steps Six and Seven, they do a lot to raise the threshold of what they consider normal. Many patients make an ecstatic discovery that "normal" can be much brighter, much happier, and much more positive than it's ever been before. At the same time, they can learn how to avoid those deep pits of acute depression, which they are prone to fall into from time to time.

The following are some assessment statements to help you reflect on low-grade chronic depression and discover if this is in any way part of your personality make-up. Check the statements below that apply to you.

_____ 1. I always see myself as the victim of unfortunate circumstances.

_____ 2. I have stopped hoping. It is difficult to believe that things can and will get better.

_____ 3. I feel paralyzed by the grip of depression much of the time. The weight of this depression is so great that I'm moving in slow motion in contrast to the world around me.

_____ 4. There is a strange safety and security to my depression. I have come to rely on the numbness that depression brings to my feelings. I hide be-

hind the safety shield of my depression as a means
of avoiding the necessary risk-taking in life.

_____ 5. In the spirit of Step Six: I am entirely ready to
have God remove this painful companion, this illusion of safety. I am entirely ready to have God
address and heal my depressive personality.

2. *The chronically anxious personality* is driven by fear.
At worst, this kind of person is unconsciously trembling in
his boots; at best he is worrying almost all of the time.
When we get to Step Six, we are always concerned about
people who have this personality flaw because there is a
tendency to focus on, "What is wrong in me that is hurting
others?" There is the temptation to forget about something like anxiety, which is often almost 99 percent self-
punishing. It may not spill out on others to harm them,
but it is still a dangerous personality defect because it
severely limits you and who you can become.

Three premises apply to the chronically anxious personality. First, it is one of the most uncomfortable states
anyone can ever experience. To be constantly worried and
anxious puts you under tremendous stress.

Second, many addictions are efforts to somehow self-
medicate this ongoing anxiety. We may do it directly by
popping tranquilizer pills or downing alcohol, but there
are many other approaches. For example, a compulsive
hand washer will set up an exaggerated anxious situation
in his mind and then sit there fearful that his hands are
becoming contaminated. He runs quickly to the rest room
and compulsively washes them for the eighty-eighth time
that day, temporarily giving him a sense of tranquiliza-
tion. Ten minutes later, however, he is imagining a new
anxious situation and again imagines that he has touched
the wrong thing and has contaminated his hands. Again,
he is off to the rest room for a few minutes of peace and
tranquility at the wash basin.

Third, chronic anxiety can often lead to an ever higher

threshold of tolerated anxiety. As patients with chronic anxiety reach a midway point through recovery—around Step Six or Seven—they may have a break-through. They haven't realized that even when things were going "pretty well," they were in a state of simmering, churning anxiousness that was there twenty-four-hours-a-day. Now they begin to enjoy a few isolated pockets of genuine serenity when, as the old popular song puts it, they can "leave their worries on the doorstep."

When Andy returned to see Dr. Hemfelt for his next counseling session, he had picked chronic anxiety as one of his possible personality flaws. Before he decided to take Step One and go into a recovery program, if Andy had been asked, "Do you suffer from anxiety, do you worry much?" he would have said, "No." Andy believed that he had life under control, that he did all the right things, that he was an entrepreneur on the way up. Before recovery, Andy didn't realize his workaholism, perfectionism, and legalism were all efforts to try to outrun the low-grade anxiety that burned within him. After all, if he could just stay busy enough, he wouldn't have to feel whatever it was that was vaguely bothering him.

"What made you realize that chronic anxiety might be one of your personality flaws?" Dr. Hemfelt asked.

"Well," said Andy, "to be truthful, I didn't exactly figure it out with any deep thinking. The day after my last appointment I turned my ankle while running and I haven't been able to exercise at all ever since. After four or five days of just sitting around, I began having these strange, anxious feelings flooding over me and it seemed to me that maybe I do have some kind of anxiety flaw after all."

"Andy," said Dr. Hemfelt with a smile, "ever since the early part of your recovery program, everyone who has worked with you has been trying to tell you there is a scared, fearful little boy inside who is running like mad to stay ahead of his fear. All of your obsessive-compulsive behavior is an attempt to control the world around you and relieve those fears. Now that you've been forced to slow down for even just a few days, what you are feeling is kind of a withdrawal symptom. Turning your ankle was a good thing, really, because it helped you realize you're going to have to face that underlying bed of fear and deal with it as you go through Steps Six and Seven."

Next Dr. Hemfelt had Andy go over the assessment statements dealing with the anxious personality. He found several that applied to him to a certain degree. What about you?

_____ 1. I awaken each morning with a knot in the pit of my stomach and a sense of dread about what the day will bring.

_____ 2. Every decision, large or small, is a crisis, because I feel so fearful about the outcome.

_____ 3. A nameless, faceless, shapeless cloud of doubt and insecurity seems to hang over me much of the time.

_____ 4. I have tried countless techniques, from breathing exercises to pills to exotic forms of meditation to chase these fears, but nothing has touched the real core of my anxiety.

_____ 5. Therefore, in the spirit of Step Six, I am entirely ready to trust God, surrender this anxiety, and believe that life can be lived in a relatively tranquil, serene and peaceful manner.

3. *The naive/passive personality* sees the glass as not just half full—the glass as always at the brim and running over. We sometimes call this the Mr. Magoo syndrome. Mr. Magoo is so naive he can step off the curb into a mud puddle and pretend that he's on the French Riviera as he talks about the sand and water feeling warm between his toes. Fundamentally, what this person is doing is avoiding some of the authentic challenges of life by blindly and naively assuming that "everything's okay."

Usually there are three ways the naive/passive personality can operate: (1) as a partner or enabler; (2) in a special community, such as a cult; (3) through some kind of religious addiction that says, "Everything is going to be okay and God will handle it all and spare me from pain."

An important part of the population that is affected by the naive, passive personality defect is made up of all the codependents living side by side with other addicts in the family. The key example here, of course, is alcoholism, but many other addictions apply. Codependency becomes its own kind of addiction, and very often we find the wife of the alcoholic or workaholic man in a very passive mode. Seemingly she can't set any boundaries, she can't expect him to be home, she can't do anything. Her sole function is to cover up and enable the ongoing addiction of her spouse and pretend to herself and to the outside world that everything is okay.

If you suspect that you may have naive/passive personality flaws, see how many of these assessment statements may apply to you.

_____ 1. I have clung to a legalistic religion or to an extreme belief system as a lifetime security blanket.

_____ 2. There is someone (spouse, parent, employer, pastor) to whom I have handed over almost total responsibility for my life.

_____ 3. It is terrifying to imagine taking back some responsibility for my own thoughts, feelings, and actions.

_____ 4. I have even begun to rely on some diagnosis of physical illness or emotional illness as an excuse to be exempt from life's responsibilities.

_____ 5. I avoid reading newspapers and watching TV news because the real world is simply too harsh for me to confront.

_____ 6. Therefore, in the spirit of Step Six, I am entirely ready to ask God to give me back my fair share of

responsibility for addressing the pain and suffering around me.

4. *The compulsive/controlling/driven personality* is
specifically seen in the obsessive-compulsive behavior displayed by the workaholic, the control-aholic, the perfectionist, and the busy-aholic. The driven person believes:
"The only worth or identity I have must come from my
accomplishments and performance, and to perform well I
must be in control."

As he grappled with Step Six, Andy tended at first to
view his addictions, not as weaknesses, but as his greatest assets. Andy also showed a good deal of what we see in
many workaholics—the tongue-in-cheek syndrome. Alcoholics get to a certain point in their recovery therapy
and learn to parrot all of the appropriate phrases. Yes,
they know that what they do is "damaging themselves
and others," and they know "it's all counter-productive."
In Andy's case, he even admitted it was a kind of idolatry
with which God could not be pleased. And yet, underneath all of the right phrases, Andy's counselors could
sense that he was still getting a certain braggadocio en-
joyment out of his workaholism.

Finally, Dr. Hemfelt confronted Andy and asked him to
go over the following assessment questions as a means of
helping him realize that what he was really doing was
bragging about his workaholism and refusing to see it as
a real addiction or admit the character defects that were
causing it.

If you believe that you might fit in the compulsive,
driven, controlling personality category, see how many of
these assessment statements may apply to you.

_____ 1. I always feel driven to do more and be more in
an effort to fill the emptiness inside of me.

_____ 2. The pace of my busy-ness serves to outrun the
pain that gnaws inside of me.

_____ 3. I am only comfortable when I feel that I am in control of persons around me—my spouse, my family, my co-workers.

_____ 4. I am constantly trying to perfect certain aspects of behavior, and I am constantly plagued with guilt for falling short of these expectations.

_____ 5. Therefore, in the spirit of Step Six, I am entirely ready to ask God to remove my reliance on external achievement and to guide me to a new authentic source of identity and value.

5. *The anger/explosive personality* is almost always found in the rageaholic. Anger seems to pay off for the rageaholic in three ways:

First, it's an effective way to control others. If you bellow, scream, and explode, it pushes people into line around you. Some of them may disappear, but the masochists will remain and put up with you.

Second, anger covers up a great deal of insecurity, which is the core issue beneath all the bombast and explosions. An example we sometimes give our patients is the wizard in the children's story, *The Wizard of Oz*. Dorothy and her friends finally get an audience with the wizard and arrive in a huge chamber where they are confronted by a giant mechanical apparition with a booming voice belching fire, smoke, and lightning bolts. At first they are terrified, but with the help of Toto, Dorothy's dog, they pull back a curtain and find a little old white-haired man who is also scared and lost.

We use this image to help rageaholic patients see that behind their angry, abusive facade is a frightened little person trying to get back to someplace that they know is more secure. We tell them, "Behind that part of you that can be so abusive to others is a hurting, scared person who is trying to find some way to gain control."

Third, angry explosions are an indirect and inefficient way of trying to grieve out pain. Many times rageaholics are trying to say that they are lonely, scared, or hurting, but they don't know how. Or perhaps they can't give themselves permission to express their feelings, so all those feelings get converted into anger, which eventually comes exploding out.

The following are assessment statements to help the anger/explosive personality face his flaws. If anger is a problem for you, see how many of these statements apply to your behavior:

_____ 1. I stay angry most of the time. It seems that people and circumstances around me are constantly conspiring to "push my button."

_____ 2. I hold my anger in for long periods and save it up for a "justifiable" explosion.

_____ 3. I have come to depend on my anger as a weapon that allows me to control or dominate others.

_____ 4. I am filled with righteous indignation and find myself constantly giving others (and myself) a thousand different reasons why my anger is necessary or justified.

_____ 5. More and more people have confronted me about the damage my anger has done to certain relationships.

_____ 6. Therefore, in the spirit of Step Six, I am entirely ready to have God direct me into new (perhaps painful) avenues for the expression of my emotions besides exploding my frustrations onto others.

_____ 7. I am entirely ready to ask God to demonstrate to me and to others the tender, vulnerable side of me that has been hidden behind this mask of rage.

6. *The pathologically dishonest personality* is reflected at two levels: One, we call "cash-register honesty," which means you tell the truth about *facts*. The second level of

honesty is what we call "emotional or self-identity honesty," which involves accurately sharing about your *feelings*.

We find that many patients are cash-register honest. They may, for example, drive ten miles back to return a dollar too much change, but these same patients will practice blatant emotional dishonesty, being unwilling (or unable) to tell the truth about their feelings and what is going on inside.

If you have this personality flaw, you must acknowledge it in Step Six, and seek to eradicate it in Step Seven, because it contributes to a dangerous character defect that can strongly influence how well you conquer a particular addiction. As they like to say in A.A., "If you sober up a drunken horse thief, what you have is a sober horse thief."

In our counseling we see that perhaps 10 percent of those who have trouble with pathological dishonesty are at the cash-register level. Ninety percent of the pathological dishonesty we treat is in the emotional area. Often, it is here that the therapist must confront the patient by being bluntly honest.

By the time Andy got to Step Six, one of his main challenges was realizing that the reason he had lost Jennifer was not simply because of his workaholism. True, he wasn't physically there a lot of the time. But it gradually dawned on him that, even when he and Jennifer were together, he wasn't really there because he had emotionally checked out. Andy had to see that he was unconsciously putting her off because he didn't want to commit to her. Andy was a perfect example of emotional dishonesty by default. He wasn't consciously or openly misrepresenting his feelings to Jennifer, but he was so out of touch with his own feelings that he was emotionally A.W.O.L. much of the time. We will look much more closely at Andy's twisted relationship with Jennifer when we discuss relationship dysfunctions in Steps Eight and Nine.

Before leaving this personality defect, however, here is

a list of assessment statements to help you determine if you may be struggling with pathological dishonesty, particularly at the emotional level.

_____ 1. I have difficulty being honest with myself and others about my true feelings.

_____ 2. I constantly edit my reactions to others based on what I think they want to hear. (I am a chronic people pleaser.)

_____ 3. I have been "stuffing my feelings" (pushing them deeper and deeper within, like stuffing leaves in a garbage bag) instead of acknowledging my feelings and expressing them appropriately. I have done this for so long that even I don't know what I feel or want.

_____ 4. Although I consider myself to be a moral person, I catch myself telling frequent white lies to cover what I imagine are my flaws or shortcomings.

_____ 5. I feel so "less than" on the inside that I constantly embellish, brag on, or expand what I am on the outside to look better and sound better.

_____ 6. Therefore, in the spirit of Step Six, I am entirely ready to take off the mask that I have been wearing in family, romantic, and business relationships. I am entirely ready to make rigorous honesty the foundation of all of my key relationships.

The Key to Step Six is Balance

As we deal with patients, we find them reacting so severely to their character defects that they swing 180 degrees in the opposite direction. For example, I may have abused my sexuality and be, in fact, a sexual addict. So, to get rid of this defect I go to the opposite extreme and start believing my whole sexuality is bad. I start asking God to give me a "sexuality-ectomy"—to remove my sexuality completely.

The goal is not to destroy or eliminate our God-given needs, appetites, or instincts. Our goal is to find balanced fulfillment for these needs.

The obvious question that many patients ask next is "What is balance anyway? How do I know when I'm balanced?" Rather than try to do the impossible and give each individual a precise definition of "balance," we prefer to answer this question in two ways:

First, a big part of Step Six (as well as Step Four) is to identify and admit areas where you know or suspect you are out of balance. When Andy, for example, dealt with his personality defects, it didn't result in his knowing precisely how to find the perfect counter-balance. What he did know, however, was that the pendulum had swung much too far in different areas of his life and he had to get back toward center.

Andy's life was way out of balance due to his reliance on external achievement, which resulted in his workaholism, perfectionism, and legalistic outlook on life. That's all Andy really needed to know. The location of precise center was not the issue. Being *willing to have God correct his character defects* was his real goal in Step Six. He would tackle getting rid of these defects in Step Seven.

Second, just as Rome wasn't built in a day, character defects are not removed quickly or easily. For most of us it is a lifetime struggle. What Step Six involves is coming to the point where you are entirely ready and willing to have God remove your defects. That is not to say that God is going to do this in the next five minutes. By now it has probably occurred to you that you don't achieve or finish any of the Twelve Steps, *you practice them.*

Step Seven

Humbly asked Him to remove our shortcomings.

Andy sat in Dr. Hemfelt's office with his head in his hands. "I really did Step Six, Doctor. I was and I am still willing to have God remove all my character defects. But I don't know what to do. I can't run any faster than I am. I can't work any harder than I am. I'm stretched to the limit and nothing works. Why won't it work for me? I don't see what more I can do."

Dr. Hemfelt pointed to Andy's journal. "Look back at the list of character defects you made in your Step Six work." Andy turned to the page. "As you read those, I want you to look at them as your attempts to deal with your low self-esteem in your own way. Do you remember the old Frank Sinatra song, 'I Did It My Way'? But the good news is that you don't have to do it your way, and you don't have to do it in your strength. Look at Step Seven; 'Humbly asked Him.' That's the key; going to God in humility and saying, 'Let's do it Your way.'"

"But it seems to me that I have to do something," Andy replied. "I can't expect to sit back and do nothing while God magically takes care of everything."

"Andy, I don't believe God ever 'magically' does anything, but He does do miracles if we are humble enough to let Him."

Why Humility Is so Necessary

The 12 × 12 says the whole emphasis of Step Seven is on humility. In our work with patients at the clinics across the country, we stress that there are at least three reasons why humility is necessary if we want to achieve spiritual release of character defects—in other words, our shortcomings.

First, our shortcomings—character defects—are major, not just minor mistakes or weaknesses. Anyone with an addiction may have a real problem with seeing how serious his or her shortcomings are. As A.A. mentor Chuck C. says, "We must discover how to see everyone and everything around us through 'a new pair of glasses.' "[1] That new pair of glasses is humility. So often the addict has been looking at life through the distorted lenses of grandiosity—a pompous tendency to see oneself as far more magnificent and grand than one really is.

Even though we may not like the idea of "being humble," our addiction can drive us to our knees and help us see that our grandiosity has been stupid and non-productive. Martin, the alcoholic history professor, approached Step Seven purely from the standpoint of sheer necessity.

"Right," he told Dr. Fowler. "I have these character flaws. I acknowledge that. They have driven me to become a problem drinker. If I don't get rid of them sooner or later I'll retreat into alcoholism again. I understand that. So I see the necessity of humility. But I don't like it very much."

"But aren't you ready to admit that lack of humility is what led you drinking in the first place?"

Martin ducked his head with a wry smile. "Okay, I get the point—what do I have to lose? I guess I'm willing to try suffering a new way. I can hardly claim that the show's been so great under my own direction. I don't think I've told you yet, but my drinking has cost me my job after all. My department head told me yesterday my contract is not being renewed. The academic dean decided he didn't want to take a chance on having me relapse and not show up for classes again this fall. They're sorry, but they know I'll understand."

There was dead silence as Dr. Fowler absorbed the news of Martin's firing. He got up, walked over to the window, and stood staring out for what seemed a long time. Finally, he turned, fixed Martin with a compassionate gaze and said, "Martin, I am so sorry. That has to be a tremendous blow after getting all the way through Step Five. Unfortunately, you aren't the first one to go into recovery and then get fired. It is typical for an employer to just be too afraid to take a chance, particularly when alcohol has been involved."

"Well, maybe getting fired will help me learn to be humble. Right now, I have to admit I feel lower than the proverbial snake's bootheels."

"Martin, I've got to give you credit for being able to joke about something this serious, but, at the same time, I don't want you to confuse humility with humiliation. Humility does *not* equal low self-esteem. Another one of those paradoxes of recovery is the fact that low self-esteem produces grandiosity and false pride, while the better our self-image becomes, the more humble we will be."

Martin nodded as if he understood but as he left his session with Dr. Fowler, he knew he had a lot more work to do before he would get used to being "confidently humble."

Second, *human power alone is very limited to deal with character defects*. We cannot call on God's help until we have fully acknowledged our own limitations.

Helena, Kathryn's sponsor, told her story, especially her struggle with Step Seven, at a meeting one night: "I always thought my mind was the answer. I was sure that if I could just understand, I'd have it made. Before I did Step Four I didn't *know* I was angry. When I reached that great understanding I thought, 'Okay, now I know. Now I can deal with it.' But I couldn't. I hadn't surrendered a thing. I was just working my head off in my own strength.

I wanted to be Miss A.A. of Dallas—you see, I was still all ego.

"My alcoholism was removed in one of those Damascus Road experiences like Bill Wilson's, but my smoking wasn't, my overeating wasn't, my compulsive spending wasn't. I was just running around stark raving sober!"

Third, *humility helps us appreciate the immensity of God's power to transform our lives.* To paraphrase a verse from the Old Testament, "Not by might nor by power, but by My Spirit, says the Lord of hosts."[2]

The 12 × 12 says "During this process of learning more about humility, the most profound thought of all was the change in our attitude toward God . . . we began to get over the idea that the Higher Power was a sort of bush-league pinch hitter, to be called upon only in an emergency. The notion that we would still live our own lives, God helping a little now and then, began to evaporate."[3]

Humility, then, tells us that our shortcomings are glaringly huge. If we hope to make progress, we must make God a full partner. In fact, He must be *senior* partner. Humility admits that God calls the shots.

A Nine Point Plan to Remove Defects

As our patients come to the end of Step Six and begin Step Seven, they usually face a practical problem: Yes, they have become willing to let God deal with their defects. Yes, they have humbly asked Him to remove those defects, *but* the defects are still there. What do they do now? They still have these "stuck places." How and when do they get them *unstuck?*

We tell our patients that because our human power is so limited, we do not have unlimited access to God's unlimited power. In other words, we aren't God. We are limited human beings, and we can tap into His power only as our limitations allow us to do so. A father with an epileptic son no one seemed to be able to help put it well when he told Jesus, "Lord, I believe; help my unbelief."[4]

God *does* help our unbelief as we work at believing harder. As the Apostle Paul told his Philippian believers, we need to work out our salvation with fear and trembling because God is working in us to will and to do of His good pleasure.[5] What anyone in recovery must try to do is take his or her limited power and wed it to God's limitless divine power. Then, a day at a time, a minute at a time, or even at fifteen seconds at a time, you can know victory over the character defects that have plagued you for so long.

A Nine Point Plan

To help our patients achieve this joining of their human power with God's divine power, we have worked out a nine point plan for this day by day, hour by hour, battle. Almost daily (sometimes more than once a day) we need to do the following:

1. *Continue to re-acknowledge your basic character or personality defects.* Patients need to restate these to themselves as a way of pushing back the veil of denial that has kept them from seeing these defects in the first place. A patient cannot re-acknowledge his defects too often.

Andy, for example, must continue to acknowledge his chronic anxiety, which is a symptom of his fear and insecurity; his compulsive drivenness, which keeps him trying to do more and more so he won't be less and less; and his pathological dishonesty at an emotional level, which he showed and continues to show toward Jennifer as he attempts to re-establish their relationship because deep down he doesn't want to commit to her.

2. *Hand the defects back over to God's care.* Different people do this in different ways. For some, it's enough to do it verbally in prayer. Andy might pray: "Dear God, I acknowledge there's this part of me that never feels good on the inside unless I'm doing something on the outside. I

hand this over to You for Your care over the next twenty-four hours. Take this from me, relieve me of it."

In other cases, the words may not be enough and sometimes we ask our patients to use some visual imagery that can be a picture or symbol of the character defects. Again, using Andy as an example, he might picture in his mind a miniature treadmill with a little mouse running on it. He might imagine taking this mouse off the treadmill, wrapping it up in paper, and tying it with a string. Then he might literally see himself handing that "gift" over to God. In the final frame of this scenario, Andy would see God accepting the mouse and the treadmill from him. With this kind of visual imagery, Andy could see himself handing over his workaholism to God's care.

3. *Specify very carefully what needs to be changed for just this one day.* We stress to patients that it's extremely important to be *specific* about what needs to be changed and focus on changing it for just this day. In some cases, if people are really struggling, we have them break them down into even smaller segments of time. For example, "What needs to be transformed within you for the next three hours this morning?" This technique is most effective when done as a dialogue between the patient and God. It closely parallels a technique called "Part Acts," which we adopted from an organization called Recovery, Inc.[6] What this means is that, if I wake up in the morning and say, "I should never ever be compulsive again and I promise I never will," I am doomed to disappointment. It just isn't going to work.

I will be much more successful, however, if I can break my defect down into a small manageable period of time and say, "Dear Lord, I want to spend the first three hours of this morning following my schedule instead of compulsively cramming more into it than I've already scheduled." With this kind of prayer, you are taking a lifetime problem and breaking it down into something you can work with over the next three hours only. That's what "Part Acts" means. The key is to break down your major defects into partial actions and cut an overwhelming foe into smaller, more manageable pieces.

The Part Acts technique can be very useful to someone who struggles with an anger/explosive personality. Perhaps, for example, this person stays chronically angry at his boss. In setting up his Part Act for the morning, he could pray, "Lord, help me to go to the office and to make it to mid-morning coffee break without slipping into my obsession about how unfair my boss is. Give me ninety minutes this morning when I'm free from that."

Whenever we pray a prayer that asks God to help us with a "Part Act," we must be specific in two ways. First, we must specify what needs to be changed. Instead of asking, "Make me a better person," we focus tightly on the *specific* personality defects that need correcting. Second, instead of making a blanket request that covers an indefinite amount of time, we break our requests down into small, digestible bits of personal effort—today, this morning, the next ninety minutes, or even, "the next sixty seconds."

4. *With great specificity, ask God to touch the parts of you that need to be healed or transformed.* For example, you may need to ask Him to touch your mind or your heart (the center of your emotions). Or you may need to ask Him to touch some part of your physical body. If, for example, you have a knot in the pit of your stomach every time you walk into the office and have to deal with your boss, you can ask God specifically to touch you in this area, relieve the tension, and help you to be relaxed.

Note that in taking Step Seven, you have humbly invited God to remove your shortcomings, but right here, in point four, you are going one step further. You are asking Him to touch you mentally, emotionally, or physically to bring about that extra dimension of healing that you can never achieve through your own human efforts.

As Andy struggles with his workaholism, for example, he may have earlier in the day specifically prayed, "Dear God, help me to honor the eight-hour time limit that I have committed to for this day and not work one moment longer." As the clock ticks toward the end of his eight-hour day, Andy can feel tension in the pit of his stomach. He almost has a sense of guilt that tells him, "I can't walk out the door. I can't stop working. I've got to keep it all before me and finish everything before I leave." At that moment, Andy would ask God to do several specific things:

> "Lord, please remove this knot in my stomach. Calm my twisted places.
>
> "Lord, touch my mind and still that obsessive voice that tells me I have to do more and be more.
>
> "Finally, Lord, touch my emotions and help me to have some sense of calmness and tranquility as I lock up shop and walk out the door."

5. *Act your way into better thinking and feeling.* Making these changes is seldom easy, particularly at first. Even though you've handed it over to God, even though you've invited Him to touch your mind, emotions, and body to make it possible, there will still be a part of you that almost recoils against the whole idea.

As Andy walks out of that office at 5:00 P.M. and locks the door behind him, there will be a part of him that just won't feel right about what he's doing. We have to repeatedly tell patients that at first it will feel awkward and even wrong to go through the motions of doing what you know is the proper action to weed out the old character defects. But—and it is a very big *but*—if you will take the proper action over and over again, the good feelings will gradually catch up with you.

An informal oral slogan used in many Twelve-Step recovery groups is, "Fake it until you make it." And a similar slogan that comes out of Recovery, Inc., is simply, "Make muscles move." What both these slogans are talking about is that you may not be able to control your thoughts or your feelings, but you can control your muscles.

When Andy comes to the end of the day and is flooded with guilty feelings about stopping work, we know that he can't just reach in, flip a switch, and feel differently. He does, however, have control over his feet and legs. Even though it doesn't "feel right," and even though he has thoughts telling him to do the opposite, he can stop to ask God for strength to literally force his muscles to move. *He can walk out of the office and lock the door behind him.*

6. *Being willing to bear discomfort* is another concept adapted from Recovery, Inc. Any time you're trying to change something as ingrained as a personality defect, it will feel awkward and even bad for a certain period of time. Making this change just won't feel "normal" because normal has meant something totally different to this point. Changing the normal setting will inevitably lead to some—maybe a lot of—discomfort.

No matter what your addiction may be—and, like Andy, your problems may have nothing to do with drugs or chemicals—you will probably go through some sort of withdrawal. You must be willing to bear the discomfort if you want to take Step Seven in its fullest sense. At several points we have emphasized that when taking the Twelve Steps, human willpower alone won't work. But here in point six of our nine point plan (as well as back in point five), you can use willpower to an important degree.

With persistent determination, you can make your muscles move. By courageously "gritting your teeth," you can bear the necessary discomfort. In fact, you must use your willpower or be doomed to failure.

Here is where your partnership with God comes into play. He is the Senior Partner, in fact, He is the Boss—but He is not going to move you with some magic flying carpet. Your muscles must do that. He is not going to take away the withdrawal symptoms. You will have to wait those out and as long as you are trusting God for help, *willpower will work!*

7. *Thinking secure thoughts,* another technique of Recovery, Inc., will help counterbalance the flood of negative self-messages that are saying, "This won't work . . . you can't make it . . . it doesn't really matter anyway. . . ."

This kind of negative self-talk is to be expected, especially in the wake of feeling discomfort and pain due to withdrawal from the addictive agent, whatever it might be. When you go into withdrawal, your personality defects fight back with self-protective, built-in messages. The moment you try to deal with them, all kinds of false warning signals and negative messages go off. To jam this false warning system, you need to do some intentional positive thinking, not "pie in the sky," but reassuring positive messages that will help you "fake it until you make it."

We sometimes have patients deal with their negative self-talk by writing out a series of positive counter-messages on three by five inch notecards, which they carry in their pocket or purse. In Andy's case, those messages might read: "Going home at 5:00 is a positive step in my recovery. People I trust, such as my therapist and support group, have encouraged me to draw a line on work hours and stick to it. In the long run I'm laying the foundation for having a better relationship with Jennifer."

Andy knows these positive message cards work because he has tried them. One evening after he shut his office door at 5:00 P.M., he had severe difficulties but was still able to make his muscles move and get as far as the parking lot. Then, however, he literally felt his knees go weak as a shame attack hit him head on. He unlocked his car, got in behind the wheel and, as he warmed up the engine, he pulled out a three by five card containing one of his personal series of positive secure thought messages:

"My business will ultimately do better if I take care of me rather than exhaust myself with overwork."

"I have to admit I really didn't think the card would do much good," Andy told his therapist. "But I was surprised at how powerful a positive message can be. It reminded me of what I was really trying to do and of the benefits that would come if I could only hang in there. After a few minutes, I was able to back out of my parking space and drive on home. I didn't go back to the office until the next morning."

Was Andy "faking it"? Absolutely, but he was nonetheless "making it" a step at a time, and that's where victory lies.

8. *Develop new habits and patterns with repetition.* You may need to fake it until you can make it day after day, week after week, and, in some cases, month after month, until you can really see results. This is where humility plays such an important role. Your personality defects will keep sending their negative messages to remind you that you have "pride and dignity." That is when you must come to grips with what being humble is really about.

A principle from the A.A. *Big Book* is you get stronger with repetition. Dealing with personality and character defects is much like dealing with bad habits. You have to replace the old with something new. To change your behavior you will have to take positive steps over and over in order to get new patterns grooved in and allow for the old discomfort to slip away.

9. *At the end of the day, stop and thank God for any and all of the smallest incremental changes.* This last point in the plan is crucial. As weeks and even months go by, patients can become discouraged. They come to their therapist and say, "I've done these points for forty-five days and I still don't see any change. I'm still struggling with the same defects."

In many cases, these patients have been looking for giant leaps of progress too soon. That's why it's important to take time at the end of the day to acknowledge to yourself even the tiniest sense of progress. In some cases, when a patient is going up against a sticky intransigent personality defect, perhaps the best that patient can hope for at first is to be able to commend himself about the fact that he has spent one more day battling his defect with God's help. That in itself is a victory because at least he has been involved in the contest and committed to the struggle.

Reaching a State of Amazing Grace

When we give patients the nine point plan to use in their Step Seven work, some of them protest, "Sounds like I'm pulling myself up with my own bootstraps. Where does God fit in?" Our answer is, "Without being humble enough to ask for God's direction and strength, taking Step Seven will be impossible." Early A.A. members realized this when they wrote Step Seven and included that all-important phrase, "Humbly ask Him (God) to remove our shortcomings."

The nine point plan for removing character defects is helpful, but without God's empowerment it will have limited effect. We often liken taking Step Seven to "reaching a state of grace." *The 12 × 12* says, "We would like to be assured that the grace of God can do for us what we cannot do for ourselves."[7]

At several points in his letters, the Apostle Paul wrote of having a defect of some kind. It may have been physical, or it could have had something to do with his emotions and personality. Whatever Paul's problem was, after he pleaded with the Lord three times to have the defect removed, God said to him: "My grace is sufficient for you, for My strength is made perfect in weakness"[8] That was enough for Paul and it should be enough for us. When we know we are weak and cannot do it without God's help, it is then that we become strong.

Step Eight

Made a list of all persons we had harmed, and became willing to make amends to them all.

Kathryn sat with her notebook on her knees, a neatly penned "People I Have Harmed" at the top of a page that contained only one name so far: "Henry"—but even that was followed by a question mark. She sat there for a full five minutes longer, then tossed the book on her bed, picked up the phone, and dialed a familiar number. Helena answered on the third ring.

"Helena, I suppose this must sound as if I'm in some kind of denial, but I really can't get going with Step Eight. I honestly can't think of anybody I've *really* harmed. I know that back when I did my inventory I admitted to overmothering the children and covering too much for Henry, but I'm still the one that's submissive. I'm the one who's always trying to keep the lid on and make this family work. I thought I was in ACOA because I see to everyone else's needs too much instead of taking care of my own."

On the other end of the line, Helena was silent, playing her role as a good listener. Finally, she said, "Kathryn, it is not wrong to love your family and to try to take care of them, but the pendulum can swing too far, especially with someone like you."

"What do you mean, 'someone like me'?"

"Kathryn, you've been a practicing codependent rescuer who's been loving her family and picking up their messes for a long time. The way you take care of Henry is bad enough because by not confronting him you're just letting him blunder along in his alcoholic haze. But I'm thinking even more about how you always move in to take care of your kids—in fact, you overwhelm them. You don't let Polly be the adult wife and mother that she is. She's even told you that you make her feel like a child, or at least a teen-ager, who isn't old enough to be married and have a family of her own. And as for Jason, you won't let him grow up. The other day you told me you even help him pick out his clothes! Kathryn, Jason is sixteen! That's incredible!"

"He seems to appreciate my help and I like to do it for him. Everything I do for my kids I do out of love . . ."

"Kathryn, listen to me carefully. You know, it is possible to *love people to death.* Do you remember the night I came over after Jason got caught stealing? You really didn't want to deal with that, but as far as I'm concerned Jason was sending you a message that said, 'Mom, I've had it with being smothered . . . I rebel!'"

The phone was silent for the next ten seconds, then Kathryn said, "Helena, you've been very honest with me, and, while some of it hurts, I appreciate it. And I think I see my problem. Back in Steps Four and Five, I admitted that I tried to rescue Henry and that I'm overprotective of the children, but I guess I never fully realized the *harm* I've been doing."

"Kathryn, I'm sorry if some of it hurt, but I could see you were in a real blind spot with making out this list of people that you may have harmed. What I've been trying to tell you is that in loving your kids so much, in a very real sense you have been harming them. I was just trying to shake your thinking loose. The key to making out this list for Step Eight is being *willing* to make amends, even if you're not quite sure who did the hurting and why."

"Thanks so much, Helena. What would I do without you?"

"Well, if you didn't have me, you'd have someone else, but I'm glad it's me. The longer I'm in ACOA, the more I realize how we get to know ourselves from knowing each other. We learn how to love. We get our healing energy from each other and from God." She paused to catch her breath. "Well, enough of that, that's just to say I love you, and God bless you."

Making Restitution Takes Responsibility

In Steps Six and Seven (as well as in Step Four), we examined our defects—the root causes of where we have gone wrong. We focused on our obsessions and compulsions, our own hurts and resentments, and how to submit ourselves to God's guidance and control.

Steps Eight and Nine are another couplet that points us in a new direction. Now the focus changes to rebuilding relationships we may have destroyed or damaged. We want to let go of our need to hold on to the past and blame others for our misfortune. Instead, we begin accepting full responsibility for our lives.

Love Does Mean Saying "I'm Sorry"

One of the key principles that we stress in Step Eight is that *attitude is all-important.* The key is our *willingness* to make amends to others for hurting their feelings, offending them, and in some cases causing them inconvenience, pain, and even harm.

Twenty years after Ali MacGraw recovered from her alcohol dependency, a reporter asked her if the famous line from her hit movie, "Love Story," was really true. "Does love mean never having to say you're sorry?" the reporter wanted to know.

"It's quite the opposite," Ali replied. In her book *Moving Pictures,* Ali comments, "Making amends is a powerful experience. It involves taking a cold, hard look at my behavior toward other people all these years, and then taking full responsibility for everything I have said and done. It is often painful, even shaming. It is absolutely necessary in the great garbage-cleaning process called recovery."[1]

Making Your List

Keep Helena's advice to Kathryn in mind as you work on your own Step Eight list. Don't worry about the actual amends-making. Don't get caught up in mental pictures of yourself going to another person with some deep dark confession or slogging for months or years in a second job to earn enough money to pay someone back.

Your list must be completely uncensored—everyone you've harmed, or think you may have harmed, dead or alive, living next door or in China. If you become your own editor by analyzing whether or not it's possible to make amends to each person you think of, you can get stuck in Step Eight. Just ask God to give you a willing heart.

As you ask the question, "Who have I harmed?" it's good to remember the hurts you can't see are usually the deeper ones, the ones for which amends really need to be made.

You will want your list to include anyone to whom you owe a financial debt, a physical debt, or an emotional debt. Four areas in which to look for names are:

1. *Victims of your addictions:* Anyone physically harmed when you were drunk, anyone with financial losses from your overspending, anyone you abused in a rage, anyone harmed from a commitment you didn't fulfill because you were indulging your addiction. In earlier steps we have urged you to examine specific incidents for the purpose of finding a pattern; here the important point is the specific incident. Think of your behavior patterns to help call specific incidents to mind. Did you miss your son's seventh birthday party because you spent too long in

a business meeting? Look back at the list you made in Step Five on page 121. Mention those three names here: Do you need to add any others? If so, list them below.

Who I Harmed   How I Harmed Them

1._____   _____

2._____   _____

3._____   _____

2. Closely associated to victims of your addictions are all persons harmed by situations listed in your Step Four Relationships Survey. As a general rule, many people on that Step Four Relationship list will need to be on your "To Make Amends" list as well. Use the spaces below to list some of the key figures you may have harmed in some way:

Family of Origin   How Harmed

1._____   _____

2._____   _____

3._____   _____

4._____   _____

5._____   _____

Spouse and Other Mem-
bers of the Opposite Sex   How Harmed

1._____   _____

2._____   _____

3._____   _____

4._____   _____

5._____   _____

3. A third key category is what we call *members of the next generation*. Here we are concerned especially with

children who may have been affected by your addictions or obsessive-compulsive behavior. The harm done may not be showing up yet, but nonetheless damage was done and amends need to be made. Use the spaces below to catalogue any harms you may have done to the generations who will be following you:

My Children   How Harmed

1._____   _____

2._____   _____

3._____   _____

My Grandchildren   How Harmed

1._____   _____

2._____   _____

3._____   _____

4. The fourth category includes other "family" groups such as your work family, church family, and organizations. Don't overlook anyone here; there could be some very significant persons to whom you need to make amends:

Work Family   How Harmed

1._____   _____

2._____   _____

3._____   _____

Church Family   How Harmed

1._____   _____

2._____   _____

3._____   _____

Other Special "Families"
or Communities   How Harmed

1._____   _____

2._____   _____

3._____   _____

The All-important "Second List"

When Kathryn returned to see Dr. Meier, she showed him the list of names she had put down as part of her work on Step Eight. "I know this doesn't look like much," she said, "but it was a lot of work to compile this. My sponsor, Helena, gave me some help, and I think I'm ready to say I've completed Step Eight."

"This is excellent," Dr. Meier beamed. "Many patients just don't realize how difficult making a simple list like this can be. Getting it down in black and white makes all the difference in the world. There is, however, one more list I would like you to make before you totally put Step Eight to bed."

"Oh, no," Kathryn groaned. "More work? What list is that? Step Eight says to list everybody to whom you should make amends. Isn't that enough?"

"Well, it is enough at one level," Dr. Meier admitted, "but we like to help patients prepare for Step Nine by making one additional list that helps them better understand why the need for amends is there in the first place."

And with that introduction, Dr. Meier spent most of the session with Kathryn explaining the need for a second list when doing Step Eight. While working with clinic patients, we point out that the superficial way of doing Step Eight is to simply make a "list of damages." For example: "I knocked over a table at Uncle Henry's birthday party two years ago in an angry rage, and I need to apologize to him for ruining his party."

As important as making that admission is, you can make Step Eight even more comprehensive and meaning-

ful if you are willing to go beneath the surface and find
the patterns that have caused relationship dysfunctions
in the past. What are the reasons for the anger that
ruined Uncle Henry's party? Or, to get back to Kathryn,
what is behind her need to overinvolve herself in the lives
of her children?

To make this second list of relationship dysfunctions,
we need to look closely at two key words: *harm* and
boundaries. Harm is simply what I have done to hurt others while pursuing my addiction or obsessive-compulsive
behavior. Sometimes that harm can be very direct, such
as smashing Uncle Henry's table. Or, perhaps I could
have attacked Uncle Henry physically or verbally. But
harm can also be done indirectly, as Kathryn learned
when Helena pointed out her overcontrolling ways with
her children.

The point we try to make is that *anytime something is
not working in one of my relationships, I am harmed and
the other person is harmed.* Even if it's seemingly the
other person who is doing most of the harming, I am still
playing some part. My response to that other person (or
my lack of being willing to respond or confront) may ultimately harm him. When a relationship suffers, both parties are harmed in the long run. That's why we push our
patients to gain a broader understanding of Step Eight by
listing ways they may be harming others or allowing others to harm them.

We find that as a general rule, harm can be caused in
one of four ways:

1. I violate the boundaries of others.
2. I allow others to violate my boundaries without giving them feedback.
3. My boundaries are too thick and no one can get
through.
4. My boundaries are fragile or non-existent. I am so
lacking in identity I am not even sure when one of my
boundaries is crossed.

The key word in the four statements above is *bound-aries*. It must be understood that in this context, a bound-ary is not some kind of fence or wall, but instead, it is more like a gate, which can be opened or closed. Any rela-tionship boundary is a two-way regulator. I may close this boundary to keep people out or at an appropriate dis-tance. I can also open up this same boundary to invite people into my confidence and affection. In dealing with our patients, we find that invariably harm is caused in a relationship when boundaries are abused. We have them ask four questions:

1. "Do I Violate the Boundaries of Others?"

Violating the boundaries of others involves several ma-jor patterns:

I may be overly possessive of someone else. One obvious pattern has already been described in Kathryn's behavior with her children. Her adult daughter, Polly, has suppos-edly left the nest, yet Kathryn keeps second-guessing the decisions Polly is making in her adult life. As for sixteen-year-old Jason who still lives at home, Kathryn is con-stantly smother-mothering him and not allowing him to grow up and take adult responsibilities. Jason's stealing incident was his own desperate effort to confront this boundary violation. He was not a discipline problem in school; he had never even had a traffic ticket. He was simply trying to get his mother's attention.

I relate to others through chronic conflict—constantly fighting and bickering. In the best of relationships there is some conflict and even some fighting. But functional peo-ple work it through and fighting is not their norm for re-lating to one another. If, however, I'm in a relationship where the main style of dealing with each other is to al-ways be fighting or at war, it means I'm locked into a pattern of constantly challenging and assaulting someone else's boundaries.

I constantly criticize or give constructive criticism. I may not be fighting or arguing with others, but my basic stance most of the time is to note where they are not quite measuring up. I sit over them in righteous judgment and let them know when they are failing to meet the proper standards (mine). I simply can't leave them within their own boundaries and give them space to exist in peace.

I am overcontrolling of others. In this relationship, I always have to be the top dog, the one in charge, commander of the ship. A classic pattern we see in marriage counseling is that the controller marries the pleaser. Usually the husband is the controller, the wife the pleaser, but the order can be reversed in some relationships. In Kathryn's case, Henry was the controller, but he usually did it quietly by staying in a non-communicative shell. Only occasionally would he pop out to rage a bit, but Kathryn always knew he was in charge so she constantly lived to please Henry and placate him.

I am verbally, physically, emotionally, or spiritually abusive of others. To find examples of this behavior, you may need to go no further than back to your Step Four inventory to see what kind of abuses you have experienced while growing up. Simply turn all that around and ask yourself, "Do I perpetuate any of these kinds of abuses against my spouse, children, friends, or co-workers?"

The following are seven assessment statements that will help you determine how and why you may violate the boundaries of others. To identify certain traits or patterns, it may help to rate yourself from 1 (not true of me) to 10 (very true of me).

_____ 1. I fear that unless I am pulling the strings of people and situations around me, my needs will not be met.

_____ 2. Although I reject the notion, I've had one or more people in my life accuse me of being manipulative.

_____ 3. I am heavily invested in someone else's life, and

I allow my own ambitions and frustrations to spill over into his or her life.

_____ 4. I have lost significant friendships over power struggles, over debates about who is right and wrong.

_____ 5. I have a very strong sense of what is right and wrong, and I don't hesitate to impose those values on all the people around me.

_____ 6. I usually need to win an argument.

_____ 7. If anyone challenges my control, I feel threatened and I retaliate.

2. "Do I Allow Others to Violate My Boundaries?"

We cannot overemphasize that as one person allows another to repeatedly violate his or her boundaries, it keeps both people in a nonworking, dysfunctional relationship. And, eventually, the person being violated will save up so much resentment that it will come spilling out in one form or another, perhaps years later. Again, we see several major patterns that usually surface when one person is allowing the other to violate boundaries.

I am overly submissive or passive toward someone else. I allow this person to tell me what to do. I just stand on the sidelines and seldom comment or offer an opinion. I am not necessarily in abject submission to others, but I certainly don't initiate much. I hold myself in reserve.

I play the martyr role and get a tremendous payoff from having my boundaries violated. I actually relish being hurt, harmed or damaged. My identity springs from this role of being the long-suffering martyr.

I play the chronic victim role, which is different from martyr. As a victim, I always see myself being swindled, tricked, or overrun by someone else. I don't like it and I really don't get any "payoff" from it, but there seems to be little I can do about it and it just seems to be my normal way of life.

Kathryn fits to a "T" the role of someone whose boundaries are being violated because she has put up with intolerable behavior on Henry's part. A passive personality when she married Henry, she soon became overly submissive to him in her efforts to please. As the years went by, she felt more and more like a victim and eventually she slid into becoming a martyr. She began to relish her task of trying to appease Henry and that spilled over into becoming overinvolved in the lives of her children. She saw herself as someone who is always being taken advantage of, always going out of her way to make life easier for her family but getting little in return.

An example of another person who allowed his boundaries to be violated was Andy, who, as an adult, was still very submissive to his parents and very much under their control. As he did his work on Step Eight, Andy realized that he had always thought he was the victim—the one being violated by his parents, particularly his rageaholic father. Now, however, he could see that by allowing his parents to be overcontrolling, he actually had been harming them.

The following assessment statements will help you ascertain how often your boundaries may be violated. Again, it may be helpful to score yourself (1–10) as to how true these statements are of you.

_____ 1. I am often plagued with self-doubts and indecisions when I'm dealing with people.

_____ 2. I frequently look to someone else to take charge of me or take charge of the situation.

_____ 3. I am a people-pleaser. I will do almost anything to avoid a fight or conflict.

_____ 4. There is someone in my life who has a great deal of power or influence over me, and I don't seem to be able to challenge this person or say no to this person.

_____ 5. On the surface I appear very easy-going and willing to please, but beneath the surface I hold

deep resentments about the way people have
steam-rollered over me.

_____ 6. I always seem to end up being the victim in
relationships, especially in relationships with the
opposite sex or relationships with authority figures. I always seem to come out on the short end of
the stick.

3. "Are My Boundaries Too Thick or Rigid?"

When a person's boundaries are too thick or too rigid, it
surfaces in several kinds of behavior. At the very base is a
strong fear of abandonment. Way down inside I fear that
if you really knew me or got to know the real me, you'd
reject me. I feel that I'm basically unlovable and so, as a
buffer against this fear of rejection and abandonment, I
keep a fairly thick wall between me and other people.
This can surface in a number of ways, including the failure to establish a committed, adult sexual union.

Perhaps my boundaries have been so thick I have never
been able to allow myself to think of marriage. The
thought of being that intimate with someone else is just
too threatening. Or perhaps, even though I've gotten married, I have never allowed myself to know complete physical or emotional intimacy with my spouse.

The reverse side of the sexual coin is sexual promiscuity, which is another way of keeping up a very thick
boundary. I run from intimacy by relating to people as
physical objects. I use people sexually, but I don't go beyond that into intimacy.

Another behavior that is characteristic of having thick
boundaries is isolation, which often originates as an early
safety mechanism in life. If I have grown up in a family
where I was hurt or violated or where family intimacy
seemed painful to me, I learned at a very early age to pull
back or withdraw in much the same way a turtle reflex-
ively pulls back into its shell.

There are two types of isolation: (1) "Isolated isolation"

means there are literally few people in my world and I live something of a hermit-like existence. (2) The more common type of isolation is the "lonely in a crowd" syndrome. There may be a lot of people around me, but I don't feel connected to them. I have some automatic relationship patterns that keep me a step removed from all of the key people around me.

The following assessment statements will help you see if you have any boundaries that are too thick or rigid. Are any of the following true of you to any degree? In what way?

_____ 1. I'd like to move closer to certain people but every time I take the first step in that direction, I'm flooded with fear that they will not like me.

_____ 2. I'm convinced that if you really got to know me, you wouldn't want to know me.

_____ 3. My intimacy life has been stalled for a long time. I've got the safety brake on. (For example, maybe I've never allowed myself to marry or, if I am married, I've sexually or emotionally pulled far back from my partner.)

_____ 4. There seems to be an invisible shield around me that separates me from other people.

_____ 5. Everyone else has some opportunity for closeness and intimacy. I always seem to be on the outside looking in.

_____ 6. I have at least a vague awareness that I've used certain parts of my personality or even my body to push people away. (For example, my quick temper or my cold body language or the extra 75 pounds of weight I carry, are all messages that say, "Keep your distance.")

_____ 7. I have trouble allowing people to give to me or nurture me.

_____ 8. I fear that I have little to give, emotionally,

physically, spiritually, that another person would want or value.

4. "Are My Boundaries Too Fragile or Perhaps Non-existent?"

The most basic relationship dysfunction that we find in the area of boundaries that are too thin or non-existent is the person living the "non-authentic" or "non-chosen" life. My boundaries are so fragile or seemingly non-existent that I am uncertain and insecure about who and what I am. I have to borrow or copy someone else's interpretation of what I should be.

When my boundaries are too fragile or thin, I will usually do one of two things: (1) Mesh or intertwine my personality with someone else—literally mold into who they are. (2) Hang tightly to some institution, some body of rules to which I can go for my identity and security.

Kathryn is an example of the first category. Henry violated her boundaries, and she tried to fix everything by fixing him. She became so obsessive over taking care of Henry that she intertwined her personality with his and in so doing she leaned on him for something that just wasn't there. Ironically, Henry, the very person from whom she was trying to draw strength and identity, was very sick, cold, and emotionally unavailable and withdrawn. Kathryn's situation was really desperate—like a person dying of thirst who has nothing to drink but salt water. The more she drank, the worse her situation became.

Andy, the workaholic perfectionist, is a good example of someone clinging tightly to a body of rules for identity and security. His religious legalism comes out of the fact that he isn't really sure of who he is or even what he truly believes. As firm as his faith appears to be, Andy isn't even sure of his personal relationship to God. That's why his workaholism and perfectionism keep driving him to achieve. In this way he hopes to please his parents but also God as well. His strict religious beliefs are like a shell, which protects and covers what is so fragile on the inside.

The following assessment statements will help you determine if your boundaries may be too thin. Perhaps you're not even sure they are there at all. As in the other three main boundary categories, it may help to give yourself an approximate rating on each statement and to make notes when something applies directly to you. Remember that you are not trying to tally up any certain score. You're merely trying to identify patterns that you can work on as you complete Steps Eight and Nine.

_____ 1. I have spent so much of my life trying to second-guess what other people want me to do or be that I've lost sight of who I am.

_____ 2. I can't imagine life apart from my spouse or dating partner. If he or she were not a part of my life, I'd cease to exist.

_____ 3. I sometimes wonder who I really am, what my identity is. My worth, value, and identity seem to be totally wrapped up in someone else or something else (my spouse, my boyfriend, my girlfriend, my job, my church).

_____ 4. I have to admit that I am so unsure of myself that I keep a very tight grip on some key person in my life. (For example, I'm anxious if my husband has to be away from home on business for a few days, or, I'm anxious if my wife is not at the front door to greet me every night of the week.)

_____ 5. I feel helpless in many areas of my life. I've become overly dependent on someone else to manage those parts of my life. (For example, I depend on someone else to manage my money or pick the style of my clothing or dictate what my relationship with God should be.)

_____ 6. Since I don't really know who I am and I don't trust my ability to say yes or no to people around me, I find it hard to trust others. In fact, this lack of trust has grown into a deep suspicion, almost a feeling of paranoia about the people around me.

Now that you've looked at the four boundary violations, go back and add up your score in each area. In what particular area or areas are your relationships suffering? We will give you some ways to correct these relationships in Step Nine.

As You Move Toward Step Nine

As you finish Step Eight and begin to consider Step Nine, you should have two lists ready.

The first list contains "historical facts," which identify the people that you believe you have harmed in the past. Your goal in making this basic list has been to put down anyone who comes to mind and then to ask God to make you willing to make amends to those that He would help you single out. In Step Nine you will learn how to single them out and how to go about making your Historical Amends with care and sincerity.

Your second list categorizes the boundary violations (relationship dysfunctions) that reveal certain patterns of behavior that cause you to do harm to others. This second list not only helps you understand better just how and why you have done harm to others, but it will also be extremely useful as you complete Step Nine and look at the all-important concept of Living Amends—continuing to live in a Christ-like spirit which will bear fruit in the future.

When doing Steps Eight and Nine, it is good to remember that the same God who helped you with Steps Six and Seven is ready to help you here. It took humility to become ready to ask God to remove your defects. It will take even more humility to go to people you have harmed to make amends.

As we said at the beginning of this chapter, the key, as

always, is attitude—a humble attitude. Keep in mind that while restitution and amends are somewhat alike, there is one important difference. Restitution is something that can be paid, much like a bill, a fine, or a penalty. I can make restitution but not necessarily have a change of heart.

In the Old Testament book of Leviticus, someone who had stolen, taken something through extortion, or who had sworn falsely, had to make restitution in full and add a fifth of the value as well.[2] In Old Testament examples like this, we see restitution as something to be paid back with an additional twenty percent added for good measure.

In the New Testament, however, we find another dimension, which is described in the story of Zacchaeus, the short-statured tax collector who wanted to see Jesus so badly he climbed a tree to look over the crowd. As Jesus came by, He looked up, saw Zacchaeus, and invited him to come down. The huge crowd, mostly Jews, was dismayed at Jesus' kindness toward a hated tax collector. Zacchaeus, a Jew himself, was working for the Roman government and that made him a traitor in the eyes of his countrymen. In addition, tax collectors were well-known for overcharging the people and keeping the excess.

Zacchaeus was wealthy, but he was a despised and unpopular man. Yet Jesus told him, "This very day I must stay at your house." As you read this story (see Luke 19:1–10), you see no mention that Jesus demands that Zacchaeus pay any restitution or reparation for all the cheating he has done in the past. Jesus doesn't have to say anything because Zacchaeus's heart has already been changed.

Even as the crowd is murmuring about the Lord's strange willingness to associate with a man who is such a great sinner, Zacchaeus says, "Look, Lord, I give half of my goods to the poor; and if I have taken anything from anyone by false accusation, I restore fourfold."[3]

Zacchaeus was so willing to make amends to those he

had swindled, he offered to pay four times the amount, far more than what the law demanded. In Zacchaeus we see a model of what Steps Eight and Nine are really all about. Even if it proves to be costly, we are willing to make amends because our hearts—not the law—lead us to do so. In Step Nine we will look at how to make amends with courage—and compassion.

Step Nine

Made direct amends to such people wherever possible, except when to do so would injure them or others.

"**W**ell, I've made my two lists," Kathryn told Dr. Meier. "Henry, Polly, and Jason are right at the top of my list of people I've offended or harmed. I let Henry violate my boundaries with his drinking and raging, and I've tried to placate him and take responsibility for his problems. In addition, I've violated my kids' boundaries by getting overinvolved in their lives."

"You've made great progress!" said Dr. Meier. "Now you're ready to make two kinds of amends. First, we'll concentrate on making the Historical Amends to the people you've harmed or offended. Later, we'll look at making Living Amends—how you can change your relationship patterns and avoid violating boundaries in the future."

"I'm ready to begin, but I confess I have a big problem . . ."

"What is that?"

"I guess I'm a coward. I'm having trouble working up courage to speak to my children, not to mention Henry."

"That's not surprising," Dr. Meier smiled. "It happens to many patients when they come to Step Nine. What they're really struggling with is their shame base. All compulsive, addictive behavior is based on shame, and we've looked at your shame base several times in other sessions. For example, one reason you have such a tight grip on your children is that you had so much happen during your own childhood. We talked about how your mother and dad were not very involved in your life; also, your father had numerous sexual affairs. Then there was your grandmother's very judgmental religion, which gave you a warped view of God. Finally, we have all those years of tolerating Henry's abuse."

"Yes, we've talked about all this, but surely I don't have to bring all these things up when I'm making amends?"

"Of course not, but you should be aware that your shame base is a key part of your codependency. Your over-dependence on others and overinvolvement in their lives are typical patterns for someone in a codependent relationship. You've been telling yourself that if you could just be a better wife to Henry, you could fix him, and if you could just love your kids to death, that will compensate for what Henry hasn't given them."

"It's still hard to accept . . . by trying to help Henry and the children, I've actually been harming them. Even if I can work up enough courage, is there any way I can ever make enough amends?"

"If there's anything we want to avoid in Step Nine, it's getting trapped into some kind of legalistic or mechanical formula—if I can just apologize well enough, if I can do things the right way, somehow I could pay off my shame debt. But trying to pay off a lifelong shame debt all at once is like trying to pay off the national debt at twenty dollars a month."

"Then my making amends doesn't necessarily solve everything?"

"No, it doesn't, but I want you to keep coming back to the key issue—the attitudinal shift that is going on inside of you. You're moving away from the old fears and resentments to an attitude of wanting to make peace with the world, wanting to offer amends for whatever you contributed to the discord. In essence, that's what it means to take Steps Eight and Nine. But it's not something you can quantify. You can't say, 'I took Steps Eight and Nine because I made so many phone calls, wrote so many letters of apology, had so many face-to-face conversations.'"

"Well, I certainly want the right attitude. I want this making of amends to go well—especially with the children."

"Kathryn, I know how you feel right here, but I think it's best if you just keep it simple. First make your Historical Amends—say you're sorry for what's happened in the past. All your kids need to hear from you is that you recognize that you've done some damage and that you are sincerely sorry. Don't make some big pledge that you'll never interfere or be overcontrolling again because it isn't that simple. But just let them know that you do realize you've been overinvolved in their lives and that you're working very hard at changing your style of being a mom."

"And Henry? What about Henry?"

"Well, strange as it sounds, you do owe some Historical Amends to Henry. But for right now, let's put that on a back burner. We'll get to Henry a little later."

Why Make Amends?

In making amends, the goal is three-fold: to be reconciled with our own conscience, to be reconciled with other persons, and to be reconciled with God.

1. *Being reconciled with your own conscience* reinforces your earlier decisions to surrender and change your defects of character, which you identified in Steps Six and Seven, as well as the relationship dysfunctions (boundary violations) you discovered in Step Eight. By making restitution, you clear away a lot of the shame and guilt of what could be called "the relationship wreckage of the past."

In addition, making peace with your own conscience by making Historical Amends sets the stage for your work on Living Amends—changing your style of relating to others so you don't slip right back into the same harmful patterns. After you clear away the wreckage that you may have caused, you will have a clear conscience and be able to do your very best to build new and better relationships.

2. *Being reconciled to others* is at the heart of making amends and is accomplished by sincerely offering apologies for past harm. *Never underestimate the power of "I'm sorry."* Sometimes we may be dealing with great wrongs that we have done and merely saying, "I'm sorry" seems so banal and perfunctory that it's hardly worth the bother. Yet the greater the harm, the more likely it is that saying, "I'm sorry," is all we can really do.

As we reconcile to others, we build bridges for our positive future relationships. Making Historical Amends—what's happened in the past—clears the way for making Living Amends—building better relationships in the future.

As part of taking Step Nine, Martin went back to apologize to Gordon Thomas, his old department head, as well as his former boss, the academic dean. Dean Walters politely, and warmly, accepted Martin's apology, but he didn't offer Martin his job back. Actually, the position had been filled, but even if the job had been open, the dean really wasn't ready to have Martin return.

Even though there was no mention of getting his job back, Martin never considered the amends he made that day to be a waste of time. "I still don't have a job," he told Dr. Fowler at his next session, "but whenever I run into Dean Walters or Gordon while out shopping or doing research at the library, I can look them in the eye and greet them as old friends. All isn't lost by a long shot. They both appreciated my sincerity and have promised to write good recommendations for me when I apply for another position. I'm not out of the woods yet, but I'd say I'm on the right trail."

3. *Reconciling with God* is the capstone on making amends. Some might say it should be the foundation—that we should reconcile with God first. In one sense, we do this when we go to God and ask His forgiveness for

what we've done. This gives us the courage and conviction to go out and make our amends to others. According to Jesus' own teachings, this is the final step in being reconciled to God.

As Jesus taught His Jewish followers one day, He referred to the sacrificial system they still used to underline the importance of being reconciled to others in order to be reconciled to God. Jesus drew a simple word picture for His listeners by asking them to imagine bringing a sacrificial gift to the altar of the Temple, but while bringing it, they would remember that someone (in their family, a friend, anyone with whom they have a relationship) had something against them. According to Jesus, they should put their gift aside, go find that person, and be reconciled. Then they could come back, offer their gift, and be reconciled to God as well.[1]

As William Barclay says concerning this passage: "We sometimes wonder why there is a barrier between us and God; we sometimes wonder why our prayers seem unavailing. The reason may well be that we ourselves have erected that barrier, because we are at variance with our fellowmen, or because we have wronged someone and have done nothing to put things right."[2]

Guidelines for Making Historical Amends

Following Dr. Meier's advice, Kathryn called Helena and asked if they could get together and go over her list of those to whom she believed she owed amends. "I'd like some help on who to contact first and the best way to go about it," Kathryn said.

"I'll be glad to help." Helena's voice sounded eager. "Meet you for coffee in an hour in the usual place."

By asking Helena for help deciding who to see first to make amends, Kathryn was following the spirit of Step Nine. We are to make direct amends to as many people as possible, *except when to do so might injure them or others.* Because the truth can be used to injure as well as to heal, we must use good judgment and a careful sense of timing in deciding when, how, and to whom to make amends. Based on our clinical experience with patients using the Twelve-Step program, we have identified at least five categories of people and timings to consider when contemplating the offering of amends:

1. *First, those to whom we may turn immediately to make complete amends.* In Kathryn's case, Polly, her married daughter, and Jason, her sixteen-year-old son, were at the top of her list. As she had coffee with Helena, they talked about who Kathryn might contact first. They decided that Polly was the best candidate. Kathryn would take Polly to lunch and tell her, "I want to make amends to you for the way I've been overmothering and even interfering in your life. For everything I've said that may have sounded meddling or controlling, I ask your forgiveness. And I'm going to work on moderating my approach in the future. I want you to help me and let me know when you hear me doing it again."

Over that same cup of coffee, Kathryn determined that Jason would be next on the list. When Jason wasn't dashing out the door to go somewhere, she would sit him down for a casual talk. She would start by telling him she was proud of the way he was developing into a fine young man and how she realized at times she was too much of a smother-mother.

"I'll tell him that I'm sorry and I want to avoid overmothering in the future," Kathryn told Helena. "And just as I'll do with Polly, I'll let Jason know that next time I get out of line, he is free to tell me."

On the lines provided below, why not list those you might want to contact immediately? Please put them down here, and then check your choices with your sponsor, a good friend, your pastor, or your therapist before going ahead.

People I Can Turn to Immediately to Offer Historical
Amends

Person 1: _____

Person 2: _____

Person 3: _____

2. *Those persons to whom amends should be made at a
later date, perhaps at a time when they will be more recep-
tive to your amends or you will have the perspective of time
to help you make the proper amends.* This would especially
be true in any case where the harm was recently done, or
if you or the other person is given to reacting in rage. The
proper passage of time may give an opportunity for healing. Also, you may need to grow stronger and heal your
own resentments before you face this person to make your
amends.

As Kathryn talked with Helena, Henry's name came
up. Helena agreed that Kathryn should wait to talk to
Henry because in making amends she would have to confront him with his own harmful behavior toward her. As
Dr. Meier had said, this was something to be put on the
back burner and dealt with when Kathryn learned more
about how to make Living Amends (to be discussed later
in this chapter).

Are there those to whom you should make amends at a
later date? Write their names below:

People to Whom I Should Make Historical Amends
at a Later Date When the Timing Is Better

Person 1: _____

Person 2: _____

Person 3: _____

3. *Persons who should never be contacted because doing
so would only open up old relationship doors that need to
stay closed.* Dr. Fowler had a patient who was in such a

situation. This man had been acting out a sexual addiction for several years. When Dr. Fowler explained Step Nine to him, his eyes began to light up: "You mean I get to go back and contact all my old girlfriends—apologize to them in person?"

"Absolutely not," Dr. Fowler responded. "Such an encounter would upset their equilibrium and very likely damage your present relationships, as well as move you right back into your old addictions."

Always the question to ask yourself is: "Am I making my amends at the cost of another person's security, privacy, confidentiality, or even that person's morality?" If you answer affirmatively to any of these categories, you should not make direct amends.

The 12 × 12 points out that there is "the occasional situation where to make a full revelation would seriously harm the one to whom we are making amends. Or—quite as important—other people. We cannot, for example, unload a detailed account of extramarital adventuring upon the shoulders of our unsuspecting wife or husband. And even in those cases where such a matter must be discussed, let's try to avoid harming third parties, whoever they may be. It does not lighten our burden when we recklessly make the crosses of others heavier."[3]

People Who Should Not Be Contacted Because Making Amends Could Only Make Things Worse

Person 1: _____

Person 2: _____

Person 3: _____

4. *Those who cannot be directly contacted because they have died, become too ill to see anyone, or you have simply lost track of them and have no way of finding them.* In such a situation, we recommend using one of three techniques for making your amends. One is called the empty chair technique. Sit next to an empty chair, imagine the

person is sitting there, and have a dialogue with him or her.

Another technique is writing letters that are never sent. Even though the letters will never be received, you may find yourself making amends through the very process of writing them down.

Finally, there is the graveside dialogue in which you go back and visit the grave of the deceased person, usually a family member, and talk with the memory of him or her. Somehow, just the memory of being there at the grave can be a very powerful catalyst for amends-making dialogue.

In completing Step Nine, Kathryn began feeling very guilty for refusing to attend the bedside of a dying great aunt who had never approved of her marriage to Henry. Telling Dr. Meier how she handled making amends to a deceased family member, Kathryn said, "Helena, bless her, suggested I visit Aunt Penny's grave. I went early in the morning to be sure I'd have privacy. And it wasn't at all as if I were in a cemetery, it was just like it was twenty years ago. Aunt Penny and I were sitting out on the porch by her big maple tree, and I said, 'Remember how you always loved the birds in the morning, Aunt Penny? You called it the dawn chorus and said they were praising God —or sometimes that it was God sending a message of love to us. You taught me to love the sound of singing birds, Aunt Penny. And to this day I never hear a bird without thinking of you and remembering those times together. Thank you so much. No one else would ever have taught me to listen to birds or to think of God when I heard one.

" 'Aunt Penny, please forgive me for not being there when you needed me at the end. I know God must have been with you and made it all right for you, but I'll never be able to replace what I missed, that one last time we could have listened to the birds together. Forgive me for the anger I felt toward you—so much of it was because I secretly knew you were right but wouldn't admit it to myself. I guess the words *God bless you* are a silly thing to say to someone in heaven, but, God bless you, Aunt Penny.'

"When I turned to leave, a bird was singing."

Additional Pointers on Historical Amends

It's essential to understand that amends are one-directional. They do not require mutual reciprocation. There may be people to whom you make amends who will not respond positively. They may refuse to forgive you, or they may refuse to ask your forgiveness if they have hurt you. If this happens, it should not matter. You are responsible for your own behavior and your own recovery. You are responsible to do the right thing as God has directed and pray that He will lead others to do the right thing also, but only in His good time.

If you go into an amends-making situation expecting or demanding reciprocation from the other party, you can be fairly certain your underlying resentments have not been resolved. In order for you to make genuine amends to someone who has offended you, it is very important that you first work on grieving out the resentment, the hurt, the pain, and the anger about the past offense. Otherwise, you are trying to put a bandage on a festering, cancerous sore. You must remove the toxicity first. Then you can forgive (and possibly be forgiven) with a high degree of integrity.

As *The 12 × 12* says, "Good judgment, a careful sense of timing, courage, and prudence—these are all qualities we shall need when we take Step Nine."[4] The basic process of making Historical Amends—searching out those whom you have harmed or offended and asking their forgiveness —can be painful, but it is the only way to continued growth and recovery.

As Helena told Kathryn, "The world is so much bigger than you think it is when you're in pain. When you're in pain you think there's no solution, but when you work Step Nine you realize there are solutions after all. And see that there are NO problems God doesn't have solutions for."

A Nine Point Plan to Make Living Amends

While making Historical Amends is the obvious first part of Step Nine, we also try to help patients understand the importance of making Living Amends. Many patients —if not *most* patients—come to a point in their recovery where they seem to have their initial addiction or obsessive-compulsive behavior well in hand. Because they seem to have these under control and because they've even dealt with some of their personality defects, which are at the center of their addictive behavior, they think they have cleared up over 90 percent of their problems. What they fail to see, however, is that while they have the obvious addictions under control, they still have underlying relationship patterns that are damaging and dangerous, even though their central addiction may be well on the way to recovery.

This is where Living Amends comes in. By Living Amends we simply mean changing the very pattern of our relationships in an ongoing, day to day, hour to hour, sometimes minute to minute way. We sometimes compare these kinds of changes to changing the course of a river. It can be done, but we must remember that a river is accustomed to flowing in its natural course, and that means literally damming something over here and carving out a new alternative river bed over there.

As a tool patients can use to work on Living Amends, we developed a nine point plan, which helps them use the Boundaries Inventory they took in Step Eight—that "second list" that Dr. Meier kept mentioning to Kathryn. The Boundaries Inventory includes four areas:

1. How I violate the boundaries of others.
2. How I allow others to violate my boundaries.
3. How I may have boundaries that are too thick.

4. How my boundaries may be too fragile, thin, or even non-existent.

Once I make my Boundaries Inventory, I can use the following nine point plan as an ongoing way of making Living Amends in all my relationships. To help the person in recovery stay centered on the real problem, we put the nine point plan statements in first person to help the patient focus directly on what "I need to do."

1. *I need to identify specific roles that I play out repeatedly in the key relationships of my life.* These roles vary, according to the patient's basic problem. Familiar roles we see at the clinic include victimizer, controller, rager, pleaser, caretaker, victim, or martyr. Step Eight gave you a sense of what is wrong with your boundary keeping, and you may have already identified the roles that you frequently play. Here in Step Nine we want you to think about how you play out your key roles in daily interaction with certain key people.

In Kathryn's case, she allowed her boundaries to be violated again and again by Henry and wound up playing the role of chronic victim, and, to a great extent, chronic martyr. While Kathryn didn't like being victimized by Henry, she had to admit that deep down there really was a payoff. By acting as Henry's caretaker, she would get tremendous sympathy from her friends who would tell her no Christian martyr had ever suffered more, that she was such a sweetheart to put up with Henry and his boorish ways.

2. *With the roles I play clearly in mind, I need to identify the specific persons and situations that seem to trigger these roles.* If, for example, I am a victim, with which people do I play out that role? What are the "trigger situations" that turn me into a victim almost instantly?

In Kathryn's case, whenever Henry raised his voice, which he was prone to do, drunk or sober, it was a trigger that turned her into a victim/martyr. Even though Kathryn would try to discount Henry's anger by telling herself, "Well, he's just drunk and blowing off steam," his loud voice still collapsed her boundaries. The minute Henry's voice went up in volume, she suddenly became a scared little girl and her boundaries were gone.

3. *I need to give myself permission to set new boundaries with trigger persons and situations so I can act out new healthier roles.* Kathryn decided to give herself permission to set new boundaries whenever Henry began raising his voice. Part of setting those new boundaries was telling herself: "That's about him, not about me. That's his alcoholism and his rage. It's not my fault, not my guilt, and not my responsibility."

Equally important, however, were the new physical boundaries that Kathryn set for herself. Whenever Henry went into one of his rages, minor or major, she would leave the room. If he followed her, she would walk out of the house. If he followed her out of the house, she would get in the car and drive to her sponsor's house, or perhaps drive over to the park and just sit there for awhile to disconnect from the situation.

Kathryn's strategy was simple. She would not allow herself to stay in the same physical proximity with the old trigger events that would put her back in the old role of victim/martyr. She set internal boundaries (what she would tell herself when Henry raged) and external boundaries (what she would do when Henry started raising his voice).

4. *I need to use "I" messages to declare my new boundaries and new roles to significant persons around me.* A key phrase here is "significant persons." In minor or peripheral relationships, there is little need to go and announce to someone, "I'm going to act differently in relating to you in the future." Instead, all that is really necessary is to start living out a different role. With key people, however, for example a spouse, a parent, or a child, it is better to have an understanding.

Kathryn waited for a calm moment when Henry wasn't drunk or particularly angry and told him, "As I've been going through recovery, I realize I've done some things that are really damaging to our relationship. I have acted irresponsibly at times in tolerating behavior from you that I shouldn't have. I have also tried to be your nurse and caretaker and now I need to let you know as a loving wife, for your well-being and mine, I'm choosing not to play those roles any more."

This kind of "I" message is much different than a "you" message, which would sound something like this: "You, Henry, made me a victim. You abused me and you forced me to take care of you, and I'm going to change all that." Any time we use "you" messages we make it very hard for the other person to really hear what we are saying. We have a much better chance of communicating if we use "I" messages.

5. *I need to remember that I can change my role regardless of the situation and regardless of the other person's reaction.* Whenever we make changes in our own behavior, we hope the person to whom we are relating will respond and make some changes too. But if that does not happen, it should not limit or diminish the changes we make. Unfortunately, when other key persons don't respond to changes by someone in recovery, a lot of the old thick layers of codependency may come into play.

As Kathryn moved through Step Nine, Dr. Meier had to caution her. "At first, deep down, you may be telling yourself, 'Yes, I can do all this and I want to do all this, but I can only do it if Henry will change. If Henry responds visibly, then I'll be able to be stronger with my boundaries and able to let go of my resentments.' Don't fall into that trap. Even if Henry gets worse—and he just might—you still have the freedom to stop your part of the codependent dance that's been going on between the two of you for years."

Something else Dr. Meier emphasized to Kathryn was the word, *detachment.* In essence, point five is the process of detachment. Twelve-Step groups, like Al-Anon and Alcoholics Anonymous, use a phrase they call, "practicing detachment with love." All this means is, "I love you, I'm committed to you, I care about you, but I love you enough to want to unhook from the sick or dysfunctional roles you and I have been playing out together."

Detachment does not mean abandonment, rejection, or even aloofness. It means not putting the same heavy emotional investment in the other person's sick behavior that you have in the past. Detachment means, "The next time you pull the trigger, I simply won't dance to your tune."

6. *Day by day, hour by hour, minute by minute, I need to draw on God's supernatural power as I set my new boundaries, play my new roles, and practice the appropriate kind of detachment.* This is where the rubber must meet the road. The next time that Henry raises his voice, Kathryn may have fear in the pit of her stomach. There may be a voice that says, "Stay right here and appease him, or try to please him in some way to change his anger." Instead, Kathryn must pause, close her eyes, and possibly step into the next room to pray: "Dear God, I can do all things through Christ who strengthens me. Right now help me detach from Henry's anger. Help me not to feel responsible for how he is acting. And please give me strength to walk out of this situation for the next few minutes."

Strengthened by her brief prayer, Kathryn can grab her car keys, walk calmly to the garage, get in the car, and go to the grocery store for an hour, or the park—anywhere away from the trigger that would send her back to being a victim and a martyr.

7. *I need to make frequent contact with my support network—my sponsor, good friends I can trust, my pastor, or my therapist.* I want to make these contacts for three reasons: (1) to receive frequent doses of unconditional love; (2) to receive specific support for the changes I'm trying to make in my new roles; and (3) to receive feedback and loving confrontation if I'm slipping back into the old dysfunctional roles.

Besides calling on God for help, we need to allow God to

work through other people. Because we've asked God's help, He will send those we need. It may be a sponsor, a Codependents Anonymous group, or a men's prayer breakfast. Whatever the setting, there are people who know what you are trying to change, relationship-wise, in your life, and you need their wisdom and counsel as well as their words of encouragement. Always make use of your support network as a sounding board. Invite their feedback even if it must be critical at times. It is seldom easy to see your own obsessive-compulsive behavior starting to spring up. That's why you need a trusted support friend or group to bring it to your attention.

8. *I need to verbally affirm to myself my new role and the appropriate detachment that I desire.* Affirmation, written or spoken, is a powerful tool. As we might easily predict, Henry did not change when Kathryn started confronting him with "I" messages and detaching behavior. In fact, his drinking got worse and his rages escalated. Henry was testing Kathryn's detachment, thinking, "If I can get sick enough, or drunk enough, or angry enough, I can force her back into taking care of me and doing things my way."

Kathryn had to get alone any number of times a day and tell herself aloud, "I am not a victim. *I am not a victim.* I will not choose to play the victim's role. I do not have to be victimized by Henry. *I have a choice!*"

Not only did she walk around muttering these affirmations to herself, she also wrote a few key ones down on three by five cards and put them in places like her purse, the visor of her car, and even inside the medicine chest in her bathroom. That way at different times during the day, she would be forced to look again at an affirmation in her own handwriting, confirming the new direction she had taken. Some of the statements Kathryn used included:

"I am no longer a victim in this marriage."
"I choose to be a co-equal partner in this marriage."

"I deserve my husband's love and his respect of my boundaries."

A technique we teach at our clinics is to make affirmation statements even more powerful by attaching an appropriate Scripture verse.[5] One of the main reasons to memorize Scripture is to have God's Word in mind for crisis situations. Just about any affirmation statement you wish to make can be supported by Scripture. For example, "I am no longer a victim" is supported nicely by 1 Peter 5:7: "casting all your care upon Him, for He cares for you."

"I choose to be a co-equal partner in this marriage" is supported by Ephesians 5:21(NIV): "Submit to one another out of reverence to Christ," or Galatians 3:28: "for you are all one in Christ Jesus."

As for "I deserve my husband's love and respect," a good verse is Ephesians 5:25: "Husbands, love your wives, just as Christ also loved the church and gave Himself for it."

9. *Finally, I need to take healthy risks as I experiment in my new roles.* We encourage patients to set daily and weekly goals that help them experiment with their new roles and their new boundaries. In Kathryn's case, one thing Henry did to make her a little crazy was to be very irregular about showing up for the evening meal. Sometimes he'd be late, sometimes he wouldn't. Sometimes he'd call, and sometimes he didn't. But no matter when he arrived, he always wanted his dinner warm and perfectly cooked.

As part of her experimental risk-taking, Kathryn decided to leave Henry notes before he left for work, telling him what time they would be eating that evening. If plans changed, she would telephone to let him know when dinner would be served.

If Henry continued in his old patterns and did not get home on time, she and Jason would go ahead and eat and she would put his meal in the oven. When he got home, he could serve himself and clear his own dishes afterward.

The first few times Kathryn tried her new plan, Henry tried to rage and complain bitterly, but she simply walked away from his rage and would not listen. Eventually, he became much more prompt about getting home on time for dinner and even started calling her to let her know he would be late.

Opportunities to experiment with new boundaries are limitless. But the key is to go ahead and experiment. Don't wait for a crisis that will force you to make a stand. Step out and plan a situation where you can put your new boundaries to the test. That way you will grow and recover all the faster.

Tool for a Lifetime of Relating

The nine point plan above is just one more tool for fighting the day to day, sometimes hour to hour, battle of recovery. Making Living Amends will help you take Step Nine and go beyond to improve your relationships and style of relating.

As Andy walked through Step Nine, the restitution step, he mustered up the courage to call Jennifer. Fully expecting her to hang up on him he considered several alternatives, such as writing her a letter, leaving a message on her answering machine, or merely showing up on her doorstep unannounced. Finally, he decided the very least he owed her was good manners, so he called and asked her to allow him to come over and talk to her. "I know you don't really want to see me, Jenny. I promise not to take much of your time or make a nuisance of myself, but I really do need to talk to you for—say half an hour, maybe?"

He couldn't believe how readily she agreed, even if her voice was cool. And when he arrived at her apartment, he couldn't believe how lovely she looked in her blue cotton dress. It was enough to make him forget his promise not to be a nuisance.

They sat at opposite ends of the sofa, and Andy recited

the apology he had practiced all the way over to her house. Without going into maudlin detail he told her briefly of his counseling with Dr. Hemfelt and his work with his Twelve-Step group, of the progress he had made, and the areas of his life that still needed modification. "I spend less time working and running, but it's still more than I should," he admitted. "I'm trying to change that. But at least I'm doing these things for different reasons now—because I enjoy doing them, not to fill a void inside myself. When I look back, I'm amazed that you put up with me as long as you did, and first I want to thank you for that. The big thing is, however, that I want to apologize for all the times I hurt you and stood you up and was just plain rude, because I was so selfishly busy seeing to my own needs. I couldn't really see anyone else—even someone as beautiful as you."

He sat for a moment. "So, that's it. Thank you for listening. I just came to say that I'm sorry. I've always been so terrified of committing errors that my drive for perfection made me make the worst mistakes of my life."

After another moment of silence Andy stood to go.

"No, wait." Jenny held out her hand to stop him. "I'm thinking. When someone says, 'Sorry,' you're supposed to say, 'That's okay, I forgive you.' I think I do, but I want to be sure. I had no idea about anything you've told me— except the selfishness part—I'd sort of figured that out." She smiled at him.

"I know something about this Twelve-Step stuff. I had an uncle who went to Alcoholics Anonymous. He had a motto in his living room—my mother had worked it for him in cross stitch when she was about my age. It said: I'D RATHER BE HAPPY THAN RIGHT. Would you like me to make one for you?"

Now it was Andy's turn to blink in astonishment. "Rather be happy than right?" He threw back his head and laughed. "What a weird concept! I'll have to think about that. If you'd like to make it for me, I'd love to have it. Of course, a person like me thinks that being perfectionistically right is part of being happy, but I'm seeing the need to change some of those beliefs. That cross stitch might help me put those words into practice."

"And you're working on letting right-brained types like me muddle through life in our own way looking at rainbows and smelling roses?"

"Please don't ever quit looking at rainbows, Jenny. And once in a while remind me to look, too. You know . . . the more I think about it, I *would* rather be happy than right!"

Step Ten

*Continued to take personal inventory
and when we were wrong
promptly admitted it.*

Martin and his family were thrilled when word came
of a small college in Southern California that had a va-
cancy for a professor of American history. He flew to Los
Angeles and three days later greeted Mary with a wide
smile when she met him at the airport.

"It isn't in the bag yet, but the interview went great!
The campus is beautiful, on a rocky point overlooking the
ocean. And there's a great beach—the kids will love it!
Everyone was so friendly and the department head assured me there would be time for me to work on my book,
too. Their system there is very supportive for creative
work. Of course, the salary is considerably less than the
one I had here."

Mary hugged him and laughed, "Well, emphasis on
had. At this point anything is a hundred percent increase,
right? Did you tell them about your A.A. work?"

"I told the dean. He said as long as I was in recovery it
was fine, but they'd want a letter from my doctor. Of
course, we can't start packing yet. It may be a month or so
until they're ready to offer a contract, but Mary, it feels so
good to be really started on a new life."

It wasn't until they were well away from the airport
and on the drive home that Martin added, "Mary, I know I

told you I'm sorry when I did Step Nine, but I haven't done an adequate job of saying, 'Thank you.' Thank you for sticking out the bad times and for continuing to work with me on this."

Mary reached over and squeezed his hand. "You know, I read the neatest thing in that Twelve-Step book for Al-Anons the other night. This woman said she thanked God that she'd had the good fortune to marry an alcoholic because she had learned so much about herself that she couldn't have learned any other way but through her Al-Anon work. It's true, you know. I guess I should thank you too."

For all his congratulations and sharing the Woodruffs' optimism, Dr. Fowler issued some serious warnings when Martin went to him two days later to ask for the letter his prospective employer had requested.

"You've made great progress," he said, "but you've got to keep on with your Twelve-Step work. Step Nine is such a major breakthrough for most people that it's not at all uncommon for them to get the idea that they've completed their recovery work—they think they're home free now. Many people quit attending meetings regularly, and that will be a real temptation if you move to a new area."

"Hmmmm, what you're saying makes a lot of sense, as usual," Martin replied. "I definitely don't want to slip after all the work we've done."

"That would really be a shame at this point because these last three steps are the important maintenance steps. They're the "New life adventure" that is talked about in *The 12 × 12*. It says that here we begin putting our A.A. way of living to practical use, day by day, in fair weather or foul."[1]

Martin nodded. "Yeah, I know. In a new job, there's bound to be some foul weather, even in Southern California."

"That's right, and foul weather is what can blow you off course. That's why Step Ten is so important. Taking personal inventory will help you correct your course and keep you going in the right direction."

Personal Inventory Includes Four Major Areas

In some ways Step Ten is a continuation of Step Four. As we take continuing inventory, we're looking for any resurgence or even a hint of the old character defects or relationship dysfunctions. As patients do their daily personal inventory work in Step Ten, we recommend that they concentrate on four areas: physical, emotional, relational, and spiritual.

1. *Physical surveying can be done quickly, but should never be ignored* because your body is a sensitive barometer of what's going on. Your body will send you warning signals when tension or anger is building within. Perhaps it would be chronic indigestion, a headache, or pains in other areas. If your addiction has been some kind of substance—alcohol, drugs, even food—you may start to get strong cravings for a drink, a fix, or a huge slab of chocolate cake with ice cream.

2. *Your emotional survey is the core of your daily inventory work* because it deals with your feelings. We emphasize to patients that they must always try to be in touch with their *authentic* feelings, that is, ask themselves what is really going on inside emotionally. Can they tell?

Patients often run into several problems here. They may have a numbness and literally not be able to "feel their feelings." Martin, the deep intellectual thinker, has this problem. He can think about feelings, but he finds it hard to actually feel.

On the other hand, Kathryn, who is highly codependent, is flooded with feelings. She often has a sense of dread as she faces her day.

As you survey your feelings, you want to look at three levels. At the first level ask, "What am I feeling right now?" At a second level, are you allowing your real feelings to surface and be expressed, or are you trying to tell yourself you feel okay, even cheerful, when you're really harboring resentments and underneath you are angry, hurt, or afraid?

At a third level, you may have unmet needs that are causing anger or fear. Do a quick check of your needs for the coming day. Your material needs for food and shelter are probably being met, but also remember needs that may arise out of your basic personality. Do you need order and structure? Or are you at the other end of the spectrum, needing freedom and the opportunity to be creative?

Even more important are the basic universal needs that are deep within all of us. We all need to matter to someone else, to have someone pay attention to us and show us love, affirmation, and affection. We need to feel significant, that we matter, that we belong. Also, we need to feel capable—that we can, indeed, handle our tasks for the day. We need a certain amount of confidence that we can go through our day anticipating a reasonable amount of success.

The reason you should always be concerned about your basic universal needs is that there is a natural tendency on the part of people who have been addictive or codependent to fall back into, and even seek out, relationships where their basic needs don't get met.

3. *When doing inventory on your relationships,* it will help to review the four boundaries discussed in Step Eight. How am I violating the boundaries of others? How are others violating my boundaries? In what ways are my boundaries too thick or rigid? In what ways are my boundaries too thin, fragile, or even non-existent?

Your daily relationships will fall into two main categories—people that you will deal with face to face or over the phone and people you won't see or talk to but perhaps are "living rent free in your mind." Sometimes this second category causes more trouble than the first.

For example, suppose I wake up one morning obsessing over the fact that Aunt Lucy, who lives fifteen hundred miles away, has written me out of her will. If I let these thoughts take control, they can dog my steps everywhere during the coming day. Instead, I must choose to appropriately release these obsessive thoughts. I need to let go of Aunt Lucy and, more important, my feelings about being "cheated" because I wasn't in her will.

4. *Last, and most important, include spiritual issues* in your daily inventory. As you go through each day, make sure to "turn it over" to the Lord. A common tendency is to become your own God and take too much responsibility for your own life. Repeat the Serenity Prayer several times and always remember that God knows the big picture, of which you are only a small part. In that larger picture, you must accept the things you cannot change, change what you can according to God's guidance, and always pray for wisdom to know the difference.

The 12 × 12 mentions the value of long range inventory work, such as occasional retreats and "annual or semi-annual housecleanings." In this chapter, however, we want to focus on your daily personal inventory because of its importance in your recovery process. By checking on yourself daily, even if only for a few minutes, you can spot problem areas where you may be getting off course and are heading back toward your addiction or compulsive behavior.

The Three Parts of Your Daily Inventory

As part of your daily inventory, *start with a brief morning quiet time,* during which you invite God to guide your day as you do a quick survey of your schedule for the next twelve hours or so. Anticipate the physical, mental, and emotional challenges that are ahead, especially the people you might be dealing with and the possible tensions that might arise. Turn all this over to God and ask for His guidance, wisdom, and patience.

Second, as you go through your day you may feel pressures beginning to build. These pressures may be external; for example, it may be obvious that your co-worker is irritated and ready to blow up. Or the pressures can be internal; you can literally feel your own blood pressure rising due to what is going on at the moment. When these major or minor crises arise, you can stop to do what Bill Wilson calls a "spot check." Right now, while you are "in the process," stop to assess the situation and how you are handling it.

One favorite approach to doing a spot check is a technique that comes out of the oral traditions of many Twelve-Step groups. Using an acrostic built around the word "HALT," ask yourself, am I:

*H*ungry?
*A*ngry?
*L*onely?
*T*ired?

Try saying "halt" to yourself as you go through the day. The way you have been taking care of (or not taking care of) yourself may be showing up in what your body and your emotions are telling you.

Good spot check questions to ask are: What is my body telling me? What are my emotions right now? Whose boundaries am I crossing, or who is violating my boundaries?

Your inventory at day's end is perhaps the most important. This is when you find a quiet place where you can unwind and review your day to see what has worked and what hasn't.

Have any of your old defects or dysfunctions surfaced? The key to your day's end inventory is honesty, but don't focus entirely on the negative. As you look back over the last eight to twelve hours, be sure to note those places where the glass is at least half full or more. You may want to make out a quick Gratitude List, which is described in more detail later in this chapter.

Recognizing Warning Signs of Relapse

One of the most important functions of Step Ten is to help you watch for any warning signs of a possible relapse back into your obsessive-compulsive behavior or using your addictive agent. We give patients five questions to focus on to determine whether or not relapse might be threatening:

1. *Is anger building inside of you?* Often a patient has resentments that are simmering close to the boiling point just beneath the surface of what seems like a placid and even happy time in his recovery. That's exactly what happened to Martin. Ironically, just a few days after returning from his trip to California for a very favorable job interview, Martin woke up feeling depressed and angry. As he began doing his Step Ten work and checking his emotions, Martin became very aware that his depression was tied to being angry at Gordon Thomas, his old department head. He couldn't stop thinking about how Gordon had "done him in" and gotten him fired from his former job.

Martin went in to see Dr. Fowler and told him what was going on. "Even though I've got a good chance at a new job, I'm still angry about what happened at my old one," he explained. "I keep thinking about the other faculty members who had their contracts renewed. None of them can hold a candle to me as a scholar. Why were they rehired and I wasn't? They know I'm in recovery and that I'm making good progress. It must have been Gordon —he must have really convinced the dean that I'd be a poor risk."

"Obviously, you have some deep resentments that aren't going to go away quickly," Dr. Fowler observed. "But I'd like you to think about something else. Why have these resentments boiled to the surface just now when things are going so well? I'm wondering if it couldn't be because you're a little bit afraid of going out to a new

An Outline for Doing Daily Inventory

Morning Quiet Time
Duration: Three to Thirty Minutes

Physically, how do I feel right now? How is my energy level? Am I ready to go?

Emotionally, what are my true feelings at the moment? Am I trying to ignore or deny how I really feel in order to put on a positive front?

Relationally, with whom will I be dealing today? What tensions may arise? How can I avoid these?

Spiritually, have I turned the day over to God? Have I reconnected with Him as the day has begun, and am I looking toward His guidance throughout the rest of the day?

Spot Check Inventories at Any Time During the Day
Duration: A Few Seconds to a Few Minutes

Physically, what am I feeling right now? Is my stomach churning? Does my head ache? Am I tired or fatigued? Do I need a short break or maybe a short walk to relax?

Emotionally, am I calm or agitated? Are my needs being met or am I being frustrated in some way?

Relationally, is someone irritating me? Am I possibly irritating someone else? Is there any way I can relieve this tension right now?

Spiritually, have I remembered to invite God into the process right now as I face this crisis, whether it's major or minor? Am I remembering to "turn it over" to God at all times?

Day's End Inventory Taken Before Retiring
Duration: Five to Sixty Minutes

Physically, am I tired and ready for sleep? Is my fatigue the healthy kind that comes from a good day's work and feeling that accomplishments have been made?

Emotionally, what am I feeling right now? Am I trying to

displace any feelings that have arisen during the day? How were my needs met or not met this day? How important was that to me? Am I harboring resentment about things, real or imagined, that happened during the past day?

Relationally, what relationships went well today and why? If I had some problems, why did they occur? What could I have done to make the relationship smoother? What went well today and why?

Did I allow anyone to "live rent free in my mind" today? Even though I didn't see them in person or talk to them on the phone, did I obsessively think about them all day and brood about something that they may or may not have done, something they may or may not have said?

Spiritually, have I been aware of God's guidance this day? Can I look back and see where I remembered to keep Him in the process and always turn it over to Him?

My Gratitude List For Today

Am I grateful to God for how the day has gone, good or bad? What were the minor or major victories I enjoyed today? Did I try something and fail or perhaps partially succeed? What did I learn from this? For whom and what do I want to thank God tonight? What do I value in myself tonight? What do I like about the way I lived and interacted with others today?

college, a new job, and having to prove yourself all over again."

"Well, I hadn't really thought about that. I don't think I'm afraid to start over but who knows?"

"You may just be resenting the big change you're facing. Remember that you're a person who likes everything in its place, tied down, no loose ends. Right now, even though you've had good news, it may mean a move across country that will be very stressing."

Whenever your resentments start to bubble up, it is likely that, like Martin, you are still carrying an old hurt that you have not identified and worked out through the grief process that was covered in Step Five. If this is the case, you may want to review the grief process and also return to your Step Four inventory for more in-depth work.

2. *Do you find yourself excessively preoccupied with your old addictive agent?* For example, Martin's primary addictive agent was alcohol, but earlier in his recovery program he had admitted to having two other obsessive-compulsive behaviors: his powerful drive to be in control and run his own show, and his compulsion to intellectualize everything.

After Martin returned from his California job interview and became depressed and angry, he couldn't stop thinking about how resentful he was toward "intellectual inferiors" who had retained their jobs while he had been let go. Unconsciously, he allowed his old secondary obsessions to creep back in.

Martin didn't sit down and say to himself: "I think I'll dredge up my old obsessions about intellectualism and wanting complete control." Instead he began dwelling on questions like: "How good am I really? How do I stack up against my peers? How can I get a sharper mental edge? What do I have to do to prove my worth?"

Martin couldn't shake his anger and depression.

And then he began to wake up thinking: "Drinking did have its positive effect. It took the edge off and kept me balanced. It really was a way I could relax, and I don't feel very relaxed right now." As Martin slipped back over the line into a secondary compulsive behavior, he started to drift dangerously close to relapsing into his primary addiction, alcohol.

3. *Do you find yourself rationalizing your old dependency?* If you find yourself looking back and thinking, "It really wasn't so bad . . . I didn't really do anything that awful," you may be on the verge of going back into denial and then into relapse. This could take you all the way back to Step One where you will have to admit that you are powerless over your addiction and that your life is really unmanageable.

Fortunately for Martin, he could sense that he was beginning to rationalize. In a session with Dr. Fowler he said, "Even though we've talked for months about the need to find unconditional love, and even though I have a support group that gives me that kind of love, I've begun to focus on having to reprove my worth in my new job. All of those feelings of being loved and supported for who I am are going out the window. I'm starting to tell myself, 'If you're going to make it in the academic arena, it will take sheer guts and brilliance.' I'm even starting to think Darwin's theory of natural selection makes a lot of sense."

"Is that the extent of your rationalizing?" asked Dr. Fowler, expecting there might be more. There was.

"What truly scares me is that I'm starting to rationalize why it would be okay to take a drink. I'm starting to tell myself, 'You're not *really* an alcoholic. Yes, you have a problem, but you just need to be careful.' And I'm also thinking that because of all the pressure I'm under right now with the move, I need to relax and what would be better than a drink or two? And third, I have just run across some articles which dispute the theory that alcoholism is an addiction. According to these writers, who seem to have some pretty fair academic credentials, alcohol is not really addicting."

In Martin's case, Dr. Fowler just let him talk because he was solving his own problem. He had sensed he was rationalizing, and when he got through the doctor said, "I think you know the answer to everything you've been saying. Rationalizing is one of your most dangerous enemies. Now that you've shared all this with me, why don't you talk all this over with your sponsor too? Then if you get any more deep desires for a drink, make an appointment to see me immediately."

4. *Are you beginning to isolate?* If you find your attendance at your Twelve-Step meetings is irregular; if you've lost touch with your sponsor or therapist; if you're finding excuses to stay home from church or Bible study; you may need to renew your commitment to living your chosen lifestyle.

As Martin did his daily inventory work, he could see signs of isolation in his behavior. He had begun attending every other A.A. meeting, and when he was there he became much quieter and more passive, listening with a detached, intellectual perspective as if he were doing research on A.A. rather than being part of it. As many Twelve-Step groups describe it, Martin had begun "auditing the course."

"And I haven't been going out with anyone after A.A. meetings for coffee either," he admitted to Dr. Fowler. "My sponsor is calling to ask me what's wrong, and Mary wonders why I've pulled back from her in spite of the excitement of our possible move to California."

5. *Have you fallen into the habit of "stinkin'*
thinkin'"? This sign of encroaching relapse is often difficult to put your finger on because it is just a

vague sense that things aren't very good. If you are going around in a funk—like the little character in the old comic strip "Li'l Abner" who walked around with a black rain cloud over his head—you may be on the verge of a "dry drunk." You are not necessarily about to go back into your primary addiction, but you are relapsing into chronic anger or depression.

For Martin "stinkin' thinkin' " came out in his militant cynicism over what had happened at his old job. He saw himself as better than others and was concentrating on ways to get back at Gordon, his old department head. Perhaps some people in the academic world would like to know about some shoddy research Gordon had done on a thesis a few years back was Martin's train of thought. Martin knew because Gordon had written on one of Martin's strongest areas and it was easy to spot.

"Stinkin' thinkin' " comes out in feelings of anger, depression, and wanting to retaliate. You see through the glass darkly, and at every point your attitude is 180 degrees from good mental health. Seeing things from a balanced perspective, being able to appreciate life's blessings, wanting the best for others, not feeling cornered or threatened—all of these positive healthy characteristics are turned upside down. Instead, you slip into paranoia, depression, hostility, and cynicism.

Dr. Fowler finally had to tell Martin, "I think you're on a dry drunk. All the warning signs are there. You still haven't touched any alcohol, but you're definitely struggling with a large part of your old addictions. We've got to break you out of this."

The Remedy for Relapse

Fortunately for Martin, he worked Step Ten and stayed in touch with his therapist as he went through his "dry drunk funk." He never had a full-fledged relapse, which would have meant taking a drink, getting intoxicated, and in the worse case scenario, winding up back in some kind of dry-out recovery program. Nonetheless, Martin's dry drunk brought him right to the edge of going on a chemical wet one, and he needed to take the same steps that we recommend for people in a full-fledged relapse. These steps include the following:

1. *I need to acknowledge to myself, another person, and to God the reality of the relapse.* I must be honest and not go into denial. If I'm a food-aholic, I must admit that I've been off my food plan for two weeks and back on my addictive agent—too many calories. I need to pray and admit this to God, as well as tell my sponsor and my peers. If I'm part of a Twelve-Step group, I need to get to a meeting immediately and share what's going on and get some compassionate support.

2. *I need to forgive myself and endorse myself.* The greatest danger in a relapse is that I will simply heap shame on myself and then wallow in that self-shame. When I engage in significant self-shaming, I simply drive myself deeper into the relapse.

This is what could have happened to Martin if he had let his dry drunk turn into a wet one. If Martin had taken a drink, it would have been quite natural for him to be flooded with waves of guilt and remorse because he had broken abstinence, and in so doing he had broken fellowship with his A.A. support groups. As he continued to tell himself what a bad person he was, he could have accelerated his self-shaming. Finally, the only way to cope with all that would have been the bottle and winding up in the gutter or a detox facility.

3. *I need to give myself permission to reset the necessary abstinence or balance boundaries with my addictive agent.* The reason I "give myself permission" to get my addiction under control, rather than make

a vow to do so, is to get out of the shame syndrome. I want to avoid the tug-of-war that usually happens when I "take the pledge this morning and find myself craving alcohol (or whatever my addictive agent might be) before nightfall."

It is much better to think, "I am giving myself permission to step back into the boundaries that are healthy and life-giving to me. I always want to see getting back into the program that controls my addiction as a gift, not a punishment or a deprivation."

4. *I need to listen to what my relapse is trying to tell me.* If I have relapsed (or as in Martin's case, come very close to a primary addiction relapse), there is a message in this. My relapse is trying to tell me that something is missing, deficient, or incomplete in my recovery. In very practical terms, there is something significant going on inside of me emotionally that I haven't been picking up in my Step Ten work. Perhaps I have been sensing something in my daily inventories, but I haven't been willing or able to deal with it and now it has sabotaged me and pulled me toward a full-blown relapse or even over the line. I need to understand the message in all of this. The message is not that I'm bad, not that I need to be shamed and hung out to dry. The message is simply: "Something is missing in my recovery—what is it?"

In Martin's case, he had failed to deal with his grandiosity—the feeling that he was intellectually superior to everyone else. Ironically, Martin's grandiosity was simply a cover-up for his severe feelings of insecurity and inferiority. The danger for Martin was that, when he slipped back into his grandiose thinking, it could lead him back toward drinking to shore up his sagging self-esteem.

5. *I need to recommit to a revitalized recovery program.* Here is where taking the pledge and making vows come into play, but I must be wise, not just

determined. My goal is to re-channel my willpower to do what I know is possible at this time.

For example, if I've gone back to drinking, I don't necessarily "swear off alcohol forever." Instead, I vow to stop drinking one day at a time, and I commit to going to three A.A. meetings a day for the next thirty days. I also might commit to talking to my sponsor twice a day and doing extensive journaling about my feelings. I need to make tangible corrective commitments to revitalize my recovery, but they must be goals that are reachable.

Count Your Blessings, Not Just Your Errors

One of the most effective tools we've found for helping patients do Step Ten is to have them periodically draw up a Gratitude List. As *The 12 × 12* reminds us, ". . . inventory taking is not always done in red ink. It's a poor day indeed when we haven't done *something* right. As a matter of fact, the waking hours are usually well filled with things that are constructive. Good intentions, good thoughts and good acts are there for us to see."[2]

A Gratitude List can be made as you start your day, but you may find it easier to do the inventory during the meditation that ends your day in the evening. Even if life hasn't been going very well, especially during the past twenty-four hours, what can you do to get in touch with and affirm even the minor victories? Don't overlook the seemingly small insignificant things. You got up and got to work on time. You received or made a friendly phone call. You tried a different kind of salad dressing at lunch and liked it. You finished a pesky job that had been stacked on your desk.

Also important is to try to see the good behind

things that may seem to be failures on the surface. The point is you tried, and even if you failed you learned from the experience. *The 12 × 12* notes: "Even when we have tried hard and failed, we may chalk that up as one of the greatest credits of all. Under these conditions, the pains of failure are converted into assets. Out of them we have received the stimulation we need to go forward."[3]

When Dr. Fowler suggested that Martin fight off his dry drunk by making a Gratitude List, the intellectual history professor balked at first. "You mean I should put down things like getting up and brushing my teeth?" he asked a little incredulously.

"Well, as a matter of fact, we do suggest that people use something even that simple to get started," Dr. Fowler replied. "But I'm sure you can find plenty of other things if you just start looking."

Martin soon got the hang of it. His Gratitude List started to grow, with items like:

Packed two boxes of books today.
Read several journals that had stacked up on me.
Contacted a realtor to list with if the job comes through.

Another key part of a Gratitude List is what we call "the basic blessings of life." If things haven't gone well today or even during the past week, you still have some underlying areas in which you can be grateful. These might include good health, a good job, a comfortable home, a loving spouse, and relatively obedient children. Martin's first thought when it came to his basic blessings was his wife Mary. He was also feeling better than he had in years because alcohol wasn't ravaging his body. And there was the strong possibility of that new job in California!

The more he thought about his basic blessings, the less threatening the possible move appeared to be. He began seeing the positive side and practically stopped thinking about Gordon and what he had supposedly done to undermine him.

One evening, as they were going out to a movie, he told Mary, "I don't know why I've been thinking lately that Gordon cost me my old job. *I* cost me my old job, but now we have a good shot at a new start. Thank God for that!"

Third on your Gratitude List should be "what you value or like in yourself." If valuing yourself sounds a bit narcissistic, remember that God made you. To fail to value yourself is to fail to value the work of the Creator. As you do your daily inventory, morning or evening, think of the good job God did when He created you. Don't fail to note what you particularly like about how you've handled yourself over the past day.

Don't overlook the trivial—and be sure to include the profound. The fact that you didn't overreact in anger when someone cut you off in traffic is definitely to be valued. The fact that you felt good about how your hair looked today is something to be valued.

On the profound side, the fact that you were sensitive to your spouse's needs today is valuable indeed. And if you can think of several times when you turned to the Lord today for guidance when the pressure mounted, that's something to be valued above all else.

As Martin looked at what he valued in himself, he decided he liked his dry sense of humor, particularly when he was able to joke with the usually dead-pan bus driver and get him to laugh. Martin had a little more difficulty thinking about something profound. "I suppose," he mused, "that I should be thankful that God made me a thinking being, that I have a mind."

And that brings us to our fourth area—"to value anything large or small that you have seen in your day that shows you how the grace of God is working in your life." What things worked out that seemed to be beyond your human power to engineer them?

Although Martin's relationship to God as he understood

Him was still tenuous at best, he told Mary one morning at breakfast, "Before I went into recovery, I would have been saying that I deserved this new job—that they're getting the best man they could possibly find. But now I know that's not true. If I do get the job, it will be a tremendous break. They'll be hiring an alcoholic who says he's stopped drinking, but how do they know what I'll do? It's a miracle they even considered me and gave me as much encouragement as they did. God must be behind this in some way and all I can do is be thankful."

Step Eleven

Sought through prayer and meditation to improve our conscious contact with God *as we understood Him,* praying *only for knowledge of* His *will for us and the power to carry that out.*

Martin did get the job at the California college. The week before he was to move he attended his home A.A. group to say goodbye to people he had once looked upon so askance, many of whom were now his best friends. He accepted their congratulations on his new job and their well-wishes for his future with an open smile. But the day after the meeting, he confided his newest problem to Dr. Fowler in their weekly session together.

"I thought you'd like to know that I did get the job in California, and I'll be leaving shortly. That's the good news, but I do have a problem."

"What is that?" Dr. Fowler wanted to know.

"Well, I've worked Step Ten fairly well. In fact, I'm still working on it, but Step Eleven has me stuck. When I came into this program I hardly believed in a god at all. I've come quite a ways since then and I've been comfortable with trying to relate to God 'as I understand Him.' Sometimes I think I have a pretty good understanding— God is a Higher Power who hears my prayers and forgives my sins. But at other times I slip back into thinking my

Twelve-Step group is my Higher Power. Sometimes I even think the steps themselves are my Higher Power."

Martin paused and then added with a wry smile, "At least I'm beyond cracking jokes about a tree being my Higher Power, but I know I've got a ways to go on this one, particularly with praying for knowledge of God's will. I'm not sure I'm ready for that."

As Martin finished his explanation, Dr. Fowler reached for his Bible and opened it to the eleventh chapter of Hebrews in the New Testament. As he showed the page to Martin he said, "I don't think you should be discouraged at all. The fact that you're sober and that you are here talking to me about Step Eleven because you are searching for a closer relationship with God—all of this indicates how far you've come in your recovery."

"That's encouraging, I guess," Martin acknowledged, "but now I'm really stuck. Step Eleven seems to be beyond what I understand about my Higher Power."

"The key to Step Eleven is that phrase 'as you understand Him.' You can't grow closer and more pleasing to a God you don't understand. We get to know God through faith in Him. Step Eleven has to be approached from a foundation of faith—even just a little bit of faith. Look at verses one and three in this chapter from Hebrews: 'Now faith is being sure of what we hoped for and certain of what we do not see. . . . By faith we understand that the worlds were framed by the Word of God, so that the things which are seen were not made of things which are visible.' Martin, you know that at this clinic 'God as we understand Him' is found in the Bible, which is the Word of God. I'd like you to consider this: If God's Word is so powerful that just His speaking it framed the worlds, think what it could do in your life."

Martin nodded slowly but said nothing.

"What I think these verses are telling us is that faith is a means to knowledge," Dr. Fowler continued. "As an historian, Martin, you know that much of our knowledge comes by faith in some authoritative person or source of information rather than by our own personal verification. Just as you can be sure of Columbus's voyage, even though you weren't there to see it, so can you be sure of Divine creation, even though you weren't there to see it, by the evidence you can see around you, what you can read in God's Word, and your own experiences with the Divine order."

"But Columbus was an historical figure," Martin pointed out, his love for debate rising up. "There are many ways to verify that he lived and did make his voyages to the New World."

"Jesus Christ is an historical figure also," Dr. Fowler pointed out quickly. "As for verifying the information on Jesus, the Bible is the most verified book in the world. It's been tested and retested, far more times than a lot of written history has."

"Yes, I suppose that's true . . ." Martin hesitated, wondering where the conversation was going next.

"Martin, all I'm trying to say is that faith is not belief in a never-never land. It is the exact opposite. These verses in Hebrews are saying that faith penetrates the superficial world of appearances to grasp the eternal reality behind what we see. Faith is not something just for children, it is at the heart of any sound philosophy. That's why Step Eleven lays out such specific means for spiritual growth. This isn't kindergarten stuff. You will note that Step Eleven is the longest step—longest in terms of words and in terms of time. In fact, you don't finish Step Eleven. It takes years and none of us can ever say we've finished growing spiritually in this life."

"Doctor, I think you've been telling me for months that there is only one authentic direction for that growth. It can't be as vague as 'some nebulous force in the cosmos.' "

"That's right, Martin. The task of Step Eleven is very straightforward. It is the task of building a personal spiritual relationship with the One true God of the universe, the Lord Jesus Christ."

Martin left the clinic building that day with a lot to

think about. He also carried with him a copy of *Mere Christianity* by C. S. Lewis, a present from Dr. Fowler who gave it to him saying, "C. S. Lewis had one of the finest minds of the twentieth century. He came to the Christian faith at about the same point in life as you are now. You might be interested in reading his thoughts on God and why He believed he found God in Jesus Christ." Martin determined to start reading that very evening.

Step Eleven is a direct outgrowth of Step Ten. Step Ten focused on recovery maintenance. Step Eleven focuses on spiritual maintenance.

Step Eleven is an invitation to move into the presence of the all-powerful God who is available in the person of the Lord Jesus Christ. In Step Two, we "came to believe that a Power greater than ourselves could restore us to sanity." Through the rest of the Twelve Steps to this point, we have been moving closer and closer to God, letting Him restore our sanity through His power. The entire journey will only be completed when we reach heaven, but now we each find ourselves at a different stage along the way. This fact alone helps us understand that Christ is a personal God because we, His creatures, are individual persons and He deals with us as such.

Dr. Fowler had guessed right that C. S. Lewis's thinking would appeal to a former agnostic like Martin. As the well-read history professor got into the early chapters of *Mere Christianity*, he was amazed at both the depth and simplicity of Lewis's arguments in defense of what he called "real Christianity." And when Martin got to the discussion of free will, he especially liked Lewis's reasoning about why God had given man a choice.

"Free will," wrote Lewis, "though it makes evil possible, is also the only thing that makes possible any love or goodness or joy worth having. A world of automata—of creatures that worked like machines—would hardly be worth creating. The happiness which God designs for His higher creatures is the happiness of being freely, voluntarily united to Him and to each other in an ecstasy of love and delight compared with which the most rapturous love between a man and a woman on this earth is mere milk and water. And for that they must be free."[1]

As Martin put his copy of *Mere Christianity* down and turned out the light, he thought, *Lewis is right. Robots would hardly be worth creating. God has given me the choice to accept or reject His love.*

Dealing with Road Blocks to Step Eleven

Many recovery patients who desire to grow closer to God through Step Eleven soon discover that the same basic fears that trigger their old addiction now resurface as road blocks to spiritual intimacy with God.

One of these basic fears is the fear of deprivation, that something is going to be taken away from me. A universal cause of addictive behavior is the fear that there will never be enough "whatever"—success, sex, food, chemical euphoria, etc. At Step Eleven this fear may be awakened. I may begin asking myself, "If my life moves more closely toward conformity with God's will, does that mean that God is going to take away some of the possessions, people, or activities that have been so important in my life?"

Another basic fear is the loss of control. I may believe that if I really take Step Eleven, I will lose my place in the driver's seat, one of the very fears that led to my addiction in the first place. My addiction creates the illusion of control, such as controlling my moods with chemicals or controlling other persons with codependent manipulations. In reality however, my addictions actually send my life spinning out of control.

The same part of my personality that feared the loss of control and reached for an addictive agent to create the illusion of control may now be the part of me that strongly resists the notion of further surrendering my will to God. I may need to reassure myself multiple times a day that the Christ who lives and dwells within me is the only trustworthy source of guidance. The irony is that giving up control of my life to Jesus is the only way I will ultimately bring my addictive lifestyle back into a state of healthy self-control.

Basic fears such as deprivation and loss of control can cause all kinds of secondary fears that become road blocks to your progress as you try to move down the path of Step Eleven. In the next section of this chapter, we will look at five of the most common road blocks and barriers to drawing closer to God. Don't be discouraged if you can see some of these barriers affecting you. The very fact that you are at Step Eleven and bumping into hidden road blocks is an indication of the progress you have made.

Remember, that by Step Eleven, the major brush fires that were attached to your addiction or compulsive behavior have been put out. Life is not an overwhelming twenty-four-hour-a-day struggle; now you're ready for the long haul, and developing your spiritual life is a big part of that long haul.

Five Common Road Blocks

1. *"God won't listen to me"* is one of the most universal of all road blocks. Use the following assessment statements to gauge how serious this might be for you. As an aid in your assessment, rate yourself 1 to 10 (1, not true of me; 10, very true of me).

_____ When I pray, I feel my words may be falling on deaf ears. I can't imagine that God actually hears my prayers.

_____ I sometimes debate with myself about how God can hear my individual prayers when millions of others are trying to speak to Him at the very same time.

_____ I wonder if God wants to hear me pray? I have been away from Him for so long and/or there is so

much in my life about which I feel ashamed. I'm
not sure I deserve to be heard.

_____ Early in my life, there was someone very important to me who didn't seem to care about me or
want to listen to me. And now I feel the same way
about God.

As we said, "fear that God won't listen" is almost universal. We can see it in all of our three main recovery
characters whose stories we have followed throughout
this book. Kathryn's father wouldn't listen to her because
he had his own switchboard tied up due to his own problems and his problems with Kathryn's mother. There was
simply no place for Kathryn to plug in and be heard. Now,
as an adult with a budding faith in Christ, Kathryn still
battles fears that God is too busy, too judgmental to listen
to her prayers.

Andy also faces the "God won't listen" road block. His
father wouldn't listen to him because he was too busy
preaching and lecturing. Andy's dialogue with his father
has always been one-sided with Dad doing all the talking.
It's natural enough, then, for this to spill over into Andy's
spiritual life and give him fears that God is a lot like his
earthly father.

And during Martin's boyhood, his father wouldn't listen
to him because he was too busy drinking himself into an
alcoholic stupor. As so often is the case, Martin followed
in his father's footsteps and became an alcoholic too, illus-
trating how God visits "the iniquity of the fathers upon
the children and the children's children to the third and
the fourth generation."[2]

Kathryn, Andy, and Martin are all from different back-
grounds, but they have one thing in common: their fathers let them down and never listened to them. As they
begin to take Step Eleven, they have varying degrees of
assurance that God is there and has power, but they all
wonder, "Can I trust Him?" Now they have to make new

application of their knowledge about their fathers to understand how it can be a barrier to their conscious growing contact with God.

One of their best weapons for countering fears that God won't listen are the promises of Scriptures, such as Psalm 91:15: "He shall call upon Me, and I will answer him;/I will be with Him in trouble;/I will deliver him and honor him." The entire ninety-first Psalm, in fact, is an excellent reminder of God's care, concern, and willingness to hear your prayers.

If you also fear that God isn't always listening or doesn't want to listen, realize that it is good to verbalize this fear but then recognize it for what it is—a false shame message, a lie that your shame base is feeding you. If you find some lingering issues regarding deep shame, it may be helpful to review the family of origin section in your Step Four inventory, which may give you some new insights as to why you don't think God is willing to listen to you.

2. *I'm not spiritual (or mystical) enough.* To assess how this barrier may or may not apply to you, rate how you fit the following statements (1, not true of me; to 10, very true of me):

_____ Whenever I try to pray, I have doubts that I may not be doing it correctly.

_____ The mystical accounts of encounters with God that I read in the Bible (Moses at the burning bush, Joseph's dreams, etc.) seem so far removed from my own experience of prayer and meditation that I become discouraged and want to give up.

_____ In the past I have tried some of the more exotic spiritual disciplines and trendy techniques, but these too seem to fall flat and short of my goal of conscious contact with God.

_____ I'm a person who likes quick and measurable results, and to be honest, I've been impatient with a prayer life that seems to work so slowly. I pray but God seems slow to answer or never answers at all.

We often deal with patients who tell us how they hear glowing accounts from their friends and acquaintances of how God seems to answer their every prayer. These people seem to have a pipeline to God, and He grants their every request immediately. "Why," a patient may wonder, "doesn't God answer *my* prayers in the same way? Why doesn't God answer at least *some* of my prayers a little more quickly and specifically?"

One answer to this rather common problem is that, while it is true that some people have dramatic answers to prayer, it is equally true that the vast majority of people down through the centuries have been much more likely to hear God's "still small voice" than to see bushes burn and seas open. We urge people in recovery to keep listening for God's voice and to be patient. They should keep in mind too, that while we say we want to pray for God's will, many times what we ask for comes out of our own willfulness and God may not grant the request for our own good.

3. *If I pray for God's will, He may do something that will be totally counter to what I want to do and be in life.* Rate yourself from 1 to 10 with the following assessment questions:

_____ I become so frustrated in trying to sort out my will from God's will that my prayer life comes to a standstill.

_____ Although I've made progress in trying to take myself out of the driver's seat, I have to admit that there are still many times when total surrender to God is still frightening to me.

_____ I fear that total yielding to God may bring an unwanted revolution in my life—for example, what if

God tells me to sell my business, take my family, and become a missionary in a foreign land?

_____ I fear that I may gain a sense of God's direction for my life and then discover that I am unwilling or unable to follow His leading.

Many people fear that if they truly pray for God's will, it will turn out to be something awful—some sort of horrible inconceivable punishment that will ruin their lives. Another very real concern is not being able to live up to God's leading. What if they can't handle what they believe is God's will? Then their shame base becomes even larger and their sense of guilt even more pervasive.

We find it is helpful to point out to people with this kind of road block that God's will is not necessarily contrary to your will. As soon as you have moved past the self-centeredness and grandiosity of your addiction or compulsive behavior—as soon as you truly desire God's will—you will find that most of your desires are God-given in the first place. You simply surrender to His will in order to gain power and guidance to reach what you and God want together.

This concept was a great release for Andy, who because of his legalistic background, was convinced that as soon as he totally opened himself to God's will, he would have to give up his career in computers and go into some kind of full-time ministry to which he was not suited.

He told his sponsor, Gene, "While I was growing up in our church, I met several people who weren't really called to what they were doing. They were just serving out their time."

"Andy, I've seen those kinds of people too, but what they do is not the point. As we give God possession of all our will, His leading comes to us, not as commands from without but through our own desires springing up from within. We will feel as though we *desire* to do something, not that we *must* do something. My own experience is that as I draw closer to God and know more and more of His will, I feel all the more free and liberated."

Gene's words didn't totally convince Andy, but they pointed him in the right direction, toward seeing how joyous life with God could be. And Andy had to admit that this was in sharp contrast to the harsh judgmental God he had known all his life.

4. *Is it okay to pray for specific things—particularly my everyday concerns that God is probably too busy to deal with?* Rate yourself from 1 to 10 with the following assessment statements:

_____I'm confused. Many of the people I know pray about specific needs. Step Eleven seems to be telling me something else.

_____I feel guilty if I take my petty concerns to God, and I question if He really wants to hear all of my needs and requests.

_____I wonder if it's okay for me to develop my own spiritual identity. On one side I hear that I'm supposed to be growing stronger and more decisive, and on the other side I keep hearing that I must give up my willfulness and yield totally to God. Which is it?

_____I question whether I should pray for specific outcomes in certain situations and relationships. If the only goal is "His will be done," then maybe I'm not supposed to have any preferences or desires about anything.

_____I fear I may lose myself and cease to exist as a real person if I totally surrender to what Step Eleven seems to be saying.

Many of the above concerns belonged to Kathryn because she had always played the rescuer role in her family. Naturally she wanted to pray for Henry and all her children, not to mention the starving millions in Asia. But she wasn't sure if it was permissible to make specific requests of God—He might think she was presumptuous.

As always, the best answers to concerns like these can be found in Scripture itself. Jesus modeled the very essence of prayer when He told His Heavenly Father in the Garden of Gethsemane the night before He was to be crucified, ". . . not what I will, but what You will"[3]

"Thy will be done" should be the theme that runs through all our prayers and petitions, not simply because it sounds pious but because we truly don't want anything outside of God's will. As the apostle John wrote in his letters: "Now this is the confidence that we have in Him, that if we ask anything according to His will, He hears us. And if we know that He hears us, whatever we ask, we know that we have the petitions that we have asked of Him"[4]

But perhaps the best assurance that it is quite all right with God to pray about health, finances, raising the kids, and any number of other concerns, is found in the words of Jesus:

> "Ask, and it will be given to you; seek, and you will find; knock, and it will be opened to you. For everyone who asks receives, and he who seeks finds, and to him who knocks it will be opened. Or what man is there among you who, if his son asks for bread, will give him a stone? Or if he asks for a fish, will he give him a serpent? If you then, being evil, know how to give good gifts to your children, how much more will your Father who is in heaven give good things to those who ask Him!"[5]

As Dr. Hemfelt talked with one patient who worried about praying too specifically, he told him of a passage in Scripture that says we can address God as "Abba, Father," which literally means we can call him "Daddy." Dr. Hemfelt told his patient of hearing his own four-year-old daughter cry out in the night with pain. He immediately went in to comfort her and ask, "Tell me where it hurts."

"God is like that," Dr. Hemfelt said. "He wants us to tell Him where it hurts, to tell Him what we need."

5. *What if I start to look or sound like some kind of naive spiritual fanatic?* Use the following assessment statements to rate yourself from 1 to 10:

_____ In the past I have been skeptical of, and even embarrassed by, "religious fanatics" who punctuate every other statement with, "God told me to . . ." and "The Lord showed me . . ." Will I become like that?

_____ I genuinely fear that I could abuse Step Eleven. I may begin to justify some of my more destructive human drives and directions by rationalizing my newfound spirituality and claiming that what I want is indeed God's will for me.

_____ So far the journey of my recovery has been one of the most important explorations of my life. However, I fear that the thorough working of Step Eleven is a step into spiritual fantasy land. Surely sophisticated, thoughtful persons don't live this way.

Martin had several of these concerns, particularly the one about winding up in some sort of fantasy land. After all, he was a scholar and an intellectual and in his field, very few people admitted to being "religious."

After Martin moved to California, he immediately contacted an A.A. group and found a new sponsor—a man about his own age named George. As he shared with George his concerns about becoming naive and fanatical by doing Step Eleven, Martin was surprised to hear, "Martin, I'm a Christian myself, but I certainly wasn't going to push it on you because you told me about your background as an agnostic. Now that you're here in Step Eleven, however, and even reading *Mere Christianity* by C. S. Lewis, you might as well go all the way and start to seriously read something important from the Bible. If you're worried about looking naive or fanatical, you might as well know what the Bible actually says."

"Well, you'll have to admit my concept of God has certainly grown since I started the Twelve Steps," Martin pointed out to his new sponsor. "But it's true that I am worried about looking silly and sounding like some kind of fanatic. So I'm doing my best to do what Step Eleven says —through prayer and meditation to improve my conscious contact with God as I understand Him."

"You're using C. S. Lewis to add to your understanding, so why don't you go the rest of the way and try the Gospel of John?" George suggested.

"Why the Gospel of John?" Martin wanted to know. "Why not Mark or Luke?"

"All the Gospels were written with different purposes," Allen explained, "but John was written to present Jesus Christ as God Himself. You're supposed to be a scholar who is intellectually curious. Why don't you see what John has to say?"

Motivated by George's challenge, Martin did start reading the Gospel of John—in fact, he read the entire Gospel at one sitting that evening. That same evening he called George and said, "Well, I read the Gospel of John as you suggested, but I don't know. I believe that Jesus was some kind of a son of God, and I believe he probably was the world's greatest Teacher—but God Himself? That's a little hard to swallow."

"Read chapter 20 again," George urged. "And when you come to verse 31, give it some thought. We'll talk more about it when we have lunch on Wednesday."

Grumbling because he was tired and wanted to get to bed, Martin did what George suggested and reread John 20. When he came to verse 31, it said: "But these are written that you may believe that Jesus is the Christ, the Son of God, and that believing you may have life in His name."

As Martin finished his day's end inventory that eve-

ning, his prayers were a jumble of confused thoughts.
Could Jesus really be the Son of God—could He be God
Himself Who came in human form? It was all too mind-
boggling. He would have to talk more about this with
George at lunch on Wednesday.

To Fight Any Fear—"Turn It Over"

As we said earlier, basic fears such as the fear of deprivation and the fear of loss of control are behind all of the
road blocks and barriers to God discussed above. Ironically however, as you draw closer to God and yield more of
your will to Him, you will actually experience a sense of
freedom and emancipation. It is like the spiritual paradox
Jesus described when He said, "For whoever desires to
save his life will lose it, and whoever loses his life for My
sake will find it"[6]

As Andy continued with Step Eleven, he discovered
that yielding more fully to God didn't mean that he had to
go deeper into the legalism that had haunted him practically all his life. In fact, it was quite the reverse. Andy
learned that the ultimate answer to legalism is total surrender, which took him out of the daily need to try to win,
perform, or prove his worthiness before God.

Total surrender is never done easily, however, and
that's why we urge patients in Twelve-Step recovery programs to use the "turn it over" technique to combat fears,
road blocks, and barriers that stand between them and
God. Begin in the morning by telling the Lord, "I turn this
day over—I yield it to you." Then through the day you
might have to give yourself a couple of booster shots with
this very same prayer. What Twelve-Steppers report is
that this kind of daily yielding, turning it over, helps
them see that they don't have to agonize over every small
twist and turn in the direction life may take for them on a
given day. They have turned it over and they really don't
have to take it back. Now they can trust that God will
guide. That is freedom indeed.

Spiritual growth starts with "turning it over." As we move on toward our goal, there are many avenues we could take, but three of the most basic ones will be highlighted in the rest of this chapter: prayer, meditation, and empowerment.

Prayer

While there is no "right way" to approach God in prayer, we advise patients that it is essential to see Him as a loving Father. For those who are just starting with spiritual growth, we recommend that they pray as a little child. Just talk to God as a Father; make it simple, make it child-like. Over time you can allow prayer to become more of a dialogue, and you can talk to God as your trusted Friend as you do a daily inventory of praise, confession, and supplications (requests).

A barrier to prayer for many people is not knowing what to say. After a few seconds, they seem to run out of words. One way to develop your prayer life is with what is called "foxhole" prayers, short, fragment-like cries to God in the heat of the battle of everyday life. Learning to turn to God at any moment for anything, no matter how small, is a key to what Brother Lawrence calls practicing the presence of God. He writes, ". . . the least little remembrance will always be most pleasing to Him. One need not cry out very loudly; He is nearer to us than we think."[7]

As she worked on Step Eleven, Kathryn soon discovered how useful foxhole prayers could be. At Helena's urging and with the support of her children and Dr. Meier, Kathryn took an enormous step toward independence by getting a job. Ignoring Henry's grumblings, she began working part-time in a china and fine housewares shop in a shopping mall just twenty minutes from her home. She loved the work but because the job made her schedule so much busier, she soon found it was putting a crimp in her devotional time.

When she complained to Dr. Meier of a lack of time to

even pray very much, he suggested, "One thing you can do is foxhole prayers. They aren't the whole answer to a good devotional life, but they can really help in your situation."

Kathryn was a bit dubious, but during her next counseling appointment she reported outstanding success. "It's the most exciting adventure! I start every day by praying in the shower and sometimes I sing too. You know, it's amazing how good 'The Doxology' sounds with running water. I also pray briefly while vacuuming and cooking—everything I do, as a matter of fact. It's become like a natural rhythm of my life, not something I have to remind myself to do."

With the simple concept of foxhole prayers, Kathryn was learning to practice the presence of God.

As useful as foxhole prayers are, there will still be times when you want to set aside time alone with God for in-depth prayer that marks a maturing relationship with Him. We have already mentioned the daily quiet time that should be part of your daily inventory work (Step Ten). A definite part of this should be spent in quiet communion with God.

Meditation

When speaking of meditation, the first thing we want to eliminate from your mind is an image of an Eastern Yogi sitting cross-legged as he chants his mantra. Christian meditation does not require exotic techniques. As Richard Foster says, "Christian meditation, very simply, is the ability to hear God's voice and obey His Word. It is that simple."[8]

While prayer involves talking to God and listening to Him, meditation involves the special skill of slowing down to better hear God and commune with Him. One way to look at meditation is as an outgrowth of your dialogue with God. When praying, most of us find that the easiest part is sending messages, telling God what we need—while the difficult part is receiving them, hearing what He wants to tell us. Meditation is a way to learn to listen better.

While Scripture never says directly that Jesus meditated, He did model much of what meditation is all about. In His humanness, with all the rush and scurry around Him, with all the pressure of the hundreds who wanted to be healed, He had to pull away and go off by Himself to pray and commune with His heavenly Father.

In many ways, meditation is not what you do but what you don't do. Meditation is a means of slowing down, of getting away from the fragmented life that is all about us. Richard Foster says, "Our Adversary majors in three things: noise, hurry and crowds. If he can keep us engaged in 'muchness' and 'manyness,' he will be satisfied. Psychiatrist Carl Jung once remarked, 'Hurry is not *of* the devil; it *is* the devil.' "[9]

Foster's "muchness" and "manyness" reminds us that the modern American reaction to any need in life is go somewhere, buy something, or eat something. The answer to getting beyond these superficialities is found in the silences of meditation, where we can encounter the Living God.

There are many ways to meditate. Many of our patients tell us they meditate while sitting for twenty or thirty minutes over a cup of coffee or while listening to soothing music. Others tell us they can meditate while jogging along at a slow pace that requires nothing more than putting one foot in front of the other.

Dr. Les Carter, who is part of the Minirth-Meier Clinic staff, tells of meditating while fishing. In fact, he has a passion for fishing, not just because he wants to catch fish but because the tranquility and engaging in a "simple task" give him the opportunity to commune with God.

Foxhole prayers were a big help to Kathryn, but she soon decided she needed something more. She began stopping by a quiet but well-patrolled park on the way home from work to spend twenty minutes focusing on a phrase from Scripture or a hymn that particularly spoke to her life.

When she told Helena about her new practice, her sponsor said, "Kathryn, I've been doing that for years, and I can testify that it really helps me to detach from the world around me and attach to the Lord. I believe it was Oswald Chambers who said until we get into this kind of meditative relationship, we are merely 'hanging on by the skin of our teeth.' We want to be doing a lot more than that!"

Step Twelve

Having had a spiritual awakening as the result of these steps, we tried to carry this message to others, and to practice these principles in all our affairs.

Martin gave Mary a nervous smile as he fished in his pocket for his rental car keys. "This is really silly," he said, "how can a teacher who lectures at least five days a week be nervous about giving another lecture?"

"That's the key," Mary said. "Think of them as a history class—it's just that you're telling *your* history, not George Washington's."

Martin clung to that thought as he stood before a large group of his old A.A. friends in the familiar room he had spent so much time in while in recovery in Texas. He and Mary had returned from California for a ten-day visit that would include a series of lectures at a local college, the speech to the open A.A. meeting, and their attendance at a wedding of some close friends. Although Martin had shared informally at many A.A. meetings, this was the first time he had ever undertaken giving what could be called a "formal speech." Formal or not, he decided to begin with the traditional greeting, "Hi, I'm Martin, I'm a grateful recovering alcoholic."

Then he stood silent, not only because the friendly faces in front of him were responding to his greeting, but also because the true meaning of what he had said really struck him. He dropped his gaze for a moment, then looked up slowly, shaking his head in wonder.

"You know—I really *mean* that! I *am* grateful! I'm grateful for my addiction because that's what propelled me into Twelve-Step recovery. As wrapped up in myself as I was, I'm certain nothing else could have brought me to this point—and it's great! I wouldn't want to be anywhere else. God only knows where I would be tonight if I hadn't gotten into the Twelve Steps with the rest of you.

"Speaking of God, many of you know that when I started here with you in this room, I seriously doubted that He even existed. But tonight, while I could speak on many topics, I want to share with you about my spiritual awakening which has blossomed into a commitment to the Christian faith."

Martin reached for his copy of *The 12 × 12*. "You know, I've read this many times, but just the other night, I really understood it. As it does so often, *The 12 × 12* really knows how to put our feelings into words."

Many heads in the room nodded as Martin continued: "Here, let me read this paragraph to you: 'When a man or a woman has a spiritual awakening, the most important meaning of it is that he has now become able to do, feel, and believe that which he could not do before on his unaided strength and resources alone. He has been granted a gift which amounts to a new state of consciousness and being. He has been set on a path which tells him he is really going somewhere, that life is not a dead end, not something to be endured or mastered. In a very real sense, he has been transformed, because he has laid hold of a source of strength which, in one way or another, he had hitherto denied himself. . . .'[1]

"Well, you can read the rest of it for yourselves, but for those of you who've finished the steps or are about to take Step Twelve, look at what this says about finding yourself in possession of a degree of honesty, tolerance, unselfishness, peace of mind, and love which you thought you'd never possess. That's so true. And aren't you grateful!"

Again, heads nodded. Before continuing with his lecture, Martin looked around the room and decided he had never felt as good as he did at this moment. He had come home in more ways than one.

The next morning, Martin was in Dr. Fowler's office, greeting his old therapist with a smile and a big bear hug. "I spoke to my old group last night and told them about my spiritual awakening. I came by this morning not only to thank you for all you've done for me in the Twelve Steps but to return your book and especially to thank you for lending it to me."

Martin held up a well-marked, dog-eared copy of *Mere Christianity* as he continued, "You remember the day I came in here struggling with Step Eleven and you read to me out of the book of Hebrews, and then suggested I read C. S. Lewis? Well, I did read it, and while I was in the middle of that my new sponsor out in California suggested that I do some reading in the Gospels as well. So at his urging I read the Gospel of John. . . ."

"It sounds like the Hound of Heaven was closing in on you," Dr. Fowler said with a chuckle. "What happened next?"

"Well, as you know, the Gospel of John clearly presents Jesus Christ as God Himself, which wasn't easy for me to accept, but I kept praying and reading and thinking. Then, one night as I was reading C. S. Lewis, I came upon one passage that must have made the difference. Lewis was talking about who Jesus was and what He did, and he brought up exactly what I'd been thinking: I was ready to accept Jesus as a great moral teacher but I didn't accept His claim to be God. Lewis pointed out that if anyone who was merely a man said the things Jesus said, he wouldn't be a great moral teacher, he'd be a lunatic, or maybe even a devil out of hell. Here, let me read what the rest of it says:

You must make your choice. Either this Man was, and is, the Son of God: or else a madman or something worse. You can shut Him up for a fool, you can spit at Him and kill Him as a demon; or You can fall at His feet and call Him Lord and God. But let us not come with any patronizing nonsense about His being a great human teacher. He has not left that open to us. He did not intend to.[2]

"And so what are you here to tell me?" Dr. Fowler asked quietly.

"I'm here to tell you that Mary and I have found a wonderful church, and we're both going to be baptized there next month. As you might expect out of an iconoclast like me, I had to find a nondenominational independent church, but it's very warm and loving and we're both planning to join. I guess what I've come to tell you is that I've become a follower of Jesus Christ!"

Your Spiritual Awakening

In our Twelve-Step recovery work, we see three basic kinds of spiritual awakenings. One is a slow progression like Martin's, who came all the way from agnosticism to a newfound faith in Christ as his personal God. The second awakening is that of someone who once believed in God— often back in childhood—but whose faith became withered and dormant. Now, through the Twelve Steps, this faith has been renewed and rekindled. Kathryn is a typical example.

A third kind of awakening can be seen in Andy, the lifetime believer who, through the Twelve Steps, moved away from legalism and ritualism to a deeper, more authentic personal relationship to God.

Step Twelve is an echo of Steps Two and Three. Back there you came to believe that a power greater than yourself could restore you to sanity, and you made a decision to turn your will and your life over to the care of God as you understood Him. We find that as people go through the Twelve Steps, their understanding of God grows proportionately. Stop for a minute and think about these three questions:

1. How did I see God before I started my Twelve-Step recovery? (In Martin's case, before recovery, God was a bad dream, practically nonexistent.)_____

_____

2. How did I see God early in my recovery—around Steps Two and Three? (At this point, Martin conceded that God was a fuzzy idea—maybe a concept. He was glad that Step Three included the phrase "God as we understood Him.")_____

_____

3. How do I see God now that I've reached Step Twelve? (Martin looked back over a long hard climb and found himself believing in God as a personal, loving Savior.)_____

_____

_____

Some might say that Martin had undergone a spiritual transformation and, to a great degree, this was true. But what Martin, and anyone who finishes the Twelve Steps must ever be aware of is that they have never reached the summit of spiritual development or total and final mastery over their addiction or compulsive behavior. Rejoice in how far you've come, but be aware that you have a lifetime to go.

Carrying the Message

Of the Twelve Steps, the last three all touch on the need for maintaining our recovery for life. Step Ten focused inward on ourselves as we continued to take personal inventory. Step Eleven focused upward on God as we concentrated on the means of spiritual growth. While Step Twelve also involves maintenance with its emphasis on practicing the key principles of recovery in all our affairs, we prefer to call it the step of "transcendence and evangelism." At Step Twelve we should be ready to turn outward as we "carry the message to others." One of the great truths expressed in the oral tradition of recovery groups is, "You can't keep it unless you give it away."

Andy caught the vision of the outreach aspect of Step Twelve and, accompanied by Jennifer, approached his pastor with the idea of starting a recovery group in their church. He showed Pastor Krueger the newspaper article that had sparked his idea. "Look, this says perhaps as many as one in four church members has been affected by alcohol or other substances, and that doesn't count people like myself whose addictions aren't chemical. Of course, we wouldn't offer actual treatment, but we could offer some really important support to people who are trying to get their lives back on track."

Jennifer, who had been sitting quietly, added, "Andy and I have talked a lot about this. I could help, too, especially with people who aren't really dependent themselves, but have been hurt by others' dependencies."

Pastor Krueger nodded. "I think to a rather large extent the whole church has been in denial about the need for recovery. I'm afraid there is a lot of 'it can't happen here' thinking. I believe, also, that we put a lot of emphasis on converting people but, as a church—the body of Christ—we haven't done enough to sustain them with long-term nurturing. Why don't you bring your proposal to the church board? Let's see if we can get some support for your idea, which I believe is a new way of carrying out the Great Commission."

The Great Commission was given by Jesus, Who told His disciples just before He ascended: "Go therefore and make disciples of all the nations, baptizing them in the name of the Father and of the Son and of the Holy Spirit, teaching them to observe all things that I have commanded you."[3]

That was all. Jesus left no alternate plan to spread the Gospel, and the same principle is true of A.A. and other Twelve-Step groups. Tradition Five of the Twelve Traditions says, "Each Alcoholics Anonymous group ought to be a spiritual entity *having but one primary purpose*—that of carrying its message to the alcoholic who still suffers." And there is no alternate plan, no media promotion, no advertising campaign. As Tradition Eleven says, "Our public relations should be guided by the principle of attraction rather than promotion."[4] We are to live our lives and tell our stories in a way that others who need the program will be attracted to it.

Pastor Krueger also noted to Andy that some Christians have unfounded apprehensions about using the Twelve Steps as recovery tools.

Because Bill Wilson did stray into some non-Christian practices, some Christians consider the Twelve Steps unsafe. We answer this concern in three ways: (1) King Solomon wrote much of the book of Proverbs, then strayed far from God, married 700 pagan wives, and died in disgrace and defeat. Yet Solomon's sins did not preclude Proverbs from becoming part of the Old Testament canon. (2) Christian doctors use penicillin, novocaine, ether, without needing to know the theology of those who discovered these valuable tools of healing. (3) God clearly uses the world's knowledge for His glory, whether it be knowledge of how to build a building or commonsense counseling. Of course, secular knowledge should always be put through the grid of Scripture and be consistent with the Bible.

In the Twelve Steps, Bill Wilson created important tools of healing and spiritual recovery. These tools can be misused through application of New Age philosophies, which is what is happening in some recovery groups today. These same tools, however, can be used with great effectiveness by Christians to bless broken lives and glorify God.

According to Dale Ryan, executive director of the National Association for Christian Recovery: "Parts of the recovery community welcome Christian input, and other segments are thoroughly hostile. Some groups have a strong New Age emphasis; others are distinctively Christian. The worst possible responses, however, would be either to caricature the movement and throw it all out as unnecessary, or to embrace it without discretion. Hundreds of people have come to Christ through first getting into the Twelve Steps and taking seriously that there really was a Higher Power in life. That's an opportunity for the Christian community if handled right."[5]

In A.A. circles, carrying the message to others is commonly referred to as "doing Twelfth Step work." *The 12 × 12* says, "Practically every A.A. member declares that no satisfaction has been deeper and no joy greater than in a Twelfth Step job well done."[6]

The three sides of the triangular A.A. symbol are labeled: Recovery, Unity, and Service. By the time we reach Step Twelve, we should be demonstrating our servant-heartedness in specific recovery work and in our daily lives in general. Answering calls for local recovery groups is one way people serve when they reach the Twelfth Step. Recovery groups are normally listed in the business sections of telephone directories and receive varying phone calls. Someone may phone in to ask, "I'm writing a research paper. Can you give me some information?" Those calls are answered as helpfully as possible, but the calls that Twelve-Steppers are really waiting for are those that begin, "I'm drunk, I'm scared, I need help."

In answer to this kind of call, A.A. sends two people to sit, talk, and share their story with the one who has asked for help. In order to avoid awkward situations, callers go out in pairs of the same sex to call on inquirers of that sex. Their approach is low-key. They don't try to "rescue, fix or preach." They simply tell of their own recovery journey— what the *Big Book* describes as sharing their "experience, strength, and hope."

The pattern for Twelfth-Step work used by A.A. groups is easily adapted to other addictions and obsessive-compulsive behaviors—for example, codependency, food addiction, and workaholism. When Kathryn got involved in Twelve-Step work, she admitted, "Nothing gets me out of my narcissism better than working with the newer, younger people who have just come into our ACOA group. I used to worry about slipping back into my old rescuer role, but Dr. Meier helped me see that I'm not doing that at all because I don't do Twelve-Step work to boost my own self-esteem. Mature recovery means reaching out to others to help them for their own sake. You can't imagine what a growth step that was for me!"

When your life has been changed, you want to tell others what happened. We see the same pattern in Scripture when Jesus healed the Gadarene demoniac. The man immediately "went his way and proclaimed throughout the whole city what great things Jesus had done for him."[7]

And after Jesus encountered the Samaritan woman at the well and changed her life, she ran to all her neighbors and said, "Come, see a Man who told me all things that I ever did. Could this be the Christ?"[8]

Sharing your life story and recovery experiences in support group meetings and personal conversations is the most effective way of passing the gift on. One way to say thank you to those who have gone before is to help those who come after. People in need are attracted to recovery and to God when they see changed lives.

Recovery literature reminds us that we don't always have to do the talking in order to help carry the message: "We sit in A.A. meetings and listen, not only to receive something ourselves, but to give the reassurance and support which our presence can bring."[9]

As Andy began giving so much of his energy to starting a recovery group in his church, he quit going to his original ACOA group where he began his recovery. "I don't feel sick anymore," Andy reasoned, "so as busy as I am with the recovery group at church, I don't see any reason to keep going to ACOA."

Then one day an old college friend came by to talk with Andy about computers and stayed to talk about his chemical dependency. "Oh, yeah, people have told me I should go to A.A. or something," Kevin offered, "but why should I go sit around and listen to a bunch of people who aren't any better off than I am? If anything would drive me back to coke, that would do it."

Andy instantly realized that he had made a mistake by quitting his ACOA meetings. Quickly he said, "Well, I made it out of my addiction. Why don't you come with me to a meeting and hear what happens?"

Kevin did go to the open meeting, and when Andy got up to talk, he looked into Kevin's face and saw the importance of letting others know that it's possible to succeed.

After the meeting, Kevin told Andy, "You weren't hooked on drugs, but in some ways you were worse off than I've been. I can see that I need help. I can't handle this alone—I want to try the Twelve Steps."

Two days later, as he shared what happened with his sponsor, Gene, Andy commented, "You know, I should have realized it. Recovered people are the ones best equipped to understand people who are still sick. If we drop out of the program, who will be there to share the healing?"

Gene just smiled. "Andy, you've hit on what has been an important principle of Twelve-Step recovery since its foundation. There is a special empathy between persons who have had similar afflictions. If I have walked in your shoes, I know what it is like, and you'll listen to me because you know that I know."

One caution we always give those involved in recovery programs is to guard against doing "Thirteenth Step" work—reaching out to someone with an ulterior motive. The most common temptations are money and romance. Twelve-Step work should never be done with a person who is looked upon as a possible source for borrowing money or taking part in an investment plan, or as someone you would like to date.

But an even more critical danger, which is pointed out at length in the *Big Book*,[10] is that of becoming militant in carrying the message. The most delicate situations usually involve our own loved ones. We can see their errors so clearly, because we have made the same mistakes. We want so desperately for them to find recovery, and we think, "If I can just talk long enough and loud enough and use the right words, they'll *have* to get it." In reality, our own desperation usually causes them to rebel.

As Joe McQ, internationally popular lecturer on recovery and author of *The Steps We Took,* says:

> The Twelfth Step is about faith. When we talk to a new person, we don't talk about anything we 'believe,' we talk about what we have *known through experience.* We talk about facts that have brought results in our lives.[11]

In Christian circles, letting your life do the talking is sometimes called "lifestyle evangelism." There is nothing more attractive than a transformed life. We must always remember that our recovery is a gift that must be passed on, but you can't give away something that you don't have. Whenever you are about to do Twelve-Step work, ask yourself, "Where is my own recovery?" And that brings us to a final and important point.

Practicing the Principles of Twelve-Step Recovery

There is a well-known joke about a man who rushed up to a cab parked on a street corner in New York City and asked breathlessly, "Quick, how do I get to Carnegie Hall?"

The cabbie looked up, smiled, and said, "Practice, man, practice!"

While the joke is old, the principle is timeless, especially for someone who has come through the Twelve Steps. How do you stay in recovery? By practicing the principles of the Twelve-Step program. In fact, the stark truth is that you will spend the rest of your life practicing your recovery.

We stress to every patient who reaches Step Twelve that recovery is an ongoing, lifelong process. No matter how often we work the Twelve Steps, the "old nature" that the apostle Paul described so aptly in Romans 7 will continue to rear its ugly head.

Martin found this to be true as he began his new job in California. Even after making his life-changing decision to embrace the Christian faith, Martin found that his first impulse when he met his new colleagues was, "I've got to show these people . . . I've got to impress them, let them know I'm smarter and more scholarly than they are."

Fortunately, Martin was continuing his daily inventory and devotional times. As he went over his relational questions to himself morning and evening, he spotted his old compulsion and determined to stop it.

"I've been learning to bite my tongue," he told Mary one night at dinner. "I don't always succeed, but I'm doing a lot better."

Martin's victory over his grandiosity was a small one, perhaps, but extremely significant. Practicing the Twelve Steps is usually a matter of confronting the smaller things, but this adds up to continued recovery and growth.

When Step Twelve mentions "practicing these principles in all our affairs," many truths embedded in the Twelve-Step program come to mind. At the core of the Twelve Steps, however, are two crucial principles that form the foundation for everything else: humility and honesty. Martin's refusal to try to impress his new colleagues was a simple reminder of his constant need for humility.

Throughout the Twelve Steps we have emphasized the absolute necessity for humility to make any progress in recovery. In large part, our addictions, obsessions, and compulsions are efforts to overcome shame. If we can maintain appropriate humility, there is much less propensity to try to artificially inflate who we are by drinking alcohol, working 100 hours a week, or consuming thousands of extra calories per day.

At its base, humility is the surrender of your will to God's. Humility is a constant lifelong yielding—what might be called a permanent Step Eleven. We gradually learn to say, "Not my will, Lord, but Yours be done," in everything we do. And then we discover there is great freedom in not having to have your own way.

Honesty goes hand in hand with humility because it takes honesty to be humble. Before Twelve-Step recovery, we were often driven to lie in order to practice our addictions or compulsions. The lying was usually to cover up what we were doing or perhaps what others close to us were doing if we were codependent. Now that we have broken free of such sham, we no longer have to worry about "keeping our story straight." As we have learned to apply strict honesty to our recovery, we can also apply it to every other area of our lives, especially our relationships.

Many of our patients report being surprised when they begin "telling the truth to shame the devil." Kathryn told Dr. Meier, "I really thought the world would come to an end—at least my marriage would or possibly Henry's career—when I quit trying to control him and cover up for his problems. Now if someone from the office calls, I put Henry on the phone, even if he's had too much to drink, or if he's depressed or in a rage. It's his problem, he'll have to deal with it.

"And I'm gradually learning to be more truthful about what I really think and feel. Last week at work a woman asked me if I thought a pastel peach china bowl matched her pink/rose dinner set. I was sure I'd lose the sale, but I told her I didn't think the colors blended well enough. She knew they really didn't and she wound up buying a beautiful crystal bowl instead!"

Assessing Your Spiritual Growth

Now that you have reached Step Twelve, you may find it useful to assess how you have grown—what is different about the way you are living your life? There are many ways to assess spiritual growth, but four major categories we often see as crucial concerns for recovery patients have to do with money, intimate relationships, support networks, and taking responsibility.

Go over these statements and rate yourself from 1 (not doing too well) to 10 (doing very well) to see where you've grown and where there is still more growing to do.

1. My growth in handling my finances

_____ As I've grown closer to God, the old ever-present fear of financial insecurity has begun to subside.

_____ As I have matured spiritually, my perspective on money has changed. I have surrendered some of the old dysfunctional uses of money, such as viewing it as an anesthesia for my pain, or as an aphrodisiac to prove my masculinity or femininity. I now view money as a constructive tool to be used under God's guidance.

_____ I seem to be making better decisions about my use of money: how much to spend, when to spend it, and how much to hold in reserve for savings. These decisions now come more readily and I spend less time remorsefully second-guessing myself.

_____ I am less likely now than before to cover my fear of "there will never be enough" with either compulsive overspending or compulsive hoarding.

_____ Somewhere in my spiritual journey, my basic view of money has changed. Instead of viewing money as a goal or an end in itself, I now genuinely see money as a means to an end, as a gift of stewardship from God to me.

_____ I am no longer embarrassed to ask for advice and guidance concerning my financial decisions. I have begun to shed some of the false pride that prevented me from asking for both human advice and divine guidance in all my financial affairs.

2. My growth in handling romantic, sexual, and intimate family relationships

_____ My most significant relationship with the opposite sex has undergone a transformation in God's hands. I no longer find it necessary to push away my spouse or friend through excessive conflict, indifferences, emotional coldness, or unwillingness to communicate.

_____ I sense a new feeling of trust growing between me and my partner. Instead of being preoccupied with what I must do to manipulate my partner into loving me, I now trust that my partner genuinely cares about me and that he or she is probably trying to love me in the best way possible.

_____ Fear of abandonment is no longer the driving force in my most intimate relationships and I no longer feel driven to possess and control those around me as a means of catering to that old fear.

_____ I am no longer afraid to be honest about my needs in a relationship and I feel new courage to ask assertively for those needs to be recognized and honored in all my relationships.

_____ I have come to view my boundaries and the boundaries of my partner as allies in our relationship. I cherish the fact that both I and my partner are entitled to boundaries.

3. My growth in support network relationships

_____ I have a dynamic and growing support network around me. I derive spiritual and recovery support from a number of sources, including my Twelve-Step group, my sponsor, my close friends, and my church community.

_____ I have begun to take healthy risks of emotional intimacy with my key support persons, such as my program sponsor or therapist. As I grow in my willingness to be transparent and open before God, I have also grown in my willingness to open my life to these support persons.

_____ That old sense of loneliness and aloneness has begun to fade away. While I still value those special moments of privacy and solitude, I know that caring persons are just a phone call or a meeting away.

_____ Isolation is no longer my defense mechanism or my anesthesia. Now when I'm under pressure or in great pain, I turn _toward_ others instead of retreating into myself.

_____ I've come to appreciate that I have very special relationship gifts I impart to others. I am gradually coming to believe that other persons value my time, my friendship, and my presence in a room or in a conversation.

4. My growth in meeting responsibilities and obligations

_____ I have reached a deep inner acceptance of the fact that I do have God-given responsibilities to serve and to care for others in appropriate ways. This new acceptance has removed much of the old re-

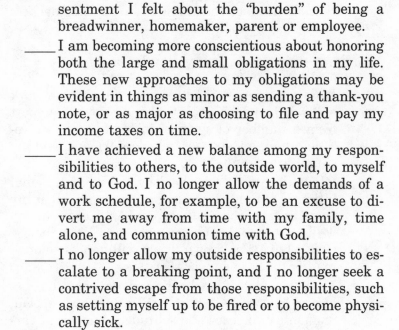

sentment I felt about the "burden" of being a
breadwinner, homemaker, parent or employee.

____ I am becoming more conscientious about honoring
both the large and small obligations in my life.
These new approaches to my obligations may be
evident in things as minor as sending a thank-you
note, or as major as choosing to file and pay my
income taxes on time.

____ I have achieved a new balance among my responsibilities to others, to the outside world, to myself
and to God. I no longer allow the demands of a
work schedule, for example, to be an excuse to di-
vert me away from time with my family, time
alone, and communion time with God.

____ I no longer allow my outside responsibilities to es-
calate to a breaking point, and I no longer seek a
contrived escape from those responsibilities, such
as setting myself up to be fired or to become physically sick.

God Turns Life Inside Out

Using the above assessment statements will probably
give you only a partial picture of where your Twelve-Step
journey has taken you. Step Twelve is well worded when
it says: "Having had a *spiritual awakening* as the result of
these steps . . ." Most people do not begin their walk
through the Twelve Steps to find a spiritual awakening.
They come because something is not working in their
lives. They come because of their pain. This pain, this
unmanageability, this dysfunction, is probably 95 percent
of the reason they show up at a Twelve-Step meeting or in
the counselor's office; they may or may not have realized
their need for spiritual growth.

This is often true, whether or not the person already
has a faith in God. It is not unusual for persons without

an active faith to question the need for a relationship with God and to doubt that their healing must be based on a spiritual foundation. But even devout Christians may think they have their spiritual lives in order and may resist the notion that further spiritual growth will be needed to combat the addiction.

Somewhere in the Twelve-Step process, however, a flip-flop occurs. Although the patients come to recovery because of their pain, they stay in, we've found, because of the spiritual growth initiated in Step Two ("Came to believe that a Power greater than ourselves could restore us to sanity"). In each successive step they continue to mature spiritually. At some point unique to their own journey, they suddenly realize they've undergone a spiritual experience. "I can't put my finger on it," they say. "But somewhere in the accumulation of all the daily work I've done in the Twelve Steps, my perspective has changed. Recovery from my addiction has become secondary. Developing a deeper relationship with God is my primary goal."

Their whole attitude has been inverted—literally turned inside out. Now their primary motivator is a desire to move toward and grow ever-closer to God and carry the message of their deliverance to others. As important as the healing of their addictions may be, this is a by-product compared to the spiritual awakening they have had through taking the Twelve Steps. They recognize that the fullest meaning of Step Twelve goes beyond mere maintenance of recovery to even more spiritual growth and transcendence.

Perhaps your own experience parallels what we have just described. Perhaps you came into the Twelve-Step program to get sober (or rid of some other addiction or obsessive compulsion), but you learned that getting sober —as important as that may be—is not the real goal of life. You also learned that sobriety is not salvation. As badly as your body and mind needed to be fixed, your soul needed fixing even more.

And because you have been touched, you want to touch

others. You want to tell your story, just as so many others have done (see Parts Three, Four, and Five for sixteen personal stories of people who have conquered addictions or who are struggling and winning through the power of Jesus Christ in their lives). Inevitably, Step Twelve moves one from transcendence to evangelism because the sign of a changed life is the willingness to carry the message to whomever will listen.

No one understood this better than The Reverend Sam Shoemaker, Rector of Calvary Episcopal Church, New York City, who had a deep influence on Bill Wilson at the time he founded Alcoholics Anonymous. In the mid-1920s, Shoemaker opened Calvary Mission at 246 East 23rd Street in New York City, and in following years it ministered to thousands who had hit bottom, including Bill Wilson himself. Sam Shoemaker's voluminous writings include many well-known books and articles, but the following poem, which he called "An Apologia for My Life," possibly best catches the spirit of Step Twelve better than anything else that could be said as we come to the end of the path to serenity.

I Stand By the Door

I stand by the door.
I neither go too far in, nor stay too far out,
The door is the most important door in the world—
It is the door through which men walk when they find
     God.
There's no use my going way inside, and staying there,
When so many are still outside and they, as much as I,
Crave to know where the door is.
And all that so many ever find
Is only the wall where a door ought to be.
They creep along the wall like blind men,
With outstretched, groping hands.
Feeling for a door, knowing there must be a door,
Yet they never find it . . .
So I stand by the door.

The most tremendous thing in the world
Is for men to find that door—the door to God.
The most important thing any man can do
Is to take hold of one of those blind, groping hands,
And put it on the latch—the latch that only clicks
And opens to the man's own touch.
Men die outside that door, as starving beggars die
On cold nights in cruel cities in the dead of winter—
Die for want of what is within their grasp.
They live, on the other side of it—live because they have
     not found it.
Nothing else matters compared to helping them find it,
And open it, and walk in, and find Him . . .
So I stand by the door. . . .

You can go in too deeply, and stay in too long,
And forget the people outside the door.
As for me, I shall take my old accustomed place,
Near enough to God to hear Him, and know He is there,
But not so far from men as not to hear them,
And remember they are there, too.
Where? Outside the door—
Thousands of them, millions of them.
But—more important for me—
One of them, two of them, ten of them,
Whose hands I am intended to put on the latch.
So I shall stand by the door and wait
For those who seek it.
"I had rather be a door-keeper . . ."
So I stand by the door.[12]

PART THREE

Those Who Are Recovering from Their Own Dependencies or Addictions: Personal Stories

She Was a Con Artist

I'm Nancy C., an alcoholic and a drug addict. I suffer from a powerlessness over people, places, and things.

As a child, when I looked out the window and watched other children play, I did not want to play. I just wanted to be able to see them clearly. I never could because I was always crying too much. I used the curtains as tissue. I didn't want to feel the inner pain and nagging, the throbbing jabs from my mother. I didn't want to feel the pain from being whipped bloody by my father.

The pill popping started when I was eleven, with the drinking soon to follow. I grew into quite a con artist, lying and stealing prescription drugs from medicine cabinets and doctors' bags. I was a fruit-bowl druggie—a little of this, a smidgen of that, a taste of this red one, a little black devil, a pink, round pill—whatever I could find and mix together, that's what I took. I didn't know the names of the pills, or care. I didn't know what I was doing to myself, and I didn't care about that either. I just wanted to be dulled and feel something other than loss.

I went to church, but I didn't really know God. In fact, by the time I got to high school, I didn't even believe in God. How could a God who was "love" allow such physical, emotional, and mental abuse to go on in my family? I even thought about suicide.

For the first five years, I always drank and drugged alone. I'd hide and no one ever thought I was involved in alcohol or drugs. Even when I told my sister, Beth, she didn't believe me at first. I was doing so well in school—teacher's pet, good grades, sports teams, student government. Oh, I put on a good show. Later, when I'd be high—out of it or throwing up consistently—Beth started to catch on.

When I got to college, a whole new world opened up. I made a lot of good friends who introduced me to the real drug world, full of fun. My favorites were hash, pot, coke, and I can't forget vodka. Needless to say, one doesn't last long mixing drugs and alcohol. I OD'd twice during my first semester.

The last time I OD'd, I had to remain in the hospital long enough to convince the psychiatrist I wouldn't OD again that week. As I lay in the emergency room and later in a ward, strapped to a bed, with gremlins taunting me and colors swirling around, I had a lot of time to think. I was sick of the games and lying. I had tried everything to get rid of the pain. I figured I didn't have anything to lose if I turned my life over to God and let Him help me out. So my long struggle to get off drugs and booze and to rely on God began. . . .

Giving up the pills was easy enough. I cried and shook and sweated and felt as if bugs were crawling all over me as I threw them all down the toilet and began withdrawal. I changed friends and didn't go to my usual parties and hangouts. I could manage life without hard drugs (at least that's what I thought) as long as I could drink. *There's nothing life threatening about a drink now and then.* What a con!

I really tried to get right with God. One day, around Thanksgiving, I was discouraged with my newfound personal relationship with Him, my school, and my job. My girlfriend, Ellen, and I bought a couple of six packs and started drinking. After a while, we decided to walk down a five-mile stretch to a church we had visited. It was cold and late at night, nearly midnight. We walked right up to the front door and loudly announced our presence. As God would have it, a deacons' meeting was ending late. The pastor came out and invited us in, with our beers in hand. He counseled us and took us to his house to sober up. It has always amazed me that he took us as we were.

My walk has taken a lot of twists and turns since then. I went back to dope a couple of times for a few years and the drinking went in swells, always getting progressively worse. When I finally came to A.A., I didn't have a problem with admitting I was powerless and my life was unmanageable. The big hurdle was Step Two: Believing that God could restore me to sanity. My entire life had been a series of insane happenings.

I discovered that God is a God of grace and mercy. He gives the gift of life. He cherishes my life, and I should too. Whatever I am, I am because of Him. He didn't have to let me live all the times I tried to die. He didn't even have to let me live all the times I was just experimenting with drugs.

It has given me courage to be the daughter of a King and to finally have a kind, gentle, loving Father. I have accepted Jesus Christ as my "higher power" because He gave up His life on the Cross for my sins and has washed me clean. I do not have to have an untimely death. Life is too precious.

God knew about my beatings, and He brought me out of that rough family. I still feel the pain from growing up in that family, but it is not a pain that God cannot heal. It is a pain I want to feel in order to feel real.

Through A.A., individual therapy, professional group therapy, self-help groups, small group Bible studies, the laying on of hands, and medication to control symptoms of severe depression, I have gotten a lot of support. Some friends and workers have not been supportive and helpful. Thank heaven, I can always count on God, though. He is there every step of the way.

He Tried to Write His Own Rules

I was probably fourteen or fifteen when I smoked my first joint. That would have been around 1973 or '74. I learned to play guitar and got into a folk rock band. Our group lied about our ages so we could play in bars. My heroes were the current rock 'n roll stars: John Lennon, Paul McCartney, Stephen Stills, and Graham Nash.

Since my heroes did drugs, it was only natural that I started experimenting. I did mostly pot and booze, then speed and an acid trip when I was sixteen or seventeen. I started working for a music store my senior year in high school. We all got high at the store every day. The summer after graduation I started snorting coke.

My folks wanted me to go to college. I wanted to get into another band and go on the road. Since I had a full-time job, I opted out of college, but I never did get into a band.

I don't remember much about that year after high school. I went into work at 10:00 A.M. or noon, worked till 8:00 P.M., went out to the bars or over to a friend's, then crashed at home. The next day I did it all again. I was high all the time and yet I remember being convinced that I was not addicted. I did spend a weekend at my older sister's home with Mom and Dad and I never smoked or snorted then, so how could I be hooked?

On May 21, 1978, I dropped a hit of acid. It was only the second time I had "tripped," and I had been looking forward to it for a long time. At first, everything was funny. Then around midnight, things started to get pretty strange.

We were sitting in a college friend's apartment, and I really started to feel lousy. So I asked my friend to take me back to my car, which was parked at another friend's house about five miles away. He said okay, but I could sense that he still wanted to party. He dinked around and dinked around until I finally stormed out of the apartment and started walking to get my car.

The fresh air made me feel better. I was walking down an old street where the trees had grown so tall they formed an arch over the pavement. I imagined that walking through the gates of heaven would be like this. Yes, I did think about heaven and God frequently. My parents had been good about taking me to church and teaching me about the Lord. Yet in the "free spirit" of the sixties, I decided that church was too confining. I started worshiping God on my own terms.

So there I was, walking down Main Street, and my friend drove by real slow. He held his hand out, palm up, and the expression on his face said, "Well, do you want a ride or not?"

I got in the car and we took off. I immediately felt lousy again. I told myself it was just the drugs, but now I wonder if there was a spiritual presence in that car. There wasn't a spirit of God, I am certain of that.

My friend had his dog, a doberman about two months old, in his lap. Suddenly I had the sensation that I was the dog, and my friend was Satan manipulating me, just like a puppet. I couldn't stand it. I had to get out of that car. We were probably going forty-five miles per hour, but I didn't think about that. I hesitated for just a second. Then I threw open the door and jumped out of the car.

The next thing I remember is being unable to move. I thought I was in hell. It is hard to describe the feeling, except to say that I felt I had really blown it and was going to be in hell for eternity.

That feeling did not last long, however. Someone

brought my mother into the room, and I thought, *Wait a minute. This can't be hell. My mother would surely never be in hell.*

Physically, my leap out of the car cost me a broken ankle, a shattered shoulder blade, a severe case of whiplash, and major cuts and abrasions. My body was pretty much healed by the end of the summer. I had not done any illegal drugs the entire summer after "the accident" (so we refer to my unfortunate incident), but I had never gone through any withdrawal. So I was still convinced that I didn't have a "drug problem." I had just got into some bad acid, I rationalized. When I went to college that fall, I started smoking dope again.

At the same time, I sensed a spiritual hunger. I decided to check out the Navigators, a Christian college campus ministry, when they sent around their questionnaire. Through my first year and a half I went to their Bible studies, but I was still smoking pot. Then they started pushing me to be on an evangelizing team, and I decided to cut out. I wanted to be a Christian—I had even asked Jesus into my heart—but I still thought I could write my own rules. And I did not think it was right to keep someone else from writing their own rules.

It's a good thing I never had much money in college or I would have killed myself doing coke. In my experience no drug makes you feel better than coke. I did a lot more drugs during my last years in college. I even tripped on acid one more time. It was another bad trip, although not as bad as the last one. Still, I never wanted to do it again.

On August 1, 1981, I smoked a joint with some people I didn't know very well. I was staying overnight with them for a big party. I don't know if the dope had PCP in it or if it was just really strong, but I started having a flashback. Sometime during the ordeal I made a promise to God that I would never smoke marijuana again. It wasn't a deal with God, like "If you help me through this, I'll never smoke dope again." It was a promise, and I knew that I would never break a promise to God.

Sounds kind of goofy, coming from a guy who writes his own rules, doesn't it? I think the Lord was working on me real hard back then.

Oh, but I was stubborn. You see, I had only made the promise about marijuana. So it was still okay to snort coke, right? That is until one night after college. I was selling advertising for a radio station, and the sales crew was at a hotel for a sales meeting. My partner-in-snuff decided he was going to drive to another party in town. We had both been drinking, and I knew if he felt anything like I did, he had no business driving a car. Try as I might, I could not convince him. I even followed him to his car, but stopped short of standing in front of the car so he couldn't drive away. I was convinced he would die that night, and I would feel guilty for the rest of my life. I tried to sleep but I couldn't. Finally, I got up and wrote down another promise to God: "I will never use cocaine again." I still have that piece of paper tucked away in a box with some of my treasures.

As far as illegal drug use goes, that is the end of my story. But my recovery is still in process. Two relationships are an important part of that journey.

First my relationship with my father. As a child and as a teenager, I hated him many times. He was the disciplinarian in our family and often very strict. When I was in high school, we rarely saw things eye-to-eye. I am sure we sometimes chose opposite sides just to antagonize each other.

Perhaps I decided I could never obtain my father's approval, so I made sure he would disapprove of everything I did. What strikes me now is that I don't remember ever saying, "I love you." Neither of us said that to the other. Maybe neither of us felt it.

Thank God, He gave us both another chance. I remember talking with my dad shortly after my "accident." He said, "I think you need to experience some successes." I wasn't exactly sure what he meant, but after I got out of my cast and sling, we rebuilt the engine of my car. Then we fixed up the body and painted it. That was the beginning of our friendship.

Now we work on woodworking and remodeling projects together. We ski together. We hug each other when we meet, and we hug again when we part. I often tell him I love him, and he tells me he loves me too. I don't believe it is ever too late to try to heal a relationship. I am so proud of my father for reaching out to me when I had failed so miserably.

The second important part of my recovery journey is my relationship with God. When I was a little boy, I remember someone in a Sunday school class talking about Jesus coming to live in your heart. I remember envisioning Jesus and God having a little tea party right behind my breastbone. Ever since, I have believed in God. Perhaps I did ask Him into my heart that day in Sunday school. Now I have studied Scripture, and I believe every word of it is true and inspired by God. I am living proof that God is faithful. Even when I was trying to hammer Him into my image, He was patient with me and carried me through the darkest period of my life.

One other scrap of paper is in my box of treasures. It says, "Each person must decide for himself what is true." I believe now that it is more accurate to say that each of us must decide whether or not we will accept that which is true.

For so long, I beat my head against a brick wall, trying to write my own rules. Now I live by the guidelines provided by the one Lord who loves me and cares for me. Instead of feeling restricted, I find that I have more freedom and happiness than ever before.

He Was Addicted to Pornography

$\mathbf{M}$y first experience with pornography came at the age of ten when I was invited over to my neighbor's house. He said he had something to show me. To my surprise he pulled out a *Playboy* magazine from underneath a bush in his backyard. A short time later I discovered that another friend's father had a collection of *Playboy* and *Penthouse* magazines. I made it a point to visit that friend often so I could sneak back to his dad's closet and tear out as many pages from these magazines as possible. I was so obsessed with the contents that I never thought of being caught—though now I'm surprised I never was. I later became so driven to have these magazines that I tore out pages of magazines on newsstands and in bookstores through our area. Again, I was never caught.

I spent my junior and senior high school years alone, depressed, discouraged, and addicted. I was terrified of girls because I was convinced that no girl in her right mind would want a no-good pervert like me. I remember going on a grand total of one date during this time, and it was a disaster. I fell asleep halfway through it.

Soon I became so intimidated by females that I began to turn to pornography as my only source of interaction with them. I felt that I could gain self-worth, power, acceptance, and importance—all of which I was desperately seeking—from pornography. I anxiously awaited my eighteenth birthday, the legal age to purchase or rent pornog-

raphy. Then I became a frequent customer at adult bookstores, go-go bars, and X-rated lateshows.

Throughout this time I was active in the church. I read
my Bible, went to Sunday school, took part in communion,
sang in the choir, acted in cantatas, worked in the church
sound booth, and prayed and prayed—and I mean prayed.
I remember spending hours on my knees, begging God to
show me a sign He loved me, a sign He cared, a sign He
wanted to help me. I also remember feeling as empty,
alone, and hopeless after those prayers as I did after leaving a go-go bar or an X-rated movie. Outwardly, I seemed
to be a very content, easy-going guy who didn't have a
care in the world when the truth was my addiction to
pornography was reaching an all-time high and my desire
to live, an all-time low.

Once I became a police officer, things got worse. Rotat-
ing shifts enabled me to dabble in pornography twenty-
four hours a day. I had hoped I was going through a normal stage and as soon as I had a girlfriend my addiction
would end. It did not! In fact, my addiction continued to
grow stronger and my will to live became weaker. While
working the overlap shift, I remember telling my wife I
was going to work, giving her a kiss good-bye, and then
changing my clothes (I had plain clothes hidden in the
trunk of my patrol car) so I could spend the next eight
hours at a go-go bar or X-rated lateshow.

During this time I hit rock bottom. I remember three
different occasions when I was sitting on the end of my
bed, watching in a mirror as I stuck my police revolver
first in my mouth and then against the side of my head
and began to pull back the trigger. It was while I was
sitting on my bed, with my .38 pressed against my head
that I heard a still, gentle voice simply say, "There is
hope." I thank God I listened to that voice and put the gun
down each time. Had it not been for the quiet voice of God
Almighty, I would have been just one of thousands who
fall prey to the deception that suicide relieves you and

everyone else of your problems. (It tears me up when I respond to a confirmed suicide as a policeman.)

In my search to find an answer to my addiction, I chose to leave two X-rated video tapes out where my wife would find them. I was afraid to confront her about my addiction, but I knew that once she found the tapes she would confront me. And she did. She immediately called me at work. When I came home that night, my first response was to lie, "It's the first time. It's just curiosity. I haven't even watched them yet."

Yet I sensed a tremendous amount of love from my wife. As I sat with her in our den it struck me that for the first time in fourteen years I had the opportunity to step out from behind the mask of deception and tell the truth! In John 8:32, Jesus spoke of knowing the truth and being set free. That night I took my first step toward freedom. I can't put into words the hope I received after I told my wife the truth. I had been isolated from all the people around me, including my wife, but now, for the first time in fourteen years, I began to feel a unity with someone—with my wife. Now someone else was praying for me, someone else knew my suffering, someone else knew the truth.

During the next six months my progress was slow and painful, but for the first time in my life I saw a light in the distance. During the second week of December 1989, my wife and I were at a fall revival at our church. As we listened to the sermon, I felt as if God was saying to me, "Satan has already robbed you of half your life. It's time to put an end to the pain, despair, and depression."

That night my wife and I went to the altar, and for the first time I pointed my finger directly at me—not at God, not at Satan, not at the people around me. Through the years I had chosen to believe that I could never give up my addiction to pornography. I had chosen to believe that I could not help myself. "The devil made me do it," I had claimed. That night I took responsibility for what I had done and for the present condition of my life. I asked God to forgive me.

I could literally feel the chains of pornography shatter the second I repented of my sins and asked God into my life. I got up from that altar a new man—a clean, honest, pure, forgiven man. I knew without a doubt that a party was being thrown in heaven in honor of my victory!

I spent the next three weeks on a spiritual and emotional high. I wanted to pay God back for all the years I had wasted. I wanted to spend every minute of every day trying to learn more and grow closer to God, Jesus Christ, and the Holy Spirit. I spent hours reading the Bible, praying, reading inspirational books, listening to sermons on the radio, and listening to old hymns.

At the end of this time I came back down to earth. At first I continued to overcome my temptation, but I felt myself growing weaker and weaker spiritually. I soon began to yield to pornographic temptations. My first response was an immeasurable sense of guilt. I could not understand why I, a saved child of God, was still falling victim to these temptations.

However, I immediately accepted responsibility for my actions and sin and asked God to forgive me. He was faithful and forgave me for my sin and the guilt that accompanied it. Each time I repented I could almost feel Jesus Christ pick me up, brush off the dirt and filth, and encourage me to continue my walk to freedom with Him.

Then on February 24, 1990, a cold winter evening, my wife and I again attended a revival at our church. The evangelist was preaching on sanctification, a term I had heard about for years, but had not really understood. He picked up an empty glove and placed it on the pulpit. Then he commanded the glove to pick up the Bible lying next to it, and of course the glove did not move. He commanded the glove a second, third, and fourth time. Still the glove did not move. Then he picked up the empty glove and filled it with his hand. He commanded the glove to pick up the Bible, and of course it did.

The evangelist went on to say, "The empty glove represents a Christian who has received salvation."

That was me since December of 1989, I decided.

"Salvation is a tremendous work of God, but much like the empty glove it is powerless in helping us to live our lives day by day. The hand represents the Holy Spirit, the source of power, strength, and ability."

That evening I went to the altar again, this time to yield my will to the Holy Spirit, the Hand of God. I felt no different physically, emotionally, mentally, and even spiritually when I got up from the altar. And in the next few days I again felt tempted by pornography. Yet Scripture verses started coming to my mind, verses I had not memorized. I began avoiding certain situations—an innocent glance at a go-go bar whose door was open, a newsstand or bookstore that carried pornographic magazines, and the channels on television that showed X-rated movies. By the grace of God I had overcome the seemingly invincible, impregnable enemy of pornography.

To God be the glory, great things He has done.

She Was Addicted to Church Work

I am recovering from being a workaholic, particularly in the church, a perfectionist, and a pleaser.

I was the second of four children. Education was very important in our house since my father was a school principal. My older sister was very smart, and I had to work hard to get Bs.

I remember my father as being very loving and spending much time with my sister and me. But my memories of my mother are harsh. I remember being screamed at and slapped so hard that red, blistering hand marks remained on my skin, being pushed across the room and having glasses of water poured on me. I seemed to be the object of my mother's rage. Yet I was an extremely shy, withdrawn child and could not remember anything I had done to deserve the punishment, except one time when I was giggling too much as I played with my dolls. (A sudden change for the better occurred when my mother had a hysterectomy during my teen years. I had a new mom. Today my mother is my best friend.)

I'm sure my early years influenced my workaholism, but I can also trace it more directly to a church I belonged to in 1980. My husband and I had both been Christians for one year. We had two daughters. Then in 1980 my husband was transferred to California. We didn't know anyone there, so we became very attached to a big church because the pastor told us it was the only church around.

This church had a lot of rules and taught that if you did not obey these rules, you were not a good Christian. We wanted to do what was "right" so we followed their rules. My children started attending their accelerated private school. I got a job at the school also. The church became our life; the people of the church, our family.

I got rid of all my slacks and spent long hours, from early morning to late at night, doing things for the church. My husband spent all his extra hours after work on church visitation, choir practice, and other duties. Our children were busy meeting the high demands of the church's Christian school. From the time they got home from school until they went to bed, they were doing school work or church work, with only a break for dinner. We had no T.V. and even thought the local Christian radio station was not good enough to listen to.

Despite all the work, we were fairly happy because we had the approval of our pastor and friends at church. Everyone thought we were such good Christians—and we thought we were pleasing God.

After six years in California, my husband's company was sold and he was without a job. So in 1986 we moved back to our hometown in Ohio. We joined a church much like the one in California and got busy right away, trying to impress the pastor and win the approval of the people.

After looking for work for about eight months, my husband decided to start his own business. We had no idea how much time and work that would be. We found it very difficult to continue with our heavy load of church work, so we talked to the pastor about getting out of some of the responsibilities. He said he would try to find someone to replace us but he never did. From the spring of 1987 to the spring of 1989, my life was filled with much inner turmoil.

Our children who were now older and in public school began questioning our standards and asking why they couldn't wear slacks, go to movies, and do other things their friends did. My mom, my sister, and other family members who used to be close to us now stayed at a distance, not feeling comfortable with our current set of standards.

The crisis occurred during a spring revival at our church in 1989. We had worked hard as members of the revival planning committee. We went to each nightly service that week dutifully. By the end of the week I knew I either had to make some drastic changes or lose my mind.

Together, my husband and I went to our pastor; we *told* him we were going to cut back (no questions asked), rather than asking him if we could do so. We also began an intensive study of the Bible to find out what we believed and why we believed it. As we walked through the Scriptures, we decided to base our lives on the Word of God, not other people's opinions or church tradition (what a difference this made!).

I also read lots of books, like *The Lies We Believe* by Dr. Chris Thurman. I realized that I was believing twenty-three lies. I wrote out Scripture memory cards with my lies on one side and the corresponding truth from Scripture on the other. On one side, for instance, I wrote: "Religious lie—'God's love must be earned.'" On the other side I wrote out Ephesians 2:8,9: "For by grace you have been saved through faith, and that not of yourselves; it is the gift of God, not of works, lest anyone should boast." Another lie I wrote on my cards was "I must be perfect!" and I countered it with 1 John 1:8: "If we say that we have no sin, we deceive ourselves, and the truth is not in us." I reviewed these cards daily as I deprogrammed my mind, substituting the truth of God's Word for my false set of beliefs, as Chris Thurman suggests. The best thing I could have done after studying the Bible was to memorize it.

As a result of my recovery program, my life slowly got back in order. The demands on my schedule eased, my priorities began to fall into place, my relationship with God became a joy. However, the more I studied the Bible, the more differences I noted between what it said and what our pastor was saying. The hardest part of my recovery was to leave this church. After all, the pastor had told us that once we joined his church we should never leave. He also made us feel guilty that we were questioning some of the church's practices although he would not answer our sincere questions about why we did what we did. Finally, our fourteen-year-old daughter liked the church and was active in the youth group. I was afraid that by changing churches we might hurt her walk with God, maybe even throw her into rebellion.

However, in December of 1990, our family returned to California for a visit, and some events that happened there made our decision final. It felt as if God was pulling us out. We finally decided to leave this church for a new loving church that was not legalistic.

My teenage daughter adjusted and truly blessed my heart when she told me, "If we had changed churches a year ago, I would have been angry. But now I can really see the good that has come from this."

We are all active in our new church but not overactive. I have learned to say "No," when asked to do things that I don't think God wants me to do. I've also stopped being a people pleaser. I still review my "pack of lies" every other day to keep them fresh in my mind. The truth of the Word of God set me free. I can't describe the exhilarating feeling the Word brought to my life. God is so good and His timing is right.

She Was Overprotected

I was raised by a loving, very protective mother and father. Yet the love they gave me was very crippling. I believe that my mother, especially, never allowed me to grow up in her own mind. She tried to live her own life through me by projecting all her fears, guilt, and anxiety onto me.

I remember two things about growing up: loneliness and quietness. Yet I don't remember being lonely until my older brother whom I loved dearly went into the air force when I was eight. After that, I remember feeling very sad and isolated until I was about fourteen years old.

I developed two addictive behaviors to cope with all of this—perfectionism and overeating. I sought my family's approval (as well as that of others) by trying to do *everything* perfect—all the time! I wanted my parents to believe that I could do something on my own. Yet when I tried to do something, I was put down by the words, "You think you know, but we are older than you and we know better than you do." I felt I was a bad person, never really succeeding at anything and always making mistakes.

I would fill my mouth with food to try to erase the feelings of failure. I soon began to eat for every reason I could think of—because I was happy or because I was having a bad day or because I needed to feel loved—whatever. My mother constantly tried to control what I ate, and . . . you guessed it: My overeating only got worse.

I believe my need for my mother's approval began in a

very unusual way. Although I knew my mother loved me, I became very confused when she said, "You don't love me. If you did, you would not hurt me." She would either cry or pretend that she was crying in reaction to something I had done. I constantly tried to please her, which led to my becoming more and more dependent. My mother would always try to hug me. Yet when I grew up I found I didn't want her even to touch me. I don't know why.

My dad was very passive, quiet (most of the time), and loving. My dad and I didn't hug all that much, but when he did hug me I felt he was a very special and wonderful dad.

I always wanted to know my dad better. He and I never shared very much, but I did mow the lawn and help in his garden. I didn't feel as much as a failure when I did things for him as I did when I tried to do things for my mom.

As a result of my parents' overprotective love, I grew up with an unrealistic idea of life. I was not given, nor did I choose, independence—freedom to be who I wanted to be or who I could be. My ultimate goal in life was to be married and have a lot of children. At the age of twenty I dropped out of college to get married. Only then did I begin to realize how totally unprepared for life I was.

I believe I married the wrong person for the wrong reasons. Since my self-esteem was rock bottom, I felt that I really couldn't find someone who was successful and intelligent. I settled for a guy who had dropped out of high school and said he had done so to support his mother and sister.

Five months after I married him I realized that he had many problems. I began to see that lying came easily to him and that he had a violent temper. Within a year, our first son, Lane, was born. By the time Lane was a year and a half old, my husband would throw him against the wall. For some reason he never abused our second son. Yet many times in the next years I was afraid for Lane. I felt guilty every time I heard him scream. I told myself I was not a good mother for allowing my husband to hurt him so.

In the next years my husband borrowed thousands of dollars from my family, always promising to pay it back. I don't know what happened to all that money. I don't know whether or not he was taking drugs; I just know he was violent at times and he lied all the time.

I looked for help but did not find any until I heard a minister preach at my dad's funeral. I had a desire to go to church, his church. There I learned of a God of love. I heard about how He wanted me to come to Him just as I was. I began to pray and ask God to help me prove that my husband was lying. He answered those prayers, and I told my husband to get out of our lives unless he got help for his problem. He refused. He said he didn't want to be married to a Christian, so he abandoned us when he could no longer abuse us.

In the months after he left, I began praying every night between my sons' beds. One night I realized what a mess I had made of my life. I was an emotional wreck and only God could heal me. That night I humbly asked Him to take over. "I can't do it myself," I admitted.

In the next weeks I began to see how God used other people to help me. A friend gave me the tape "Something Beautiful," by the Bill Gaither Trio. The lyrics of a song called "I'm Something Special" really touched me: "I'm something special. God gave me a body and a bright healthy mind."

For Christmas that year my son copied a poem at school and gave it to me as a gift, the first year we celebrated the holiday as a family of three:

What can I give Him as poor as I am,
If I were a shepherd I'd give Him a lamb.
If I were a wise man I would do my part,
What can I give Him?
I'll give Him my heart.

That poem meant more to me than anything money

could have bought. My heart was all I had to give the Lord, but I knew that was exactly what He wanted.

The boys and I prayed for a Big Brother for them. I even contacted Big Brothers, but the waiting list was so long I thought it was hopeless. One afternoon a friend called me at work and told me that a guy who worked with her, Rick, wanted to become a Big Brother. A few minutes later he called and we talked. The first question I asked him was, "If the boys misbehave, how will you handle it?" He said, "Well, I will sit them down and talk to them." I said to myself, "He's the one."

In the next months Rick spent quite a bit of time with the boys. He lived in the same apartment complex we did, but we had never seen him before. I began noticing how much love Rick had for my boys and everyone he met. Gradually I fell in love with him and he with me. We began going to church together. Soon we realized that we wanted to get married and spend the rest of our lives together. I asked God if Rick was the man He wanted for me, and I sensed more and more that the answer was, "Yes." Over the years since then, God has confirmed that He gave us to each other.

The church we joined together had many seminars, but "Healing of the Whole Person—Mind, Body, and Spirit," with the Reverend Dennis and Rita Bennett, was particularly meaningful to me. At the seminar I saw a picture in my mind of me as a child on my stick horse, standing with Jesus and asking, "Why am I so alone?" This picture led me to go to the altar at communion to be anointed with oil for healing.

As I knelt at the altar, I saw another picture in my mind. My ex-husband was standing in Lane's old bedroom. Then Jesus came into the room and bent down and took the beatings for Lane. The years of memories of his screams were healed after that prayer.

The little girl standing on her stick horse is no longer alone. Jesus stands beside her. And His children are a part of her everyday life.

She Was Addicted to a Romantic Fantasy

During the twenty-five years of our marriage my husband has always been a workaholic, imperative person. He was very spiritual in church, but he never led his family spiritually. In fact, his contact with our three children was usually very negative.

About five years ago I began to really look up to Jim, a man in our church who was the adult Sunday school teacher, the minister of music, and an elder. He showed a genuine appreciation and respect for me, and we built each other up with compliments and kindness, things I was not receiving at home and neither was he.

With time this grew into a fantasy romance. I began to visualize that I would someday become Jim's wife, after the death of both of our spouses! Our families were close friends so we went on a camping trip together, which only deepened my love and desire for Jim. My thoughts turned more and more to him until I was thinking about him day and night, obsessed. It was addictive behavior.

I had no one to talk to until we got a new pastor at our church. Soon after he arrived I began counseling with him and attempted to make myself accountable to him. He gave me wise counsel, but I wasn't ready or able to carry it all out. Something inside me still drove me until Jim went to the pastor with his and his wife's concern that there was definitely a problem between us. The pastor told them I needed help, not criticism and condemnation.

One Sunday that summer the pastor asked people in the church to go to others to share their appreciation of them or ask their forgiveness for a problem. I went to Jim's wife at the Holy Spirit's prompting and told her how sorry I was. She said she was very disappointed because I had spoiled our friendship, which increased my guilt feelings. I began praying for God to show her how to forgive me, but she has not yet been able to. Jim, I believe, has.

God had also been dealing with my husband. After the pastor's sermon he told me that he had been having fantasies about some women at church and at work. I also told him about Jim. Before this time our sex life was almost nonexistent. We were both getting our fulfillment from our fantasies, which were more real and meaningful than our marriage.

Now there has been a change in my husband. He's been open and understanding with me, so I've been able to share my daily struggles to free my mind of Jim. God has given us a love and concern for each other. We read *The Lies We Believe* aloud together, and we discuss how it applies to us. We were both believing and living out so many lies. We enjoy talking with each other and even having sexual relations with one another. I'd prayed for a new husband, but God answered my prayers differently than I had ever felt possible. Yet all things are possible with Him!

He Was a Workaholic Who Almost Lost Everything

I am an obsessive-compulsive person (alias a Type A). In other words, I'm a perfectionist and a workaholic.

I wanted so much for my parents to get along, I acted as the peacemaker in the family, trying to make them laugh, etc. Still they divorced in 1960 when I was ten years old. Both of them were hardworking individuals with strong moral and ethical traditions. They tried to bring my older brother and me up with standards like "Your word should mean a lot" and "Actions speak louder than words."

Up until the age of thirty-five I was a people pleaser, which made me very successful. I became a vice president of human resources/labor relations. Then I went through a severe depression during which I lost my job and most of my material goods—and almost lost my family. I tried almost everything for over a year. Nothing worked. Then a friend told me to try an Emotions Anonymous meeting. It probably saved my life. That was the first place I got help from others trying to survive day to day. It was so refreshing to share life experiences weekly with real people. Yet the main thing that brought me back each week was that the program was based on a Higher Power.

Spirituality has been 99.9 percent of my recovery. I had always operated as a two-dimensional being, mind and body. Then I realized that I could never get myself out of the situation I was in. It was impossible. But with God, everything is possible. As I began to get into the Bible, the spirit within me began to grow. I found I was not of the world, but in it.

Over a period of time I gradually broke the old tapes of feeling abandoned by my parents through reading the Word, something that was not stressed in church, even though I went every Sunday and was an altar boy for over twelve years.

The tools that help me in my recovery are:

- a weekly prayer group,
- individual therapy for one and a half years,
- Bible study,
- reading, reading, reading books on self-help (I have read all the Minirth-Meier books).

Since 1985 I have been trying not to rescue those I love (my family and coworkers). Jesus died upon the cross to obtain salvation for us; He is to be their Savior. Instead of trying to act like the White Knight, I try to put Jesus into my conversation with anyone who faces a crisis or appears to be lost and without hope.

It has been over six years since I began my walk with the Lord. Each day I try to increase the spiritual side of me through prayer, Christian radio or television, Scripture, or reading. My recovery has opened my eyes to the need to improve my personal relationship with God. It is hard not to try and make things happen when you have a business education background. So I begin each day with a prayer and a reminder that I do not control what will occur during that day. The first five minutes of each day I either read Scripture or a daily devotional, pray the Lord's prayer, and review the Twelve Steps of Emotions Anonymous. It has made these past six years a true blessing!

He Was Searching for a Father Figure

I'm forty years old, married, and the father of two daughters. I've played drums, guitar, bass, and keyboards part-time in bands.

My homelife was one of constant chaos when I was a child. There were no boundaries. My father always seemed angry and ready to explode. My earliest memories are of my father yelling at my mother and hitting her, and of this huge monster of a man chasing me under the table with a belt.

Except for these violent episodes, my father never paid attention to me. He always seemed to be behind his newspaper. One of my worst memories was when I wanted to help him paint a fence. He wouldn't let me, saying I would just mess it up. I cried and yelled, but I just wasn't good enough.

My mother constantly cleaned or was "sick." I remember throwing a temper tantrum and banging my head on the floor. My mother handled it by saying, "So you want to bang your head. Here, let me help you." She proceeded to bang my head against the wall. Of course, this was not the help I wanted from her.

I guess these things led me to search for a father figure, whom I found in a fifteen-year-old guy named John. I believe I was about six years old. It was great to have someone who paid attention to me. Little did I know that he was sexually abusing me. I started practicing this behavior with other males my own age and older. I finally became aware something wasn't right when John introduced me to his friends who also wanted my sexual favors. I felt betrayed and ashamed. I felt that it was my fault.

I was so angry that I proceeded to abuse two members of John's family who were four and seven. I felt that I was getting back at John for what he had done to me.

These sexual memories haunted me all through school. I was terrified that someone would find out that I was a "fag." I felt totally responsible—then and for the next twenty years.

After I was married, my wife and I began having problems. She would tell me that I needed some help, but I thought she had the problems—not me! I would often say, "That's life," to rationalize the things that I did. I took my hidden anger out on my wife, my dogs, and my new baby. And I had a constant pain in my stomach, which I now realize had its origins in my codependency, love hunger, and obsessive-compulsive behaviors (such as checking a door or a lock for over an hour).

I also vented my anger at work. If the bosses were angry about anything, I felt that I was to blame. I would jump down other people's throats if they disagreed with me and insist that my opinion was the only correct one. What I knew, I thought, was best for everyone. I also found myself trying to please my bosses at work, just as I desperately tried to please my parents.

Finally I started to talk to a pastor-therapist at my church. I went from believing I was responsible for the abuse to realizing that John had taken advantage of me over and over again. I began to see that the child in me just wanted to express my feelings to my parents for all the hurt and pain they caused.

One morning when I was delivering mail, a power came over me. It was then that I realized my purpose on earth: to share what I have learned with other people. I've changed many of my old views of life (for instance, I think we need more moral guidelines).

In my journey God, my wife, my children, my best friend, Frank, my dog, and even a jazz singer, Michael Frank, have helped me to clarify my own thoughts and feelings. I especially love the line from one of Frank's songs: "Never say die. We've got the worst behind us; if we just try, soon we'll be feeling strong."

Day by day I'm renewed and refathered by older male friends and by my dad who now does spend time doing things with me and my children. I no longer have the pain in my stomach although everything hasn't been completely resolved. I am still very angry at my mother, who still doesn't have time for me.

Yet I find help by praying and listening to Christian radio every day to gain more insight into myself and God. I've realized that I have a choice in my response to pain and sorrow. I can hate God and ask, "Why?" Or I can ask, "What changes do You have in store for me now?" I can ask, "How can I grow from this?"

He Was Haunted by His Past

I am a forty-eight-year-old man who has been happily married for twenty-three years and has three well-adjusted children. I have been—and continue to be—faithful to my wife, whom I love dearly.

Twenty-four years ago my life was a different story. During my USMC tour of duty in Vietnam, and afterward, I was promiscuous. I realized that my sexual proclivities were outside the bounds of my Christian beliefs, but I was helpless to stop them. My lifestyle caught up with me when one of my girlfriends got pregnant and refused my suggestion to get an abortion. I stayed beside her throughout the pregnancy, even though I told her I wouldn't marry her. (I had met another girl who became my wife a year later.)

I paid most of the medical expenses and even managed to tell the girl's mother of my intentions after the birth of the baby girl. That was the hardest thing I ever had to do in my life. I have remembered the hurt and tears in her eyes for the past twenty-four years.

I rejected one woman who bore my child because I didn't think I loved her. At the same time I was proving to myself and my future wife that I could beat my worldly appetites by being faithful to one who had accepted me, faults and all.

My wife and I eventually had three children whom I told about my past and the existence of an older half-

301

sister. I became active in the Right to Life movement and asked God's forgiveness for ever suggesting that my child be aborted. Yet I had periods of anger throughout these years. This anger was not necessarily directed at people I knew, but at the driver of another car on the road, for instance. Or I would curse at events and things: "Why did this blankety-blank have to happen?" Or, "Cursed car would break down now!"

Frustration, hatred, masked guilt, and sometimes fatigue were my constant companions. I didn't know why. I told myself it was the times in which we lived, the fast lane—every rationalization I could think of.

As I tried to draw closer to God, I also had increasing bouts of anger and hatred. Why? What was wrong with me? Didn't God love me? I had asked God and everyone else to forgive me, but inside my own heart I secretly, so secretly, despised myself. I was poisoning and hurting myself and my family.

During these years I did get information that my former girlfriend and her baby girl were well; she had married so my child now had a father. My conscience was relieved, but I continued to realize how bitterly I despised my failures. My present life was so at odds with my former self that I found this hatred to be only a temporary release. At times death seemed the only answer.

Just recently my daughter of those lost years contacted me. She has forgiven me. At this junction my life seems to be just beginning. I have finally given myself permission to forgive my past addiction. I sense the hand of God in this and am deeply humbled that He should release me from my self-bondage.

PART FOUR

Codependent Spouses: Personal Stories

She Learned That Men Weren't Reliable

My mother's family were migrant farm workers and sharecroppers, living in poverty and moving from southern town to southern town. She never stayed long enough in one place to have friends and rarely had a chance to say good-bye to anyone since her family usually moved in the night. She grew up afraid of not having enough and measuring people by the things they had.

We lived in a small town in rural America where only a few people seemed to have power—the doctor, the factory owner, the storekeeper, and the mayor—and power came from money. My mother was in complete awe of these people and their families. She was a working mom before that became a trend, and every penny she made was saved because there would never be enough.

Some money was spent on looking good to those in the outside world, however, because they were considered the important ones. Our house looked good from the road, but the hot water could only be turned on once a week. My parents' hoarding made it very cluttered with old magazines, books, and clothes. The only heat we had came from wood, and we didn't use that at night, so the water in a glass set on a nightstand by my bed would freeze. We never had birthday parties, picnics, vacations, or more than two toys at Christmas. Like many people, we had a nice living room that was never used, and we huddled in a much smaller room with very old furniture.

Whipping with a leather belt kept me and my brother on our toes. It hurt then and it still brings tears to my eyes. I learned only recently from my mother that her theory on child raising was, "You have to break their spirit when they're young or they'll give you trouble later." I believe it worked much too well on me.

My parents didn't have any friends, and my only friends were the kids I played with at recess. No child ever visited my home. I learned to isolate myself and distrust others as my parents did. I learned early to be ashamed of who we were.

I also learned that men weren't very reliable. My father didn't keep jobs very long because he felt he was smarter than his bosses. Women usually had to take care of men, I decided, and men could do whatever they wanted. My father drank and fought in the bars during the war, but when he and my mother married, alcohol was never allowed in our home. They divorced when I was nineteen, and they both began to drink.

Somewhere along the way I believe my teachers became very influential because I can find no other reason why I decided to go to college. I dated very little. I was elected to many student offices and I was never sure why. Someone must have seen something in me I didn't see. I was afraid they would find out I was really a stupid, bad child, but they didn't.

I didn't have my first drink until I went to college when I was nineteen. Then my ordinarily good grades and active school life disappeared. I had no self-discipline; everything had always been controlled by my mother. Alcohol made me comfortable with people who were better (richer), smarter, and prettier than I was. Sex gave me love and affection. The first boy I loved and gave myself to drank and ultimately abandoned me. I was completely alone. I had no friends because I didn't know how to have them; no family because I wanted to be as far away from them as possible; no God because the limited place He had in my family was not enough to sustain me now that I was committing all the sins that would make Him angry.

I see now that alcohol and sex were my addictions. They killed the pain and seemed the only way to fill the hole inside me. But they left me hating myself. Then I had to use them again to feel better.

I married a man I didn't know how to love. I don't know if he loved me; we communicated very little. We stayed together for ten years. We were rarely alone. We had drinking couple friends. I slept with the men. I hated myself yet I felt unable to stop what I was doing. My husband knew about the affairs, and he told me it was okay as long as I was discreet.

After ten years of no commitment and no children and too many men, too many blackouts, and too much pain, I asked for a divorce. I couldn't live with myself, and I thought getting out of the marriage would help me find what I needed. Within six months of drinking away my shame and loneliness, I met my second husband in a bar, of course. We were so drunk that night that even though he came home with me I couldn't remember his name. He was just as sick as I was and so he moved in the next week. This wounded man became my next addiction, my next god, along with alcohol.

No more affairs: My time and energy were now taken up trying to make this sad, hurting man happy. If only he could find the right job . . . If only I could help him go back to school . . . If only I were perfect, he would be happy and love me. I became addicted to his neediness, which almost felt like love—or what I thought love felt like.

I allowed my husband to use me emotionally and sexually because I feared his anger and his leaving me. I finally supported him financially. Although I was drinking, my career was going well. Drinking was accepted there, and even encouraged. Over the next five years I allowed him to have all the money I made; I didn't want him to feel badly because he wasn't making any. He took over all decision making because I wanted to make him happy and keep him. In doing so, I completely lost myself. I took him home from bars when he couldn't drive. I let him drive me when he couldn't drive. I let him sleep with my friends because he wanted to and because I had not resolved my own guilt from the same behavior. I felt I deserved this, and it would prove how much I loved him.

Finally his disease became so advanced (with my "loving" help and support) that his bouts of deep depression, talk of suicide and murder became more intense. I became obsessed with stopping him. I would call the V.A. because he said he was in Vietnam. I would call hot lines to ask about him. I would call doctors. Yet I never mentioned how much he drank. I told no one.

I finally found him a job, and we bought a house. By this time the good girl part of me had a very good job with a big title and a lot of money. Somehow I had been given the opportunity to work and advance in a business that fit me perfectly. Although my character defects—people pleasing, perfectionism, caretaking, workaholism, and I admit now, talent—weren't working at home, they seemed to pay off at work.

We decided to have a baby. I was thirty-seven and now was the time, if ever. During pregnancy I stopped drinking for the baby's sake, and my husband just drank more. We brought a precious life into the hell of our own making. He was angry all the time because I wasn't able to take care of the baby, my job, and him. We would have deep conversations (me dry, him in a blackout), and the next day I thought I was crazy because he said it never happened. Along with the depressions, there was now more talk of suicide.

I would drive home and wonder if he would be dead of a gunshot to the head. I began to sleep with a light on so I could see when he came into the bedroom; I was afraid he would shoot us all. He began to stay out all night or fly to Mexico. Still I let him have the money. Still, I allowed him to pick up the baby from the sitter, drunk. Still, I allowed him to yell at me and our child. Still, I allowed him to control our home with threats. I had no one to talk to and no God except him. Insanity.

This went on until the baby was three when he finally agreed to see our family doctor for the self-diagnosis of manic depression. Neither one of us ever admitted that alcohol was the problem, even though he was now drinking over a half gallon of scotch weekly, along with beer, wine, vodka throughout the day. I had virtually stopped drinking out of pure fear for my life, but I allowed the guns to stay in the house. Insanity.

The doctor who was a member of A.A. called me while my husband was in his office to ask how much he drank. My husband had only told him "a couple of drinks in the evening." The doctor told me to go to Al-Anon and to have my husband attend A.A. Of course, he didn't. Why should he? I was taking care of everything. I went to a couple of meetings of Al-Anon, but I wasn't ready either. (After all, they didn't tell me how to fix my husband.)

It took another year for me to hit bottom. I left the baby with him to go on a business trip. Insanity. And I realized that when I returned. The next day I was driving to work when an eerie inhuman cry came from somewhere deep inside me. I had come to the end. I called a hot line and was referred to a therapist specializing in abused women. She had no knowledge of alcoholism—amazingly—but I did begin to attend Al-Anon and was referred to Dr. Hemfelt.

I asked for help, and suddenly there was help everywhere. I began to detach enough from my fear to see that there were choices. I arranged for intervention, which didn't work for him, but did for me. The secret was out. Although everyone knew—his family and his office—no one was talking to him about it until then. Yet he didn't stick to treatment or sobriety in the next year. I asked him to go into treatment again or we would separate. He chose to separate. I chose to get better.

In Al-Anon I learned to detach with love. I learned that

I didn't cause my husband's problem. I couldn't control it, and I sure couldn't cure it. I learned that I played a part in my abuse and that I didn't have to live like that. The most important thing I learned, however, was that there was a loving God who was there for me, a God I could call my own. A God who wouldn't abandon me or abuse me. A God who could be there for me as my best friend. I learned that He forgives me and that He wants me to be happy.

Dr. Hemfelt and I explored how painful living passes from generation to generation. We learn to abuse each other and ourselves. We also explored how my longing for my distant father influenced my attraction for unavailable men. We talked about how I saw myself as two very distinct people: one who was professionally successful and the "real one" who was not as good as others (the stupid, bad child). Together we worked to find the real me who could be successful in all parts of my life.

I have just recently confronted my own alcoholism. I felt stuck in my recovery. I had not unlocked every door. I had not been rigorously honest. The time had come. For the last year I had controlled how much I drank, where I drank, what I drank, and with whom I drank. I would go months without a drink, but finally I could see that the need to control my drinking and my fear of getting drunk were not normal. My drinking never was. I had worked the Twelve Steps in Al-Anon with one big secret—my alcoholism. I had been comparing my controlled drinking with my husband's out-of-control drinking.

Now I am on a very exciting journey. I'm learning the power of being vulnerable, humble, and honest. I'm learning that I am a precious child of God, and I deserve happiness just because of that. I'm learning the power and peace of bringing God into every decision, every conversation, and every relationship. I'm learning that the promises offered by the Twelve Steps are available, even to me.

I have been trying to have an honest relationship with a kind and gentle man. We are both in recovery. Sometimes I can't be honest because I still have trouble knowing what I feel. Sometimes fear comes up, and I feel like running again. Sometimes recovery is so painful I want to give up and find someone or something easier. But I know that what I have now and who I am now are so much better than in the past. I want recovery—God and the Twelve Steps, self-examination and progress, not perfection—for the rest of my life. I have learned that sex, money, spending, alcohol, and relationships can't relieve me of empty feelings, a hollow soul, or anxiety. Only God has been able to fill me. And He was always there. I just never asked. Today I ask every day—and every day I learn something new.

She Found Serenity

After twenty years of so-called normal married life, my husband started doing things that were upsetting the whole family. Weekdays were fairly normal so we started wondering if the events of the previous weekend were actually real. Our children, who are adults, and I dreaded to think of holidays, family gatherings, and weekends, which would always be filled with tension and the scene of some major crisis. The main topic of conversation was, "What has Dad done or what is he doing?" When we confronted him about these incidents, he was able to turn the story around and put the blame on us.

Finally one of the children said, "Mom, we've got to do something about Dad's drinking." Dad's drinking? Yes, I knew he had been drinking more and more lately, but he had been drinking ever since I knew him and it had never caused a problem before. Besides he only drank on weekends. He held a good job, never missed a day's work, provided well for the family, and was a good church member. How could he have a problem with alcohol?

I talked with several of our close friends, and yes, they knew he had a drinking problem. I was the closest to him, and yet I was the last to realize what was happening. I called our doctor and talked with our pastor, and they both gave me the same advice: "Get help for yourself and the family. You can't help him unless he wants it. Attend Al-Anon meetings and read their literature."

I was so ashamed that this had happened to us. Now

that I had to go to a meeting everyone would know we had a problem. Somehow I got through the first Al-Anon meeting. Everyone was friendly and seemed to understand my problem more than anyone I had ever talked to. It was about another year, however, before I could say, "My husband is an alcoholic."

After I attended five or six Al-Anon meetings I figured I knew it all. I took several pamphlets and kept them hidden, only to read when life got rough. Two years later, I knew I needed more help so I went back to Al-Anon. They suggested that I try counseling. I was so full of hatred, resentment, frustration, and anxiety that I decided I needed all the help I could get.

After about six sessions of counseling, I decided that was enough. I was being told to think of myself, be good to myself, but how could I do these things when my husband was causing such problems? I did continue to attend Al-Anon, but I was physically, spiritually, and mentally sick of the whole thing. Oh, how I prayed that God would make my husband stop drinking, that my life would be peaceful again, and that I would start to feel like my old self.

All during this time I had tried desperately to get my husband to attend A.A. meetings or counseling. He refused any help. Finally I decided that I had to do something. So back to the counselor I went.

Between Al-Anon and counseling I began to understand such phrases as "The only person you can change is yourself"; "Let go and let God"; "Turn it over to your Higher Power." I had been brought up to believe in God, to say the Lord's Prayer, and to attend church, but something seemed to be missing. Slowly a lot of the pieces began to fall into place. I learned how to pray for courage, wisdom, and acceptance when life didn't go my way. "Thy will be done" in the Lord's Prayer had a new meaning to me.

More and more I was able to open the Bible and find the answers to my problems, like on the day we planned an intervention. I was a nervous wreck, asking questions

non-stop: "How will I get him there?" "Will he stay?"
"What if this happens?" "And what if this doesn't?"

I stopped and opened the Bible and it fell to 1 Corinthians. I glanced over the pages and came to chapter three,
verse 19: "The Lord knows the planning of the wise is
useless." I had never read this before. Then and there I
turned the planning over to my Higher Power and everything worked out beautifully.

Slowly I was beginning to realize that I was important
and that I had rights and choices. I had lived for so long
with only one important person: my husband. My whole
life revolved around what he had done, what he was doing, and what he said. I just figured that I had to put up
with my husband's drinking or leave. Now I was learning
that I could cope with the problem and still be the person
I wanted to be.

One day of my counseling changed my life. My counselor asked if there was anything I would like to do with
my life. "Yes," I replied, "I have dreamed about something
for years, but I never thought it could become a reality."
During the last couple of years I had become interested in
an old needlecraft, which was becoming very popular in
many parts of the country. I had attended several seminars and thought I would love to teach needle arts.

"Who am I to think I can do such a thing?" I asked the
counselor. "I don't own a shop or have a college education.
I feel very inferior to most people so how could I talk to
them? I wouldn't even know how to organize a class." I
had numerous excuses. But when you are told—and when
you begin to believe that you can do anything you want—
you begin to exchange negative thoughts for positive ones.

That night as I lay in bed, I thought, *O Lord, what have
I gotten myself into now? Sure I had a dream, but how
could such a thing possibly happen?* I prayed for courage.
I prayed, "Thy will be done." Surely if God wanted me to
take this step, He would show me the way.

And He did. Two weeks later I approached a shop with
several samples of my work and my plans for a class. Af-

ter listening to me for about ten or fifteen minutes, the shop owner asked, "When would you like to hold your first class?"

My first class! I could hardly believe it. Oh yes, I was anxious that day. The shop was about sixty miles away. It was pouring rain, cold, and damp. Yet the class went very well, and when it was over I was asked to hold another class in a couple of months. From that day on, one door after another opened. I was asked to demonstrate my work. I loved showing people what this creative needlework could do. I even asked if I could demonstrate during fairs and fall festivals in our area. This all happened in less than a year and now shop owners are contacting me to hold classes! Our state university has even asked me to instruct a class for a 4-H group. Two newspapers have printed articles about my work and my classes. A whole new world has begun for me! And I love every minute of it.

Yes, "I can do all things through Christ who strengthens me."[1] It has been a miracle, but miracles happen every day if we just look for them.

My husband is still drinking, but I can't change him. The only one I've been able to change is myself. I still have many upsetting situations to face, but I don't dwell on these because the new me doesn't have time or energy to waste on a ruined day. It's not always easy—and it's often discouraging—but with constant patience and many, many prayers, I have found my serenity.

Her Husband's Mid-Life Crisis Led to Alcoholism

My husband and I are both Christians who are forty-five years old. We have two boys, now sixteen and seventeen. The story of my recovery started two years ago in 1989 when I discovered that my husband was a closet drinker, consuming nearly a gallon of whiskey a week.

It all started in 1982 when my husband, an auto mechanic, became unemployed after the car dealership that employed him folded. What started out as a mid-life crisis soon progressed into heavy drinking, unbeknownst to me. He kept his stash well hidden, and I was unable to smell the liquor on his breath. But I started to notice some bizarre conversations and actions. The criticism and verbal abuse became common in the next ten years, as did his mood swings. He was constantly telling me about my faults, "for my own good." "You are the reason for my problems and my behavior," he said. Although he was only physically violent on a handful of occasions, the boys and I became very afraid of his unpredictable rages, which were an everyday occurrence. He became a recluse. Yet I desperately struggled to maintain my relationships with other people. I felt trapped in my marriage: I didn't know if I loved him, yet I didn't believe in divorce.

Slowly I became paralyzed by guilt, fear, and anger. I had always liked my job as a medical technologist, yet I could hardly get up to go to work. At home I couldn't function, except to do the laundry and cook the meals. In June of 1989 I shared my feelings and my husband's symptoms with one of my coworkers and she suggested that he might be abusing alcohol (her ex-husband had the same symptoms, she said). I went home and looked around the house with a more discerning eye. I found his stash of alcohol.

In the next six weeks, I monitored his usage. At a church prayer meeting I also blurted out what was happening in our family. Some people suspected it (they could smell the liquor on him when he ushered, they said). However, they never condemned him; they just accepted him and prayed. The pastor suggested that the boys and I confront my husband with my knowledge. When I told him what I knew, he said nothing. I then informed him that the boys and I were going to get help, regardless of what he did.

The end of July I started attending Al-Anon meetings weekly. I thoroughly resented being there, but I met people who helped me, like the gal who could laugh, even though she was living with an alcoholic. And that's what I wanted to do.

In the next months I remained open to anything God might use in my life: Al-Anon, my church family, my friends, and books. (Al-Anon gave me a total understanding of alcoholism and its affects on family members; my church family provided Christian support, love, and prayer.)

I also began to realize that I needed other help. So in October I sought the help of a Christian counselor. He showed me how to cope with my husband's rages, and we worked on issues of codependency—low self-esteem and childhood issues (lack of love, guilt, and anger). The book that had the most impact on me (I wore it out!) was *Love Is a Choice*. I read more books during that year than I had in the previous ten years (and I took notes on all of them; I didn't want to miss a thing in my healing process).

In March of 1990 my father died. In the next months my counselor and I worked through the issues that related to him. My dad was a minister—devoted to God and to us, but he spent a lot of time with church members and was very strict and undemonstrative. I was a people pleaser. I was hungry for love. I found symbols of major events in my childhood—good and bad—and then wrote a letter to my dad, as *Love Is a Choice* suggested. In it I listed five bad things, five good things, and five goals for my recovery. It was painful. I cried a lot, but it was necessary. I'd like to think that dad looked down from heaven and saw what was in that letter.

My sessions with the counselor ended in May although I still attended Al-Anon, which I did faithfully for over a year (now I attend infrequently to remind myself of my recovery process). In the process of it all, I learned to laugh!

In June of 1990 I heard a "Focus on the Family" program in which a woman who attended Al-Anon talked about how successful an intervention had been for her husband. I started to think about this seriously, and I began to realize that love is doing what is best for the other person, not necessarily what he wants. So I asked my church family to begin praying. I planned the intervention for August, just before our vacation so my husband couldn't use missing work as an excuse. I coordinated it with the program counselor in a treatment program only twenty minutes away. The intervention included the program counselor, my husband's father, the boys and myself, and two men from church whom he respected (his employer declined). Our church family prayed the whole week prior to the intervention, that very day, and that very hour. Within one hour from the time my husband arrived home to see us all gathered there, he consented to being admitted to the treatment center. The power of prayer!

My husband was in treatment for a month, receiving all kinds of cards every day from our church family, our relatives, and our friends (all the daily cards surprised the program's employees; they had never seen anybody receive that many). The day he came home from treatment I gave a workshop on codependency at a women's retreat, with his encouragement. I had set this as a goal a year earlier, as part of my own recovery.

That fall was a real struggle for my husband; he had some relapses, but I knew I had to let him work through his problems himself. Since January of this year, however, he has improved steadily. We were even able to have an exchange student in our home for three weeks this summer, and my husband enjoyed him so much. What a pleasant turnaround!

Regardless of what my husband chooses, I'm only responsible for me and my choices, and I'm only responsible to God, not to anyone else. I have chosen to love my husband (I knew he had value all along) and to be committed to our marriage (I'm not sure of his commitment at this point, but that'll be his choice).

I have backed out of my compulsive church involvements; I'm being selective about what I do to serve God (being a preacher's kid, "serving" was all I knew). I reserve my Sweet Adelines for myself. I am confident in my relationship with God, regardless of what others may think or say. Nothing can shake that.

Does my husband meet my needs yet? No. And that's okay, because God does in so many neat and creative ways.

PART FIVE

Adult Children of Dysfunctional Families Who Still Carry the After-Effects of That Emotional Legacy: Personal Stories

Her Father and Her Grandfather and Her Great-grandfather Were Addicted

My father is a recovering alcoholic. His father was an alcoholic and his only sibling is an active alcoholic. My great-grandfather was a very strict religious man who physically abused my grandfather. In our case "the sins of the fathers went into the third and fourth generations."

My mother also came from a dysfunctional family. Her father was a vagrant who had just finished hitchhiking from California when he met my grandmother. Granddad never worked longer than one year anywhere, and often went without work. My grandmother soon found solace in other men's arms. My mom lived in a small town where her father was quickly labeled a "bum," her mother a "whore."

My mom had two nervous breakdowns while the four of us children were still very small. Doctors treated her with "uppers" and she soon became addicted. When these doctors would no longer prescribe the pills for her, she went to other doctors who prescribed the then-popular diet pills, which gave her the same feeling.

We never had friends over when we were kids, because we never knew when Dad would be coming home (if he came home) or what mood Mom would be in. Very early one morning when the rest of the family was asleep, my dad put something on the stove to cook and then passed out. He nearly burned the house down. Mom would often lock him out of the bedroom at night, and he'd whine and cry like a baby. One time when I was twelve, I woke up because my whole body was numb and tingling. When I opened my eyes, Dad was on top of me, passed out. I remember how dirty and invaded I felt. I remember trying to shake off his touch. I lost all respect for Dad as early as I can remember and I resented my mother because I thought it was her fault he drank.

My older brother was the peacemaker. When Mom would start screaming and throwing things at Dad, my brother would gather the rest of us together and we would sit at the top of the stairs. He would always tell us to keep quiet and be good. My brother would also referee when the three of us fought. He was our parent. We asked him what we could or could not do; he always knew what the "mood" was.

The last day my father drank, he had been gone on a week's binge. His skin looked grey and he looked very tired. (I later learned that he had spent most of the week in a fleabag hotel, hallucinating that his room was filled with snakes.) Dad loaded his shotgun, announced that he was going to kill himself, and then went out to the barn. Mom started screaming, and he shot in the air, warning her to let him alone. I remember hearing her punching him, and then she ran toward the house, Dad coming after her.

My oldest brother had us huddled in the stairway. I broke away to come to Mom's rescue, just in time to watch my dad cock the rifle and point it at her. She threw herself down on the floor and Dad stood there with the gun pointed at me. "Pull the trigger," I screamed. I hated our family and him. Instead, he went back to the barn.

That's the last we saw of him for six weeks. Now we know that he committed himself to an inpatient treatment center. Then it was a big secret. Both sets of grandparents came to visit us during that time, but no one even mentioned Dad's name. When he came back, everything was very controlled and quiet.

Even after Dad quit drinking, he and Mom spent most of their time trying to work things out between them. I was always going out of my way to win my parents' attention. I was head majorette, held an officer's position in every club in school. I was voted outstanding sophomore, Young American, valedictorian, graduation speaker, and homecoming queen. My parents never came to any of my award ceremonies, concerts, or games.

Everything was funny to me, and I joked life's problems away. My parents could not see my emotional pain or perhaps it was very painful for them to acknowledge that we children had emotional struggles too. I tried to fill that void with witchcraft, God, boys, activities, and awards.

Whatever a potential new friend or boyfriend wanted me to be, I strived to be. Yet when the relationship intensified I would back off 100 percent. The excuse I used with girlfriends was, "I like to be free like a butterfly, not lighting anywhere for very long." With boyfriends I'd tell them, "I'm just crazy."

Then I found one boy who liked me crazy, wanted me to be crazy, and later in our marriage convinced everyone else I was crazy. I became totally dependent upon him. My senior year in high school I was anorexic and suicidal. I was 5′ 11″ and weighed 120 pounds. One day I cut off all my hair on a whim.

We married out of high school. Six months after we were married, he became verbally abusive at the same time I became pregnant with our first child. When he'd leave for work in the morning, he would mark a line behind the car tire, so he'd know if I went anywhere. Then he quit work and stayed at home. To keep us going financially (and to enhance my blue ribbon for martyrdom) I babysat five children during the day, sewed for a local clothing store on the side, and cleaned toilets at night at three different trucking terminals.

My husband constantly told me I was ugly, stupid, and crazy. He purposely did things to make me think I was nuts. He'd tell me to do something, I'd do it, then he'd slap me and ask why I did what I thought he had told me to do. After our children were born, my husband became physically and sexually abusive. I tried to leave him twice. Once he came after me as I was running down the street with the children and he tried to hit me with the car. The other time he picked me up and stuffed us back in the car, then locked me in the bedroom without my children. By now I wasn't allowed to go anywhere. This is when the bulimia began again. Each time he attacked me sexually, I quietly submitted. Then he would leave the house for hours, sometimes overnight. Once he was gone, I'd eat everything I could find and spend my evenings throwing up. It felt good to me. It was a release of my anger, frustration, and helplessness.

When he started to abuse my son, I began to make concrete plans to leave. I looked up "Women in Transition" in the phone book and arranged a meeting with one of the counselors. They told me what agencies could help me financially and helped me to locate subsidized housing in another town.

Yet, even after I left my husband, the bulimia persisted. So I went into a treatment facility, which was my first exposure to the Twelve-Step program. My counselor took me to A.A. so I could understand my father's struggles. They made me work side-by-side with a wife abuser and a sex addict so I could gain insight into those struggles. Most of all they encouraged me to get off my derriere and work on me, my addictions and compulsions—to stop blaming others for the way I acted and reacted.

The Twelve Steps gave me the courage to sit down with my parents and make peace with my childhood memories so I could sincerely forgive and forget. My father wept as he finally (after twenty-six years) had the courage to ask me if he ever sexually molested me. He wept even harder when I told him, "No, you never touched me." The Twelve

Steps were the beginning of many healing tears for my parents and me. They are foster parents and now house two or three teenagers who have active addictions and come from dysfunctional homes. Dad and Mom have nineteen years of sobriety.

My relationship with Jesus is my anchor. If I lose that, I lose my recovery. In the place of bulimia God has given me a new way to release my feelings, in song—not in sad or angry songs but in songs filled with the truths of the Word, songs built on hope and grace.

As a child my picture of God was this tall, white-haired man in a white robe who was too busy to notice me, and I saw myself as too insignificant to bother Him with my problems. Now He is my Father, my Confidant, my Comforter, and my Guide.

My church is primarily made up of ex-addicts, ex-cons, ex-victims, and ex-victimizers. Even our pastor is an ex-addict. He said someone once told him our church was just a "garbage dump." Our pastor replied, "Amen, and Jesus is the garbage collector!"

This church is my home base, filled with confronters and comforters. They encourage me to share my struggles openly and to move forward. We have Wednesday night Bible study, which is along the lines of group therapy with the Holy Spirit as a counselor and the Bible as our guide. Our pastor encourages us to get together in small groups and minister to each other instead of going to him for counsel. Often the Holy Spirit will prompt someone to pray for me, even when they don't know why, or He will prompt someone to call or visit me. We all believe that stumbling blocks are merely stepping stones to a deeper, richer relationship with Christ.

She Was Afraid of Committing the Unpardonable Sin

I am the adult child of religious addiction. While alcohol or drug abuse was not a part of our home, Bible abuse was. My father was harsh, distant, unreasonable, and disapproving in the name of Christianity. My father thought it was wrong to show affection, and I find myself still starved for a father.

By the age of seventeen I was vomiting from fear that I had committed the unpardonable sin, even though I couldn't identify exactly what that was. I felt guilty if I wore slacks or jewelry. The hair-splitting over issues (and Scripture) would almost be comical if it wasn't taken so seriously. Was it wrong for a man to wear a tie? Was it wrong to eat in a church basement? Was it evil to have life insurance? Should women have their elbows covered? Was a beard okay if you had a "conviction" for it, but sinful if you were following a trend?

Even as I write this, the tapes are playing in my head: "We must be careful to please God." "We don't want people to assume God is soft on sin." "If we allow the boundaries to weaken, we will soon be doing some real sin." I could go on. These people read about the Pharisees but somehow were not able to see themselves. Just as the Pharisees missed the Messiah, we who accept Him can terribly distort who He is.

The biggest issue for my recovery has been a need for an understanding father. How wonderful that God describes Himself in that intimate way. Yet at times I have a hard time plugging into that. I find myself becoming attached to men as father figures. Then I have to remind myself that in heaven all Christian men will be my brothers in some sense, and I won't have to strive for excessive attention.

The harshness of God in the Old Testament used to scare me until I finally did a Bible study and found Him surprisingly intimate and loving, even back then. In fact I've had to relearn how to read the Bible. Yes, God is intolerant of sin, but He is also intolerant of our making up our own list of sins.

My husband is from the same strict religious background as I am, and we find our needs for control and affection are sometimes pitted against each other. It has helped me to see that he needs to control his environment to feel worthwhile as much as I need his affection to feel worthwhile. We are learning to transfer both of those needs to Christ who willingly gives us worth.

Her Mother Abandoned
Her When She Was Two

I guess my story begins when I was two years old and my mother left my brother, then six years old, and me in a taxi cab directed to my grandmother's home. From what I know my mother was not heard from again for about a year. At the time my father was stationed in Japan, serving in the U.S. air force.

Though I do not know all of the details, my grandmother contacted my paternal grandfather, and my brother and I were sent to stay with him in New Mexico. My only memories of this are of my dad finally coming home on a train and my being so glad to see him.

When I was eleven my dad married my stepmother. I was so happy. I had wanted a mom all my life. Unfortunately things did not go well. One month after they were married my dad had a very serious heart attack and was moved to a hospital in another state for several months recovery. When he finally came home, my stepmother was always telling me not to bother him. For years she made me feel that I was the cause of his heart attack, and everything I did was likely to cause him to have another attack.

Needless to say my teen years were not happy ones. My mom would always pick the times I could have been so happy to make critical comments about what I looked like —my hairdo or whatever—or how I acted.

When I graduated from high school, I immediately got a

job and an apartment. I made new friends who were into drinking and things I had not experienced before. I basically went wild. I wanted so badly to be accepted, I can truly say I was "looking for love in all the wrong places."

I had hardly dated in high school, but before long I experienced date rape by a man I really cared for. After that I thought I had found the one thing I could do to get people (guys) to love me. As a consequence of my new behaviors I became pregnant and subsequently gave my first child up for adoption.

When I was twenty-one I met the man who was to become my husband. We began dating, and guess what? I became pregnant again. Although Marshall was hesitant, we did get married. In less than a week, he asked me, "Do you just want to be married until the baby is born or what?" I was very hurt, and I told him I hoped it would last much longer.

A few months into our marriage, a neighbor invited me to a Bible study with her. I had stopped going to church long ago—not because I didn't want to go, but because I could not go without crying. I finally gave in and went with my friend to "get her off my back." I was absolutely amazed by what I heard that day. I had never heard anything about salvation before, even though I had attended church as a child. Eventually the group leader led me to accept Christ as my Savior.

Even though I now knew Christ, circumstances in my life did not change much. My husband could see no reason for what I was experiencing, and he had no interest in the church. Yet he did allow me to go to Bible study and, eventually, to take our children to Sunday school.

I experienced bouts of deep depression and constant loneliness, even though there was no question in my life that I had the love of God. I still did not feel the love of my husband, and I felt the same guilt about the things I did before marriage. In fact the more I learned of God, the more depressed I became because I knew how far I was from Him and how I could fall away, even now, and do things which were not pleasing to Him.

I knew I needed counseling so I sought out the name of a Christian counselor who was a medical doctor as well. She was able to show me that all my life I had felt worthless because everyone had always abandoned me; at least, that was the way I saw it.

The doctor told me to visualize a mother putting a two-year-old girl into a taxi cab. She then had me think about whether I would say, "That must be a terrible little girl for her mother to leave her like that," or, "That must be a sick mother for her to leave her little girl like that." I realized for the first time that the mother in that picture was the one who was wrong, not the child. Until that time I had always felt that I must have been a terrible person for my mother to have left me. Then my stepmother didn't like me. And even my husband didn't like me (or at least that was my perception).

Besides helping me to understand I was not to blame for all the rejection I had felt during my lifetime, my counselor said it was very important for me to forgive my stepmother. I said I had forgiven her, or I thought I had. She helped me to see that I still had an awful lot of bitterness inside.

A few weekends later my youngest son was to play in a basketball tournament in a town about three hours from our home. That day at work was rather strange. I work in an accounting office, and it was tax season. Yet when I arrived that morning, my desk was pretty empty of work, while the other girl in the office had her desk piled high with files. I felt hurt, as if our boss didn't have confidence in my work. Still, I knew logically that the other girl was able to do the computer input on the files on her desk, and since I had more experience, I was supposed to work on some of the more difficult files, which were not as many that morning.

My husband picked me up from work to drive to my son's tournament. By the time we had been riding for about a half hour I was in tears. For the rest of the drive I found myself going over all the sad experiences I remembered during my lifetime, one by one. I just cried and cried, and my husband didn't even seem to be aware of my presence. At one point I thought, "There is just no answer. The only thing for me to do is to open the car door and jump out." But I knew that would hurt my kids so I didn't.

About one-half hour before our arrival at the basketball game, when I was feeling completely abandoned by everyone in my life, I realized that one person had never left: my dad! My dad had always been there, always loving and caring. It was a tiny spark of hope that I had never seen before. Once we got to the ball game I felt some better. By the next morning I felt much better and the rest of the weekend at the tournament was actually fun.

The following week my counselor explained to me that I had felt rejected once more by the lack of work I had been given that morning. During the trip I had grieved over all those hurts in my lifetime, which was necessary for me to experience. (I had unconsciously chosen a safe place to do this grieving: It was dark, my husband and I were alone, and normally we did not talk much when traveling.) As my counselor talked to me, I realized my bitterness was gone! I had finally forgiven all those people for what I felt they had done to me.

I know there will be trials ahead for me as there are for everyone. I also know I will be able to meet those trials because of the love of my Father—both fathers. I think my faith is so important to me—and my love of God so very strong—because I had a living example of God's love here on earth in my earthly father. (I later wrote to my dad and expressed those feelings.)

I am more grateful to God for my life now than I have ever been. I am like the woman who loved much because she was forgiven much. Most of all I praise my God for His love and faithfulness to us. Even when we turn away, He doesn't. I love you, Lord.

The Song in Her Heart Was Silenced One Evening

The first ten years of my life were carefree and happy. God gave me the gift of a good voice, and I sang out for the entire neighborhood from the swing in our backyard. Then, when I was ten and my sister, fourteen, she made it to the state Bible drill competition, and she and my mother were to be in another city for a few days. I was left at home in the care of a neighbor during the day and my father during the evening. I loved and trusted my father even though he rarely spoke to us unless we were getting out of line. We had talked about my love for Christ and I had asked his counsel before walking down the aisle to give my heart to Him.

That weekend my father took me to bed with him. Somehow I still loved my father very much although I did not know if I could ever trust him again. (And I did not realize how I would associate this lack of trust with my heavenly Father as well.) When I told my sister, she confided that our father had also made advances toward her. She had rejected him. I had always wondered why my dad had become so unusually cruel to my sister. Now I knew why. This was the first layer of pain I buried in my heart.

When my mother was gone, my father continued to enjoy my affections. Desire and fear entered my life. This continued for a couple of years until we moved and my father began a new job where he had to work very long hours.

At eighteen I married a boy who was just the opposite of my father. He was interested in my feelings and was my best friend. I helped him through college and he earned three degrees. We had two wonderful children. Our whole family used our talents for the Lord's service. Then after my husband and I returned from a second honeymoon, my friend, my lover, my singing partner, my husband, announced to me that he enjoyed having sex with men as well as women. He had been unfaithful to me for thirteen of the seventeen years we had been married, he said.

With the Lord's help I was able to forgive my husband, and for the next six months I worked very hard to put my family back together. During that time, however, I began to lose my fifteen-year-old son. He became unable to function in school properly. He had to be hospitalized in an institution five to six hours away. This stress, plus my husband's losing his job, ended our marriage.

I decided to take a real step in faith and move away to find a job in a larger city where I had only one friend. There were just too many memories of my husband's and my life together in the home we had shared. Two weeks after the move I had received three job offers. A loving minister of music allowed my daughter to become involved in a youth musical at our new church. God was truly blessing us each step of the way.

The first weekend in September, singles gather at Glorieta to gain spiritual renewal, and I planned to go to the gathering. I had never envisioned life as a single person so I knew God, and God alone, could help me now. While there, I met a man who was tall, strong, and very dependable—my image of a husband. Within six weeks we were married. For my new husband it was a third marriage.

Now I understand why the Lord never planned for a man and a woman to have but one husband and one wife. My husband's children were his first consideration, even though they were older and no longer under his care. This was very hard for me to accept. I turned to my daughter who was still living with us for comfort and understanding. She just wanted me to leave the marriage.

During the next years my daughter pulled further and further away from me. She was on the honor roll at school, participated in activities, and even told me at the beginning of her senior year that she did not want to become serious with any young man. Yet in the later part of the year a young man who wanted to possess all her time and affections moved into her life. He went to our church and I had known his mother and father for years. All of us sang in the church choir. By the spring of that year my daughter and this young man informed me she was pregnant. Again, pain overwhelmed my heart and soul. I cried out to God, "Couldn't you have prevented this from happening?"

The young man's parents and I supported their decision to be married. Our church family gave them a large wedding shower. The teachers at my daughter's school did all they could to help her complete the year. She graduated with honors and had a lovely church wedding. I smiled throughout the ceremony, but my heart was shattered and again I buried the pain.

My life seemed to be at a dead end. I did not know where God was now when I needed him most. Yet I remembered that my earthly father had not been very trustworthy either. Even when I thought he loved me, he had betrayed my trust.

Ever since my divorce, I occasionally had a social drink with friends from work. My profession was very stressful and everyone drank socially to relax from the tension of the day. Over the years following my daughter's marriage, I began to drink more and more. I became more and more depressed and hopeless. No matter how hard I tried, my daughter and my husband's children never became close to us, because they had too many very deep scars from the divorces. Before I realized it, my life had become unmanageable. I became an alcoholic as my grandfather, whom I had never known.

My weight was also completely out of control; I went from a size eight to a size sixteen in a three-year period. I found no fulfillment in anything, not even in my beautiful, healthy grandchild. Each day I thought how nice it would be for those I loved without me. I was so scared by these thoughts that I decided to see if someone might be able to help me.

My family physician referred me to a psychiatrist who asked if I would consider hospitalization. At the time I was fearful that my husband would use that against me. Therefore, I refused to go. He then referred me to a psychologist who told me the same thing.

Finally, after thinking about the futility of my life, I decided to enter the hospital as a day patient in the psychiatric ward. If I could learn how to have a happy life, it would be worth my efforts. If not, I could still put an end to it all. I promised the staff there that for the time of my therapy they would get 100 percent of me.

I began to open up that pain that I had buried so deeply. As layer after layer was removed, I unraveled the hurt in my soul. I did not realize the effect it was having on my relationship with God, my heavenly Father. It was absolutely necessary to grieve over the losses in my life. This gave me the freedom to separate my earthly father from my heavenly Father and to give Him complete control of my life. My heavenly Father is the only one who can meet all my needs. He has restored the song in my heart, which I lost one weekend so many years ago.

Appendix

A Guide to Twelve-Step Groups

Below is a list of Twelve-Step program offices. Some of their phones play a taped recording listing local meetings only, but for most you can leave a message and your call will be returned. Be patient: these phones are usually run by volunteers. Eventually, your call will be returned.

ACA Interim World Service
  Organization
P.O. Box 3216
Torrance, CA 90505

Alcoholics Anonymous
Box 459
Grand Central Station
New York, NY 10163
(212) 686-1100

Cocaine Anonymous
Box 1367
Culver City, CA 90232
(213) 839-1141

Co-Dependents Anonymous
Box 33577
Phoenix, AZ 85067
(602) 277-7991

Emotional Health Anonymous
2420 San Gabriel Boulevard
Rosemead, CA 91770
(818) 573-5482

Families Anonymous
Box 528
Van Nuys, CA 91408
(818) 989-7841

Gamblers Anonymous
Box 17173
Los Angeles, CA 90017
(213) 386-8789

Incest Survivors Anonymous
P.O. Box 5613
Long Beach, CA 90800

Narcotics Anonymous
Box 9999
Van Nuys, CA 91409
(818) 780-3951

Narcotics Anonymous
World Service Center
16155 Wyandotte Street
Van Nuys, CA 91406
(818) 780-3951

National Association for
Children of Alcoholics
31582 Coast Highway, Suite B
South Laguna, CA 92677
(714) 499-3889

National Clearinghouse for
Alcohol Information
P.O. Box 1908
Rockville, MD 20850

Overcomers Outreach
2290 W. Whittier Blvd.,
Suite D
La Habra, CA 90631
(213) 697-3994
(Alcoholics and adult children
    claiming Christ's promises
    and accepting His healing)

Overeaters Anonymous
Box 92870
Los Angeles, CA 90009
(213) 657-6252

Overeaters Anonymous,
World Service Office
2190 190th Street
Torrance, CA 90504
(213) 542-8363

Sexaholics Anonymous
Box 300
Simi Valley, CA 93062
(letters *only*)

For information about other Twelve-Step and self-help groups,
    call or write to:
National Self-Help Clearinghouse
City University Graduate Center
25 West 43rd Street
Room 620
New York, NY 10036
(212) 642-2944

For detailed, exhaustive information about addictions,
    codependence, and self-help groups—including Twelve-Step
    programs—see *The Recovery Resource Book* by Barbara Yoder
    (A Fireside Book, Simon & Schuster, $12.95).

The following organizations also exist. You may wish to seek
    them out locally.
Adult Children of Alcoholics Anonymous
Al-Atot
Alcoholics Victorious (Christian recovery support group)
Bulimics/Anorexics Anonymous
Child Abusers Anonymous
Cocaine Anonymous
Codependents of Sex Addicts

Parents Anonymous
Pills Anonymous
Sex Addicts Anonymous
Sexaholics Anonymous
Sex and Love Addicts Anonymous
Shoplifters Anonymous
Smokers Anonymous
Spenders Anonymous
Victims of Incest Can Emerge
Workaholics Anonymous

Notes

The Path to Serenity

1. 1 Pet. 3:7.
2. *Alcoholics Anonymous* (New York: Alcoholics Anonymous World Services, Inc., 1976), 8.
3. Bill Pittman, *A.A.: The Way It Began* (Seattle, WA: Glen Abbey Press, 1988).

Step Two

1. *Alcoholics Anonymous,* 10.
2. Chuck C., *A New Pair of Glasses* (Irvine, CA: New Look Publishing, 1984).
3. *Alcoholics Anonymous,* 569.
4. Ibid, 11.
5. Ibid, 13.
6. Ibid, 58, 59.
7. Ibid, 59.
8. Ibid, 12.
9. Ibid.

Step Three

1. *Alcoholics Anonymous,* 63.
2. Bill Wilson, *Twelve Steps and Twelve Traditions* (New York, NY: Alcoholics Anonymous World Services, Inc., 1990), 34.
3. *Alcoholics Anonymous,* 58.
4. Rom. 5:8.
5. Isa. 1:18.
6. *Alcoholics Anonymous,* 84.

Step Four

1. Exod. 20:5.
2. Robert Slatzer, *Bing Crosby—The Hollow Man.*
3. Wilson, *Twelve Steps and Twelve Traditions,* 98.
4. Rom. 8:28.
5. *Alcoholics Anonymous,* 66.

Step Five

1. Richard Foster, *Celebration of Discipline* (San Francisco, CA: Harper and Row, 1988), 151.
2. Ibid.
3. Ibid, 152.
4. Ibid, 148.

5. *The Book of Common Prayer* (New York, NY: The Seabury Press, 1977), 360.
6. John 20:23.
7. Wilson, *Twelve Steps and Twelve Traditions,* 58.
8. Ibid, 59.
9. Wilson, *Twelve Steps and Twelve Traditions,* 60.
10. 2 Cor. 4:1–2.
11. Laurie Werner, "Recovering in Public," *Dallas Times Herald,* Sept. 7–9, 1990, 4.

Step Six
1. Matt. 16:26.
2. Matt. 11:28, 29, NIV.
3. See Rom. 6:11.

Step Seven
1. Chuck C., *A New Pair of Glasses.*
2. Zech. 4:6.
3. Wilson, *Twelve Steps and Twelve Traditions,* 75.
4. Mark 9:24.
5. See Phil. 2:12, 13.
6. The Part Acts Technique as well as other techniques discussed in this chapter are presented and discussed in *Mental Health through Will-Training,* by Dr. Abraham Low (Glencoe, IL: Willett Publishing, 1984).
7. Wilson, *Twelve Steps and Twelve Traditions,* 76.
8. 2 Cor. 12:9.

Step Eight
1. Ali MacGraw, *Moving Pictures* (New York: Bantam, 1991), 207.
2. See Lev. 6:1–7.
3. Luke 19:8, *NIV.* See Luke 19:1–10 for the entire story.

Step Nine
1. See Matt. 5:23–24.
2. William Barclay, *The Gospel of Matthew, Vol. 1,* (Philadelphia: The Westminster Press, 1977), 140–1.
3. Wilson, *Twelve Steps and Twelve Traditions,* 86.
4. Ibid, 83.
5. For a good discussion of using Scripture to counter your negative self-talk, see Dr. Chris Thurman's *The Lies We Believe* (Nashville: Thomas Nelson, 1990).

Step Ten
1. Wilson, *Twelve Steps and Twelve Traditions,* 88.
2. Ibid, 93.
3. Ibid, 93.

Step Eleven

1. C. S. Lewis, *Mere Christianity* (London: Collins Clear-Type Press, Fontana Books, 1955), 49.
2. Exod. 34:7. See also Num. 14:18; Jer. 32:18.
3. Mark 14:36.
4. 1 John 5:14–15.
5. Matt. 7:7–11.
6. Matt. 16:25.
7. Brother Lawrence, *The Practice of the Presence of God* (New York: Image Books, 1977), 65.
8. Foster, *Celebration of Discipline,* 17.
9. Ibid, 15.

Step Twelve

1. Wilson, *Twelve Steps and Twelve Traditions*, 106–7.
2. Lewis, *Mere Christianity,* 52, 53.
3. Matt. 28:19, 20.
4. Wilson, *Twelve Steps and Twelve Traditions*, 180.
5. "Addiction Is in the Pew," Michael G. Maudlin, *Christianity Today,* July 22, 1991, 22.
6. Wilson, *Twelve Steps and Twelve Traditions,* 110.
7. Luke 8:39.
8. John 4:29.
9. Wilson, *Twelve Steps and Twelve Traditions,* 110.
10. Wilson, *Alcoholics Anonymous.* See especially Chapter 7, "Working with Others."
11. Joe McQ, *The Steps We Took* (Little Rock, AR: August House Publishers, 1991), 152–3.
12. Samuel Moor Shoemaker, see Helen Smith Shoemaker, *I Stand By the Door* (New York: Harper and Row, 1967), ix–x.

Codependent Spouses: Personal Stories

1. Phil. 4:13.

Bibliography

Alcoholics Anonymous, Third Edition. New York: Alcoholics Anonymous World Services, Inc., 1976.

Twelve Steps and Twelve Traditions. New York: Alcoholics Anonymous World Services, Inc., 1990.

Al-Anon's Twelve Steps & Twelve Traditions. New York: Al-Anon Family Group Headquarters, Inc., 1988.

Barclay, William. *The Daily Bible Study Series.* Philadelphia: The Westminster Press, 1977.

Beacon Bible Commentary. Kansas City, MO: Beacon Hill Press, 1969.

Beattie, Melody. *Codependent No More: How to Stop Controlling Others and Start Caring for Yourself.* Center City, MN: Hazelden, 1987.

Chambers, Oswald. *My Utmost for His Highest.* New York: Dodd, Mead, & Co., 1935.

Foster, Richard. *Celebration of Discipline.* San Francisco: Harper & Row, 1988.

Law, William. *A Serious Call to a Devout and Holy Life.* Wilton, CT: Morehouse-Barlow Co., 1981.

Lawrence, Brother. *The Practice of the Presence of God.* New York: Image Book, Doubleday, 1977.

Lewis, C. S. *Mere Christianity.* New York: Collier Books, Macmillan Publishing, 1952.

Low, Abraham A. *Mental Health Through Will-Training.* Winnetka, IL: Willett Publishing Company, 1984.

McQ, Joe. *The Steps We Took.* Little Rock, AR: August House Publishers, 1991.

Merton, Thomas. *Praying the Psalms.* Collegeville, MN: The Liturgical Press, 1956.

Ray, Veronica. *A Design for Growth.* Center City, MN: Hazelden, 1988.

Taylor, Kenneth N. *How to Grow.* Nashville: Thomas Nelson Publishers, 1985.

Twenty-Four Hours a Day. Center City, MN: Hazelden, 1989.

The Minirth-Meier Clinic Offices
"The Most Trusted Name In Christian Counseling"
ESTABLISHED IN 1976

National Headquarters
MINIRTH-MEIER CLINIC, P.A.
2100 N. Collins Blvd.
Richardson, Texas 75080
(214) 669-1733

1-800-229-3000
OUTPATIENT SERVICES
DAY TREATMENT CENTER
HOSPITAL PROGRAMS
NATIONAL MEDIA MINISTRIES

MINIRTH-MEIER TUNNELL & WILSON CLINIC
Centre Creek Office Plaza, Suite 200
1812 Centre Creek Drive
Austin, Texas 78754
(512) 339-7511

1-800-444-5751

OUTPATIENT SERVICES
DAY TREATMENT CENTER
HOSPITAL PROGRAMS

MINIRTH-MEIER CLINIC WEST
260 Newport Center Drive, Suite 430
Newport Beach, California 92660
(714) 760-3112

1-800-877-4673

OUTPATIENT SERVICES
DAY TREATMENT CENTER
HOSPITAL PROGRAMS

MINIRTH-MEIER CLINIC, P.C.
The Grove, Suite 1510
2100 Manchester Road
Wheaton, Illinois 60187
(708) 653-1717

1-800-848-8872
1-800-545-1819*
OUTPATIENT SERVICES
DAY TREATMENT CENTER
HOSPITAL PROGRAMS
*NATIONAL COMMUNICATIONS DIVISION**

MINIRTH-MEIER-RICE CLINIC, P.A.
Koger Center in the Shannon Building
10801 Executive Center Drive, Suite 305
Little Rock, Arkansas 72211
(501) 225-0576

1-800-488-4769

OUTPATIENT SERVICES
HOSPITAL PROGRAMS

MINIRTH-MEIER BYRD CLINIC, P.A.
4300 Fair Lakes Court, Suite 200
Fairfax, Virginia 22033-4231
(703) 968-3556

1-800-486-HOPE (4673)

OUTPATIENT SERVICES
DAY TREATMENT CENTER
HOSPITAL PROGRAMS

For general information about other Minirth-Meier Clinic branch offices, counseling services, educational resources and hospital programs, call toll-free
1-800-545-1819

National Headquarters: (214) 669-1733   1-800-229-3000

345